TERROR BASE UK

Neil Doyle is a renowned investigative journalist who specialises in covering the activities of terrorist groups for national newspapers and broadcasters world-wide. He is an expert in the fields of counter-terrorism, cyber-terrorism and al-Qaeda. He is also the author of *Terror Tracker*.

TERROR BASE UK

INSIDE A SECRET WAR

NEIL DOYLE

MAINSTREAM
PUBLISHING
EDINBURGH AND LONDON

First published in Great Britain in 2006 by
MAINSTREAM PUBLISHING COMPANY (EDINBURGH) LTD
7 Albany Street
Edinburgh EH1 3UG

ISBN 1 84018 994 0

All images courtesy of ND archive (www.neildoyle.com)

A catalogue record for this book is available from the British Library

Typeset in Stone Sans and Stone Serif

Printed in Great Britain by
William Clowes Ltd, Beccles, Suffolk

For Lily and Tommy

CONTENTS

AUTHOR'S NOTE

Quotations in the text are verbatim, wherever possible, especially when they have been sourced from court documents. Some of the speech of people for whom English is not their primary language looks strange, in parts. I've resisted the urge to clean up quotes and opted to preserve the mannerisms and accents of the characters as far as possible.

If you'd like to read more about any of the subjects covered here, a warm welcome awaits you at www.neildoyle.com.

PROLOGUE

JIHADI CHATTER ON THE INTERNET IN THE WEEKS LEADING UP TO THE 7 July attacks on London had been quiet. That in itself is often an ominous sign, as operatives are ordered to maintain the cyber equivalent of 'radio silence' to preserve security ahead of an impending operation. There were few clues that it would happen on home soil this time, though a head of steam had been building for over a decade.

Britain is now a land of jihad – of holy war by Muslims against unbelievers. That's long been the wish of radical Islamic preachers, most notably Abu Hamza. In his sermons, he was fond of admonishing domestic Muslims for being weak-willed and lacking the stomach to fight. He must have been delighted when several of his admirers finally went over the top in July 2005.

Hamza had been preaching the virtues of performing jihad in your own homeland for many long years. After listening to numerous hours of his speeches while researching *Terror Tracker*, I tried to sum up Hamza's predictions of future conflicts in a nutshell and concluded: 'If he was right, the streets of London would soon be littered with burnt-out buses and dotted with craters.' I also wrote a line about how, if he was serious, we would see the long-feared scenario of 'suicide bombers on Oxford Street'. I deleted that during the editing, believing it to be possibly too far-fetched and deciding to err on the side of caution.

In early 2005, however, I learnt from a TV producer friend how easily this could be done. He had been working on a documentary about al-Qaeda sleeper cells, but it had been canned. They'd set up a sleeper cell for the programme and filmed the fake al-Qaeda operatives training and preparing in a safe house. They even set out on a fictional mission to commit a terrorist atrocity in Leicester Square, wearing imitation explosive belts. They were successful, in that they mingled with the crowds without raising any suspicions, despite a heavy police presence.

I sat down to lunch recently with an influential Asian foreign affairs analyst based in London and, in the midst of war chat, he threw up his arms and claimed, with a smile on his face, that there's no point in denying that the 'war on terrorism' is a clash of civilisations, because that is exactly what it is, from whatever angle you look at it. I have to agree that it does look like it's threatening to shape up into a conflict of biblical proportions. On the Internet, you can often find chatter referring to Osama bin Laden as the 'al-Mahdi', an Islamic term meaning a saviour figure, and the emerging caliph of all Muslims.

These are the lines that Hamza was thinking along when he said on one of the tapes covered in the previous book that bin Laden is a 'beautiful man' who has been framed for the 9/11 attacks. 'Allah sends every 100 years for this ummah [whole community of Muslims] somebody to renew its religion. It could be a person, it could be many people, it could be a group . . . the only people who are renewing the religion are the Mujahideen [guerrilla fighters] and the scholars who are saying the truth, even if they get killed for it.'

One of the gifts that bin Laden gave the Taliban's supreme leader Mullah Mohammed Omar was a brown cloak that's said to have been worn by Muhammad. The Taliban leader can be seen holding it up to a crowd in a rare video of him addressing a public gathering, and the people frenziedly clamour to touch it. Bin Laden himself is increasingly looking more like a statesman than a military leader in his more recent video addresses.

When he did finally admit to 9/11, he went out of his way not to take the ultimate credit. He may have planned it, but it was Allah who had the final call on whether it would be successful. It was a powerful display; he was acting in concert with Allah in a righteous battle against the infidels to rescue the Islamic nation. It should be no surprise that in the wider Muslim world, ruined by corruption, poverty and illiteracy, he is seen as their leader in exile.

Some whisper that he had been deliberately left alone by the Western military to prevent him being elevated to an epic position in the public mind. Another rumour is that the consequences of liquidating him would have been grave for the West, as those vying to succeed him would seek to out-do his acts of terrorism in their leadership struggles.

There are also outstanding questions surrounding the reasons why al-Qaeda has not mounted more attacks on the US mainland since 9/11. Neo-conservative types have suggested that this is because the US administration has privately warned that it will not hesitate to destroy Mecca in a nuclear strike if something like that happens again. Maybe the recent unexplained flurry of jihadi propaganda images featuring mushroom clouds over New York City was a reaction to that. I've seen no evidence of preparations being made for a nuclear terror strike, nor would there be any, but the lack of signs of al-Qaeda activity in the States is slightly puzzling.

The authorities there have been searching for sleeper cells in the USA since the attacks and they've found very little. Meanwhile, according to the latest statistics from the US National Counterterrorism Center, the number of terrorist incidents outside the country's borders recorded last year was triple the total in the preceding year, though officials insisted that they are winning the war. I think the answer may be that al-Qaeda is biding its time.

I did intend to include a 'pre-9/11' timeline here of all the missed intelligence warnings, but I abandoned it halfway through because it would have taken up way too much space. It reads like the script to the mother of all Keystone Kops movies, because the threat to the USA was identified and known decades ago. One of the final entries on the timeline would have been a previously undisclosed Federal Aviation Administration report published in February 2005 which revealed that airlines had received no fewer than fifty-two different reports relating to al-Qaeda activities over the five months prior to the attacks.

According to bin Laden, 1982 is the year when the idea of crashing aircraft into tall buildings occurred to him. He claimed, in a video address on the eve of the 2004 US presidential election, that the inspiration came to him as he watched television pictures of Israeli aircraft bombing high-rise residential tower blocks in Beirut, during the US-aided invasion of Lebanon.

The potential use of such weapons was raised at the highest levels in the US military's 1963 Operation Northwoods fake terrorism plan. The danger of real terrorists using airliners came to the fore nine years later. A high-level US government panel had been set up in 1972 to develop plans to protect the country from attacks from Arab terrorists. The group was formed by president Richard Nixon after

Palestinian militants killed 11 Israeli athletes at the Munich Olympic Games.

The subsequent 1977 report by the Cabinet Committee to Combat Terrorism highlighted a range of threat scenarios, including radiological 'dirty bombs' and terrorists hijacking aircraft with the intention of destroying them. Key figures on the committee, which was later absorbed by the National Security Council, included Henry Kissinger and Rudolph Giuliani.

Documents that were produced by the committee were only declassified in January 2005 and many of the concerns that were raised over three decades ago remain the same today. One 1972 assessment mentions that 'rumors and unconfirmed reports indicate that a Palestinian cell dedicated to violence is in place in the USA'. It continues: 'It is estimated that the threat of hijacking of international flights accompanied by acts of terrorism will continue until a satisfactory solution to the Palestinian problem in the Middle East is found and peace is negotiated in the Middle East.'

In 1972, the USA had a detailed plan that might have prevented the 9/11 attacks from taking place. One of the group's first recommendations was for increased security checks on airline passengers – '100 per cent passenger inspection is now required' – but a White House memo says in response that airlines and airports would 'scream bloody murder' over the costs involved. If the plan for screening and profiling passengers and thorough baggage and security checks had been enacted and become ingrained in the workings of the industry, then maybe using airliners as missiles wouldn't have been such an attractive option in the twenty-first century.

Another 1972 report raises the possibility of the use of dirty bombs and mentions that procedures were being developed 'for protecting nuclear raw materials which, if captured by terrorists, can be made into crude atomic bombs or exploded to cause contamination. (This is a real threat, not science fiction).'

A report in the following year, from Secretary of State William Rogers to President Nixon, outlines the progress that had already been made: 'Since atomic materials could afford mind-boggling possibilities for terrorists . . . the shipment of all radioactive materials is now being escorted by guards.'

Reading the material, it seems fair to say that there was more concern about the possible use of unconventional weapons by Arab terrorist groups than airliners being hijacked. Minutes of a 1976

14

meeting refer to studies under way to 'examine the problem of possible terrorist threats or attacks involving nuclear, chemical or biological weapons of mass destruction'.

The body of the work done by the cabinet group looks spookily similar to the recommendations produced by the inquiry into the 9/11 attacks by the National Commission on Terrorist Attacks Upon the United States. A 1976 group meeting included comments from group member Rudolph Giuliani, then a Justice Department official, that raised the issue of the reluctance of the various arms of government to coordinate anti-terrorism activities and to share intelligence findings.

It was poignant to read his early concerns about in-fighting between government agencies, especially as he would have had no idea that years later he would be at the very epicentre of the most spectacular terrorist attack ever seen. His observation about agencies being reluctant to cooperate was prophetic, as the 9/11 inquiry highlighted the rivalry between the CIA and the FBI as the chief reason why the hijackers were able to slip into the USA and operate without hindrance.

The 1976 document quotes Giuliani as saying: 'Close coordination is necessary, however, between FBI and CIA when foreign terrorists come to the United States.' The CIA told the 9/11 inquiry that it had informed the Bureau about the entry of one suspected al-Qaeda operative in 'early 2000', though the FBI disputed this. It said it was only told about the movements of hijackers Khalid al-Mihdhar and Nawaf al-Hazmi on 23 August 2001 and there wasn't enough time to locate them.

I've stuck my neck out previously and said that we'd be seeing around 14 suicide bombings a day, on average, before we knew that a clash of the civilisations was in full-swing. That was based on Abu Hamza's estimate of 500,000 martyrs being required to gain control of the planet in the name of Islam, divided by a military assessment predicting a 100-year conflict. The multiple car-bomb attacks that we see in Iraq on an almost daily basis are pushing the numbers in that direction, and there are other signs of increased activities.

I also pinned my colours to the mast and presented evidence indicating that the leadership was working to a three-phase overall battle plan. Both of these headlines were proven in March 2005 when I read a new al-Qaeda book called *The Management of Barbarism*, written by their military strategist Abu Bakr Naji and published on the Net. The title refers to a predicted period of chaos immediately after the collapse of a superpower and the book is a 113-page in-depth analysis of al-Qaeda's plans and intentions. It officially confirms that they are indeed working to a three-phase plan (the 'disruption and exhaustion' phase, the 'management of barbarism' phase and the 'empowerment phase') and on the assumption that 'our long struggle will require half a million Mujahideen'.

neil@neildoyle.com

WEB WAR ONE

AL-QAEDA HAS BEEN ACTIVE IN CYBERSPACE SINCE THE EARLY 1990S, although Western propaganda in the build-up to the Afghanistan war made no distinction between the terror network and the Taliban. Most people were left with an image of this new enemy as a ridiculously turbaned, quasi-Stone Age group who got around in wrecked cars pulled along by donkeys. People living in caves surely couldn't be sending emails?

That was the misconception, even though bin Laden's network had been using email to distribute jihad manuals, for example, for over a decade. Much of the planning for the 9/11 attacks took place on a covert website, where the hijackers and the coordinators interacted via coded, seemingly innocent messages in a guest book.

Al-Qaeda's counter-attack to the West's propaganda, I quickly discovered, was being broadcast from the UK, from a website run by an outfit called Azzam Publications. The clue was in whom the website was named after: Sheikh Abdullah Azzam was regarded as the godfather of the modern global jihad and the founder of what is now known as al-Qaeda. The site appeared to be an English-language news agency devoted to coverage of the activities of the Taliban and al-Qaeda. Its output was carried on a number of key militant websites, as it promised it was 'the source of authentic news about the Jihad and the Mujahideen'.

It was a bit of a surprise to discover that al-Qaeda's media operation was being run from Britain – Birmingham, to be exact. We were on the brink of war, yet this group appeared to be running without any interference from officialdom. Of course, I wondered why, and set out to judge just how authentic this 'news agency' was.

It looked like the site had been operating since at least 1999, though there was a statement there that claimed it had been going since 1996. I think I must have navigated to the site on 11 September 2001, because it came up high in my search results, though I didn't start combing through it in detail until a couple of weeks later. It was claiming to be attracting five million visitors a day and I thought that was very unlikely, but traffic was bound to be high, as most people were on a steep learning curve then.

I don't know why I wasn't shocked; maybe it was just another case of Internet-myopia – having something significant right in front of your eyes yet it doesn't register in the brain, as if it refuses to accept that you've hit the jackpot so easily. It was just post-9/11, yet Azzam.com was carrying instructions for training for jihad and giving advice to new recruits wanting to travel to the 'jihad lands' of Chechnya and Afghanistan. There was also a step-by-step guide on how to ferry large sums of cash to the Taliban in Afghanistan and a sample letter of introduction to get you over the border. It even had a list of a dozen Taliban field commanders and their telephone numbers.

At the time, it wasn't clear to me that this was illegal, as I was struggling to think of what law might be broken by encouraging people to put themselves in the line of fire in foreign hellholes – accessory to murder, possibly, but this had clearly been going on for some years and the site looked to be thriving. One article told the story of one of its reporters who had travelled from the UK and been killed fighting in Chechnya.

It reported that 'Masood al-Benin' was killed on 12 April 2000. His obituary said that his mother was French, his father from Benin, and he'd settled in London to undertake a degree in business studies, where he soon became radicalised. It went on:

> Upon hearing a lecture on the importance of jihad and subsequently meeting ex-Mujahideen veterans, Masood had become surprisingly alarmed of how the Muslims had neglected the duty of Jihad, during a period in which Muslims were being slaughtered in large numbers across the globe. And so in a small way, he attempted to redress the balance, and made an intention to travel to Afghanistan (with his brother Mu'adh), whereby he could undergo military training.

A week prior to his departure, Masood and Mu'adh had met a 'brother' in the UK called Abu Azzam, and he persuaded them to join him in Chechnya instead. He made arrangements for the three to travel there, entering the country via 'a safe corridor'. Masood spent much of his time working on IT projects and setting up a computer centre, before he undertook 'advanced warfare training' and started participating in Mujahideen raids, acting as a cameraman.

> The fruits of his works and patience culminated in a mighty reward: his presence during the commencement of the fiercest fighting in the history of the foreign Mujahideen. After the conclusion of each military operation, Masood's duties included video editing, adding titles, etc. to the footage of the operations. The videos edited by Masood are currently in circulation all over the world.

He sustained a serious leg injury when his group came under mortar attack during an operation in the mountains above a town called Duba Yurt. He and two other injured Mujahideen were being transported in the back of a Toyota pick-up to receive medical attention when it was stopped at a Russian army checkpoint. A firefight ensued until they were overwhelmed and killed. The only weapon Masood had with him was a Makarov handgun. A colleague recalled that he'd left behind a pregnant wife:

> My advice, to all the Muslims of the world, is that we should follow the path of the Prophet Muhammad, his companions and the pious predecessors. After them, Masood is amongst the rare examples of Muslims of our age who held fast to this path. We too insha-Allah will strive to follow the path that he took.
>
> My advice to the Muslims is that a person should not be afraid of his soul. Jihad is far more besides the act of fighting on the front line. Masood al-Benin (may Allah have mercy on him) demonstrated this.

I watched one of Masood's videos, which appeared to be very popular in jihad circles, if not top of the charts. It was a fundamentally shocking example of man's inhumanity to man. I could almost smell the singed and rotting flesh each time it zoomed in on yet another dead and butchered Russian soldier. Other scenes showed rocket attacks on army tanks and trucks, and I could see people being thrown high into the air by the blasts. The word 'bestial' sticks in my mind as the best description of what I saw.

Entering this hell on earth was the goal of a great many people, as even at this early stage I was aware that the Chechen militants operated something akin to the Foreign Legion in their efforts to push back the Russian forces and establish an Islamic state there. Links with al-Qaeda were strongly suspected, though these were downplayed, as it suited the militants to be seen as insurgents fighting a regional skirmish rather than being regarded as a transnational terrorism threat, which might risk Russia seeking international assistance. Indeed, during the subsequent US-led invasion of Afghanistan, al-Qaeda and Taliban spokesmen repeatedly denied that there were any Chechens among their ranks, despite plenty of evidence to the contrary.

There were around 50 messages from all around the world at the end of the article about Masood, all hailing him as an Islamic hero. I wondered who in London was responsible for persuading Masood to follow the path of violence and what the nature of the lecture he'd attended was. To underline the fact that Azzam's operation had serious connections, there was a message of endorsement from the commander of the Islamic International Forces in Chechnya, a fearsome-looking Afghan Mujahideen veteran and associate of bin Laden called Ibn-ul-Khattab. His immediate boss was the notoriously ruthless Shamil Basayev, the overall leader of the Chechen militants.

Khattab died in 2002, after he opened a letter that had been doped with a poison and had apparently been sent by the Russian security service, the FSB, though some have speculated that, angered by a number of strategic failures, bin Laden was behind it.

This November 2000 message of thanks on the site explicitly reveals the global nature of Azzam.com's operation:

> We would also like to say thank you to the following (not in any particular order):
> To Abu Ayub (UAE) and Tarek for staying up in the night to translate the latest news
> To Abu Whalid and his team (Germany) for providing the streaming video space and helping us keep the site up and running when things were difficult
> To Sister Delila and her friends (Sweden) for the Swedish website and helping to host the Bosnian site once it developed problems

To Sister Umm Ismael (UAE) for the Italian web-site

To Abu Ubaidah (Germany) for the Bosnian web-site

To Brother Wael and the Latin American Muslim Unity (USA)
   for the Spanish web-site

To Abu Muslim (Malaysia) for the Malay web-site

To Sister Ptichka for working on the Russian web-site

To Ali and his brothers (Germany) for the Turkish web-site

To Sami, Abu Muslim and Abu Saifudeen (France) for the
   French web-site

To Lutfi and Olsi for the Albanian web-site

To Brother Ipul (Indonesia) for the Indonesian web-site

To Andrei for the Ukrainian web-site

To Abdul-Hakeem for working on the Somali web-site

To Ashraf for providing the money for the high-specification
   web server

To Sister UM from Canada whose e-mail was the inspiration to
   start the E-Mails of Support Section

To Martin and Hayley at Swiftnet for being excellent business
   people

To Sisters SN, SB and SH from Bradford, UK for their e-mails
   and letters of support

To Sister Asiya for her articles, suggestions and hard work

Brother Tahir N (USA) and Abu B (Lebanon) for their regular
   supply of e-mails of support

There was a guide to DIY jihad training there also, which advised readers: 'Military Training is an Islamic Obligation not an Option'. There was criticism of the British media: 'When tabloid journalism mistakenly informs the masses that Jihad is "to commit illegal acts of terror", they are revealing the lack of their research and the extent of their unprofessional approach to the subject.'

   Potential jihadis were told that training must be undertaken in secrecy and it detailed a strict physical training schedule to help new recruits to build up their fitness and stamina:

> It is better to go to the gym with another brother if possible, or go at a time when there are as few women as possible. Public gymnasiums are generally un-Islamic places with loud music and improperly dressed men and women. Such an atmosphere is not befitting for the training of a Mujahid.

The next two stages were martial-arts training and an outdoors survival course, before the fun bit: firearms training. It advised the trainee to join a shooting club and practise with an AK-47-type weapon, if possible, depending on the local laws. It warned:

> Recently we heard many reports circulating in the British media about certain Muslim personalities claiming the presence of jihad training camps in the UK in which firearms training is given with live ammunition before sending the trainees for jihad. We would like to inform both Muslim and non-Muslim readers of this article that there are NO such training camps within the UK. Rather, statements such as these are made by Muslim personalities and individuals propped up by Western Intelligence agencies in order to frighten the local population from Muslims.

That didn't mean that there weren't any training camps in the UK. After pointing out in no uncertain terms that Azzam was unable to and would refuse to respond to queries about travelling abroad for jihad training, it had mellowed by the end of the document into a bit of a nudge-nudge-wink-wink line:

> There are some countries where one can obtain jihad training but we are not in a position to comment on the suitability or insuitability of any particular country. Contact individuals you know and trust and they will be able to advise you better. If you are true to Allah, Allah will be true to you and He will find you a way to do what you want to do.

Much dodgier, I thought, was a statement titled 'TALIBAN: ALLAH'S BLESSING ON AFGHANISTAN'. It completely contradicted the advice in the jihad training guide, as it was specifically urging sympathisers to travel to Afghanistan. It contained detailed instructions on ferrying cash donations into the country and delivering them directly into the hands of Taliban commanders.

It started off by pointing out that the Russian authorities had recently confiscated $3 million in donations destined for the Chechen Mujahideen, so great care would need to be taken by would-be cash couriers to Afghanistan. It described the Taliban as 'the only Muslim government in the world that has refused to bow down to pressure from the enemies of Allah, despite sanctions, negative publicity, isolation and military strikes'.

It continued: 'Due to the emergency situation in Afghanistan and the imminent joint US/Russian chemical strike expected there, we urge the Muslim organisations around the world to directly convey their donations and monetary assistance to the Islamic Taliban government in Afghanistan.'

Donations should be collected at mosques through Friday prayer collections and special fund-raising events, then 'two or three wealthy, trustworthy and respected members of the community or organisation' should collect the cash together and convert it into US dollars. At the end of each month, they should travel to Karachi in Pakistan with a letter of introduction. An example was even included:

> To Whom it May Concern:
> We would like to introduce our official delegation from the Islamic Centre of South Arlington who are carrying monetary assistance for the suffering people of Afghanistan. The members of this delegation are listed below:
>   1. Abdullah Muhammad Saeed, American Passport Holder
>   2. Ishaq Mansoor al-Katib, American Passport Holder
>   3. Muhammad Abdur-Rasheed, Canadian Passport Holder
> They are carrying a quantity of cash donations which have been collected by the Muslim community of South Arlington and are to help the suffering people of Afghanistan. We request all those whom it may concern to allow the bearers of this letter to pass freely without let or hindrance and to provide them such assistance and protection as may be necessary.
>   Please do not hesitate to contact myself at any time for any further information in this regard.
>   We thank you in advance for your assistance and cooperation.
>   Yours sincerely
>   [Signed]
>   Chairman of the Islamic Centre of South Arlington, USA

It warned that under no circumstances should cash be handed to an official at the airport. Couriers should head straight for the Taliban consulate and hand the money over to the consul-general. As well as the consul's name, it even gave the address of the building and a telephone number, including a phone number for the embassy in Islamabad, in case there should be any problems. Calling from a public call box to make an appointment before travelling was preferable, to avoid the risk of monitoring by intelligence agencies inside Pakistan. The minimum donation was $20,000.

> Once you meet the Consul, hand over the money to him in cash and he will issue you with an official receipt from the Taliban Islamic Movement of Afghanistan in whatever name you wish. In this meeting, you will also have the opportunity to request anything specific you would like the money to be used for (if possible), ask questions about their current needs and perhaps arrange a visit into Afghanistan if you have time.

Azzam really came into prominence when it started to provide a near real-time flow of 'news' from the frontlines in Afghanistan. I put news in quotation marks because there was very little that was authentic about it. There were wild claims about hundreds of US soldiers who'd been slaughtered by al-Qaeda/Taliban forces and whose bodies were being secretly stockpiled in giant freezers inside an airbase in Pakistan to avoid American national panic at the sight of lots of body-bags being flown back home and shown from all angles by the 24-hour rolling news media.

One report released the names of Britons who'd reportedly been captured while fighting US forces in Afghanistan – all of them were false – while the USA was secretly using chemical weapons, supposedly. Following a spate of helicopter accidents, I wouldn't have been surprised to see an announcement that Taliban scientists had finally perfected the tractor beam, or the jet pack.

Another report claimed that a British woman had killed six soldiers in a suicide-bomb attack during the uprising of al-Qaeda fighters at the Qala-i-Janghi fort in Afghanistan:

> In Mazar-i-Sharif, a Muslim sister from Britain detonated explosives wrapped around her waist in a martyrdom operation, killing two American and four [Northern] Alliance troops. She had been captured by Alliance troops and was being taken in a car with American soldiers for interrogation when she detonated a belt of explosives strapped around her waist. Her captors did not discover the belt, thinking she was pregnant.

It was referring to the incident where al-Qaeda prisoners overpowered their captors at the fort, which was being used as a prison. CIA operative Johnny 'Mike' Spann was killed during the uprising and a long siege ensued, until John Walker Lindh (the 'American Taliban') and a handful of survivors finally emerged, blackened, from the basement of the fort. Northern Alliance troops had tried to flood it with water, then burning oil, in an attempt to smoke out the remaining diehards. The area was swarming with media and there had been reports of two suicide bombings, including a grenade attack that injured ITN journalist Andrea Catherwood, though a female suicide bomber was not specifically mentioned.

The story went on to claim that the Koran encourages women to fight jihad and pointed out that female suicide bombers had been used by Islamic groups in the past. It referred to: 'Shaheedah Hawaa Barayev . . . martyred recently in Chechnya during a solo martyrdom operation in which 27 Russians were killed and numerous others injured.'

In the wake of the 9/11 attacks, a civilian Western jihad research community had sprung up, and some among them were irked by the apparent lack of official action against websites such as this and decided to bring people-power to bear in the matter. A researcher called Jonathan Galt, for instance, described Azzam as 'the queen termite of all jihad sites'. An organised campaign of letter-writing to companies hosting the website resulted in a long game, as one company pulled the plug on the site and it re-emerged elsewhere, and the cycle went on. Apparently feeling the heat after being chased around the Net, the operators claimed to have thrown in the towel and posted a farewell message. It said that audio-visual materials produced by them would soon be available from the Maktabah Al-Ansar bookshop in Birmingham, which was also distributing recordings of inflammatory sermons given by Hamza.

The tale had even reached the ears of *Newsweek*, and it was the first indication that officialdom had started to stir from its slumbers. The magazine reported in December 2001 that British and US intelligence sources believed that photos and graphics on the site might be embedded with secret coded messages and instructions. It also reported that European computer hackers had found a subscription list on Azzam's German site that included the email address of Said Bahaji, a fugitive who was believed to be a member of the 9/11 cell based in Hamburg, Germany.

The site soon became highly notorious, but little was known about who was actually operating it. Some insight into the nature of Azzam's audience came a few years later, when a contact flagged up a link in an email. He'd found out that the visitor statistics to one main UK militant discussion site had been left open to public access. Normally, this potentially sensitive information would be password-protected, but the site administrator had forgotten to do that.

A government-sponsored study later estimated that there were around 10,000 hard-core al-Qaeda supporters in the UK and the traffic figures seemed to back that. That's not to say that they were all terrorists, far from it, but there was an extensive support network available. Scale that up and it wasn't difficult to appreciate the size of the audience that was being reached and the support that bin Laden now enjoyed globally. And these sites appeared to be expanding in number exponentially.

The UK discussion site, which was registered to a probably false address in Ilford, east London, was one of the main distributors of Azzam articles. Its statistics revealed that it had over 30,000 visitors in the previous month and 3,000 external websites linked to it. The numbers would have been more impressive had it not been abandoned as a main venue of discussion for British jihadis a few months previously, due to concerns that the site was being monitored by the Security Service. It had been the first site on the Web to publish bin Laden statements on at least two occasions.

The people on the site, who had included Abu Hamza in the past, appeared to know that they'd been rumbled and were under observation. One recent posting was on the subject of 'Why I Support Sheikh Usama bin Laden'. In response, a fellow user said: 'Brothers, I totally agree with you, but would like to advise you to find somewhere else where to discuss these issues. This Web forum is not what it used to be anymore. It is dangerous to talk or discuss these issues in here.'

By 2002, Azzam Publications had ceased to be the centre of the jihad propaganda drive and it faded from the lexicon – until the arrest of a 30-year-old Briton on 5 August 2004 in South Kensington on terrorism charges. Babar Ahmad, from Tooting in south London, was taken into custody on an American extradition warrant to face allegations of supporting terrorist organisations. The 39-page warrant claimed that he administered and operated Azzam Publication's websites on a Web server based in Connecticut and so the case fell under US jurisdiction.

The charge sheet started by alleging that from around 1998 until 2003, Ahmad:

> did unlawfully and wilfully combine, conspire, confederate, and agree with others to provide material support and resources to persons, groups, and organizations (including the Taliban and Chechen Mujahideen groups led by Ibn Khattab and Shamil Basayev), and to conceal and disguise the nature, location, source and ownership of such material support and resources, knowing and intending they were to be used in preparation for and in carrying out a violation of Title 18, United States Code, Section 956 (conspiracy to kill, maim, or damage property in a foreign country) . . .

That wasn't the end of it, either; there was also aiding/abetting/causing the commission of a federal offence, involvement in money-laundering, providing material support to terrorists, conspiring to kill people in a foreign country and conspiracy to break economic sanctions.

Ahmad, described as 'working with computers' at Imperial College London, was said to be entirely responsible for administering and maintaining the content of the Azzam website. The testimony of US Department of Homeland Security special agent and computer investigative specialist Craig Bowling was used in the warrant to outline the evidence against him. As well as operating the sites and soliciting cash donations, Ahmad was accused of laundering money by transferring funds from the United States to the Taliban and Chechen Mujahideen 'in support of the military and violent operations'.

He said Internet domain name and registration documents were routed through a post-office box number in west London and that his enquires had established that it had been in use since 1994. It was rented under the name 'D. Karim'. That was also the service address for a company that Ahmad had set up, called Optica Import Export Limited. The agent noted that Imperial College had confirmed that he was a student at this time and he and a fellow student named Karim Dallal were based in the same halls of residence.

When Ahmad's locked room at the university was raided, they found documents recording payments for Internet services made out in the name of 'Dr Karim'. The money order used was obtained from

Barclays Bank in Portman Square, London, where Ahmad also maintained an account for another company he'd set up, called Psychro.

Special agent Bowling also obtained records from two Internet service providers (ISPs) and claimed that these proved that Ahmad administered the Azzam sites, as log file entries from one ISP showed that administrative access to Azzam.com had been obtained by someone using an Imperial College Web server. One account, though registered to his company Optica, was paid for on Ahmad's personal MasterCard from May 1998 to August 2001.

British law enforcement authorities had later found a deleted 'electronic version of a letter' in his office (Room 419 in the 'Hut') at Imperial's Visualisation Centre, which discussed the registration of a mirror site – a cloned copy of a website operating on a separate Web server – called Qoqaz.net. The letter showed that, according to the Americans, he was using the aliases 'Dr D. Karim' and 'Ms Palsemo' to administer and maintain the site.

When the computers in his office were examined, investigators found that he was making heavy use of encryption when operating the site. In their report, the investigators pointed to this as a possible indication of guilt, as the sole use of such software is to prevent monitoring by third parties. It sounds damning on paper, but technically I knew that this wasn't a slam dunk. Encryption systems are also used by innocent members of the public, normally freedom-of-speech advocates, who object to the possibility that governments may be systematically monitoring their electronic communications.

Data on a hard drive recovered from Ahmad's office was also protected by an encryption program and, when it was decrypted by the authorities, Web pages and documents relating to Azzam.com were found there. A software program that's used for creating website pages – Dreamweaver – was also on the same hard disk. Further examination showed that it was last used to create a page dedicated to the memory of an Azzam correspondent who was killed during fighting between al-Qaeda/Taliban and the US/Northern Alliance at Tora Bora in Afghanistan.

The testimony of the DHS agent also highlighted passages from a section on the site that explained the purpose of Azzam Publications:

Azzam Publications has been set up for the purpose of propagating the call for jihad among the Muslims who are sitting down, ignorant of this vital duty . . . Thus the purpose of Azzam Publications is to 'incite the believers' and also secondly to raise some money for the brothers.

Written in a question-and-answer format, the website continued: 'What can I do to help jihad and the Mujahideen?' The answer was: 'Obviously the best way of helping Jihad and the Mujahideen is by actually going to the lands of jihad and physically fighting . . .'. It also went on to spell out that those who could not participate in fighting could support the Mujahideen by raising money or by providing support infrastructure. The Q&A section included Osama bin Laden's now infamous 1996 statement 'Declaration of War against the Americans Occupying the Land of the Two Holy Mosques'.

I recognised the next bit. It was the guide to jihad training that I'd seen on the site three years earlier, and the charge sheet was quoting large chunks of the document. I'd more than an inkling at the time that it was a bit near the wire, so it was satisfying to see my suspicions confirmed.

There was also the mention of an imminent US strike against the Taliban using chemical weapons, and the document quoted from an appeal for help, including 'large quantities of gas masks (in tens of thousands) and NBC warfare suits to the Taliban via the Taliban Embassies in Pakistan'. It also covered the guide for cash couriers that I'd seen just after 9/11. I'd tried to sell a story about that, but there was little interest, as most people felt that the Taliban's days were well and truly numbered.

The US document stated that these were posted to Azzam and its mirror site, Qoqaz.net, by an unnamed individual residing in New Jersey, USA, who by late 2001 was working as the American administrator of the sites. Agent Bowling said:

Therefore, it is evident that Ahmad worked in concert with this individual to maintain the continued operation of the Azzam sites, through the use of mirror sites, when the administrators of Azzam sites shut down the Azzam.com site after 9/11. I believe that this US individual's participation in the effort to continue the existence of Azzam website content in another form through the use of mirror sites demonstrates that a concerted effort existed between the administrators of Azzam, including Ahmad, and individuals in the USA and others to further the goals of Azzam, that is, to solicit funds for blocked organisations, namely the Taliban and the Chechen Mujahideen, in an effort to support their goals.

In spite of the site's disclaimer about being unable to accept offers of funding or assistance, investigators found that one email reply to an offer of a shipment of gas masks for the Taliban said: 'Instructions later this weekend.'

Another March 2001 offer to supply hand-warmers to the Chechen Mujahideen had been rebuffed. The guy making the offer was put out, as he claimed to be an associate of Shamil Basayev. The reply from an Azzam email account said: 'Via trusted contacts, we did make contact with Shamil Basayev himself, mentioned all your names and details to him and even showed your photographs to him, but he said he did not know you. That is what we based our information on.'

Agent Bowling noted that copies of messages sent from that email account had been found on a floppy disk among Ahmad's belongings in a room he used at his parents' house in Tooting. Azzam's rejection of the offer of hand-warmers was a mistake, because the email making the offer was traced to an individual in Connecticut who had made donations of over $10,000 to an Islamic charity called the Benevolence International Foundation, which was classified as an organisation funding terrorist groups in 2002. The charity's records showed that the donations included a $5,000 donation for 'Chechnya hand-warmers'.

One recovered hard drive included a database of customer orders for products sold on the site, which were mainly jihad-related tapes, CDs and videos. Ahmad had also apparently had a file-destroying session shortly after 9/11 and electronically 'shredded' hundreds of documents. They included a variety of Web pages and the instructions on how to transport cash to the Taliban. The hard disk also contained a letter written to Barclays Bank concerning his company bank accounts and details of three more, non-public, Azzam email accounts.

The indictment said: 'They contained correspondence concerning the shipment of equipment and funds to the Taliban and Chechen mujahideen, the vetting of personnel seeking to supply the Chechen mujahideen, and the operation of Azzam Publications websites.' A

December 2001 message found on a floppy disk in his office discussed transporting night-vision goggles to Pakistan:

> Find out if there is any secure way to receive things like night-visions into Pak. These things are available, but there is no safe way to send them to Pak at the moment. We want to air freight them and need an address etc. Can you get that?

It also discussed the establishment of another Azzam.com mirror site, waaqiah.com, to be maintained from Afghanistan to support the Taliban. A subsequent message, dated 2 December 2001, contained reports on the state of hostilities in Afghanistan and revealed the locations of Taliban forces. It contained a conversation which used coded references to Afghanistan ('Aberdeen') and the Taliban ('students').

> Q: b) Routes in and out, how easy or difficult, who can go, what about coming out, what are the risks, how risky, can someone pay their way in or out?
>
> A: For our bros, there are 100% routes, they can easily reach Shameem Alam's people except blackies.
>
> However, it is not advised for anyone to go on his own. Suppose, even if he has entered Aberdeen, he would not be knowing whether he would be welcomed by Student, or an American dog!
>
> If one os [sic] going with some expert (who knows the ways), there wont be any risks. However, this should be kept in mind that Aberdeen is at war, so there must be some risks always (bombs, encounters with the enemy).
> . . .
>
> Q: d) Do they need people, what sort of people do they need, do they need doctors?
>
> A: Yeah, they do need doctors, and out [sic] doctor can directly reach to Shameem's people. Fighters are always welcomed, though I haven't asked them specifically for fighters.
>
> Q: e) What equipment do they need? Is there a route for equipment such as tents, torches, night vision? What is the route and what are the risks of this route?
>
> A: Night visions are VERY important, as Students and Arabs, both are concentrating on special covert operations.
> . . .

Q: g) What about sending money, do they need it, how can it be sent?

A: Send it to Pakistan, and we will send it through Abdullaah (cousin of Kashif Bhai).

. . .

Q: j) What about routes from Iran, are there any? Is it safe?

A: Couldn't be able to ask, will tell you soon.

The headline charge was based on information found on another floppy disk on the same shelf in the bedroom. It contained a password-protected file dated 12 April 2001 that discussed a US Navy battle group, each of its member ships (including the guided-missile destroyer USS *Benfold*), 'the specifications and assignments of each ship, the battle group's planned movements in the Gulf, and a drawing of the group's planned formation as it passed through the Straits of Hormuz'. The document specifically noted that the battle group was tasked with enforcing sanctions against Iraq and conducting operations against Afghanistan and al-Qaeda. It also contained notes on ways that the ships might be attacked – including using rocket-propelled grenades fired from small inflatable boats: 'Navy officials have confirmed that the battle group composition, the dates and location of the movements of this battle group in the documents are accurate and were classified at the time the document appears to have been written.'

The sensational conclusion was that Ahmad had a sympathetic mole aboard USS *Benfold* and that they appeared to be conspiring to plan a USS *Cole*-style attack against the ship. One message from his informant read:

> Weakness
> They have nothing to stop a small craft with RPG etc, except their Seals' stinger missiles.
>
> Deploy ops to Gulf 29 April–04 October
>
> 29 APRIL is more likely the day through the Straits. For the whole of March is tax free – a moral booster. Many sailors do not like the Gulf.
>
> Please destroy message.

At his subsequent court appearance, it emerged that Ahmad was arrested by police in a raid in December 2003 and documents detailing formations of US warships in the Gulf were found near him. Despite this, he was released without charge after six days of questioning and detailed searches of three family properties. He claimed he was beaten up by police officers during the raid, though the Crown Prosecution Service eventually dropped the case, citing lack of evidence.

At his initial court hearing, when asked if he understood the charges against him, Ahmad replied that 'it was a bit confusing', though he declined to agree to be extradited. During a later, November 2004, court appearance, the barrister representing the US government also alleged that he had tried to obtain 5,000 tonnes of sulphur phosphate during 1997 and 1998.

In any event, the most striking aspect about the whole saga is the extraordinary glimpse it gives into how the cyber-terror underground operates. Ahmad's exact role, if any, hardly matters in this respect, and no one has suggested that the evidence against him is fabricated.

This is precisely what I meant when I said the significance of something that is on the screen right in front of your eyeballs just doesn't compute sometimes. Who would have believed that such a deep and widespread web of international mystery lay beneath one poorly designed website? I was curious to finally see the face of the unknown operator at long last, when the TV news showed Ahmad being led into court.

As I've said, the main concern among watchers of Azzam.com in the months after 9/11 was that the authorities were seemingly content to let the operation continue unhindered. This concern amounted to fury in some quarters. It seemed that it just wasn't a priority with the cops and the spooks, and that massive volumes of jihadi information were circulating on the Net without being monitored or analysed.

I erred in favour of this theory, which was bound to be compounded by the Islamic learning-curve problem that everyone was struggling with, I figured. It wasn't until November 2002 that I actually saw hard evidence that something along these lines might have been happening. It came in the form of leaked intelligence documents that were posted on a website. My eyes bulged in anticipation and I started feeling that 'Bingo!' feeling when I saw that a new addition to the site was marked 'restricted' and 'UK EYES ONLY'.

The first document didn't look that promising, at first. It contained the minutes of a meeting of something called the

Whitehall PMC Group, which was held on 16 November 1999. It was only when I scanned down the list of 15 attendees that it started to get interesting, as I could see that the MoD, Customs & Excise, Security Service, Secret Intelligence Service and Government Communications Headquarters (GCHQ) were represented. The PMC Group, I quickly learnt, was a new government unit that monitored the activities of private military companies – mercenaries.

The meeting began by indicating that the working party had been set up to prevent sanctions-busting by British mercenaries, though the scope was wide and the group could draw on a whole variety of resources, including 'Sigint' (signals intelligence) from GCHQ and information collected by the Security Service (MI5) and the Secret Intelligence Service (MI6). There was some discussion about the implications of setting up a database to collate information from all the varying sources, though the agencies argued that a legal steer was needed first, because of human-rights legislation. GCHQ's representative said the Act was already affecting the way that it could store information. The Customs & Excise man pointed out that court cases would have to be dropped if potential evidence could not be disclosed to the defence team. A defendant might also argue that the government had tacitly approved of his activities if it had not taken action on information in the database.

The MoD said the appropriate software was available off-the-shelf and proposed populating it with ten years' worth of GCHQ reports, two years of CX reports (intelligence bulletins for Cabinet ministers) and all Foreign and Commonwealth Office telegrams from then on in. It was vaguely interesting to get a glimpse inside the secret workings of government machinery, although the first message was the weakest of the batch.

Aside from this wrangling over an IT project, there was a brief but interesting expression of concern about 'non-military sanctions-busting' by mercenary groups in relation to Iraq. There was also a discussion about whether companies involved in mine-clearing operations should be covered, and the MI6 official noted that 'de-mining workers had been implicated in covert intelligence activities in Kosovo'. The first indication that the Azzam jihad recruitment network had come to the attention of the intelligence agencies came in the penultimate paragraph: '14. There was a brief discussion of Chechnya, and allegations that British citizens were going to

Chechnya to fight, inspired by religious convictions. But there was general agreement that this did not come within the PMC group's remit.'

The second document was much more revealing. It was a message from the head of counter-terrorism policy at the Foreign Office to the prime minister's special foreign policy and defence adviser, dated 20 September 2000. The summary was startling: a new computer system, called Fortress, which had been designed to distribute intelligence material, had proved to be *slower than the old paper-based system*. It was a plea for returning to old-fashioned methods, if the system couldn't be fixed.

Fortress had gone live 12 months previously, but substantial problems had arisen and the situation had reached a point where lives were being put in danger. It read:

> These problems have been exacerbated for CTPD [Counter-terrorism Policy Department] because we have attempted (but failed) to use FORTRESS not only as a mechanism to read reports but also in order to take action, particularly where the intelligence has indicated a threat to life.

The core problems were well known, it was argued, as there had been many meetings of a user group and discussion with 'a succession of consultants'. They were at their wits' end, it seems, and the man at the Foreign Office was trying to get the word out to the PM. The stunner came in this paragraph:

> the system is less reliable and often slower than paper distribution: there have been a number of occasions when immediate-threat intelligence arrived too late in CTPD, or did not arrive at all, because of technical hitches. We still receive intelligence well after most OGDs [other government departments]. Vital threat telegrams to our missions overseas have been delayed as a result, causing ambassadorial consternation (as with the pre-summer UBL threat to Brussels)

UBL is, of course, a reference to Usama/Osama bin Laden. The reference to Brussels seemed to be a reference to a plot to attack NATO headquarters, as I later found a report about German intelligence monitoring a group of militant Islamists who were working on a long-standing plan to bomb NATO. With 3,000 Americans working there, it was a prime al-Qaeda target.

The system made 'crisis-management meetings impossible' and taking action on reports received via the system was 'impractical'. The software had in-built printing constraints as a security feature, so it was impossible for a group of people to sit around a meeting table with paper copies of a report in front of them. It was 'not in the least user-friendly', meaning that many hours were wasted by simply trying to gain access to reports. It was estimated that it took five times longer to deal with reports – forty were typically dealt with each day – by computer than it did with the paper system.

It ended by complaining that the Foreign Office understood that there was no prospect of the required modifications being made. It then pointed out that the department had to use three different terminals and five different information-retrieval systems. Its operations were being gummed up by information overload.

> 7. I appreciate that the office's IT requirements are not driven by CTPD and that the Board of Management is seeking to optimise FCO systems across the board. But I felt I should warn you that, as far as we in CTPD are concerned, information handling is getting progressively more, not less, difficult.

The third document was dated 5 April 2001 and it suggested that the problems still hadn't been solved. It was a memo by the head of the Balkans desk at the Foreign Office complaining that Fortress reports weren't reaching him, because officials were presumably avoiding having to use it. 'I know Fortress is a pig, but somebody in each Section must go through the Section's material every day,' he said.

Seeing as major government IT projects are almost guaranteed to go ten times over budget, regardless of which party is in power, the mind boggles at the sums that were being spent on secret computer systems – before and after 9/11. This is no place for an analysis of the vagaries of different public procurement methods, mainly because it's very boring, but the important point to make is that the documents confirmed people's gut feeling that the wheels of officialdom were as rusty as we might have supposed.

GCHQ might have been sucking in the raw material like nobody's business, but the process of distribution downstream of that was slower than sending papers in the internal post. The introduction of new technology in this case meant a quantum leap backwards in time. It's simply baffling, unless we're looking at some kind of wilful institutional technophobia within the Civil Service. Even the brief details of discussions about intelligence-sharing between the various agencies were enlightening.

ARK ATTACK

THE FIRST SIGN OF AN AL-QAEDA RESPONSE TO THE US-LED INVASION of Iraq came 12 minutes before the expiration of the American deadline for Saddam to quit the country. President Bush issued an ultimatum on 17 March 2003, giving the dictator and his sons 48 hours to leave the country or face military action. The response came in the form of a strange audio file.

It had been uploaded to al-Qaeda's official home page on the Web. I listened to it and it was a weird mix of singing, chanting and talking in Arabic, all happening simultaneously in parts, and quite unlike previous tapes I'd heard. It was mystical and a bit trippy, even.

The US administration upped the national terror alert status to orange at the start of the war, amid fears that al-Qaeda had prepared retaliatory attacks against the American homeland. The emergence of the tape caused something akin to panic among online jihad-watchers, as it was feared that this was a coded signal of some kind. That concern was heightened by the appearance of messages in chat rooms that flagged up the location of the file, saying that close attention should be paid to the length of the recording. It was exactly three minutes and thirty seconds long and it was suggested that this was a coded instruction of some kind. Perhaps it was the pre-arranged go-ahead for sleeper cells to proceed with attacks on American soil or, more likely in my view, it related to Iraq somehow. Maybe it was nothing more than a morale-booster for the troops. The length of the tape could have suggested a date of 30 March, but that seemed too crude and obvious. I knew from previous experience that 'Boyd cycle'-type encrypted messages were likely to be used.

Combinations of ones and zeros correspond to pre-agreed terms and can contain enough information to specify the target, location, timing and method of attack in a string of sixteen numbers, like this: 1 111 1100 1 101 0101. These strings can then be easily hidden in the source code of innocent-looking image files and even music tracks.

One of the voices on the recording was suspected of being bin Laden's, not least because the file was titled 'benladen'. Two other, similar tapes emerged a few days later, which fuelled the sleeper-cell activation theory. One contact was convinced that a spectacular attack was on the cards and I could tell that he was getting into something of a frenzy over it, complaining about the authorities being slow to act and risking the annihilation of a major US city. In his estimation: 'It is considered to be a possible threat of terrorism to be committed in the USA. The first [tape] is considered to be a "get ready" signal, the second is considered to have a date associated with it. The third is very possibly the trigger.'

I'm not in the habit of swallowing other people's opinions and I didn't quite buy his unequivocal analysis, though I was forced to agree that I thought there was something strange about it. I'd grown sceptical of these claims, especially when they emerge from people who could be called fear-junkies. They can be found at the highest levels, though.

I'd discovered, from other contacts in the field, that US intelligence agencies were watching the same main jihad discussion sites on the Web that I and others were monitoring. One had noted that the orange alert coincided with the emergence of a flurry of threatening messages on these boards. One of these Arabic sites, because it was so heavily trafficked by Western law enforcement and military visitors, became known as Spook Central.

Even though the chatter could be seen – in theory – by anyone with an Internet connection, these overt communications between al-Qaeda supporters were considered classified information in intelligence circles. There was certainly a heady atmosphere online and it did appear that the war of words had stepped up a gear, with lots of talk such as, 'At last . . . at last', 'great events', 'the destruction of America is near' and 'zero hour approaches'.

The theory that bin Laden's latest tapes contained orders for sleeper cells was apparently confirmed by a self-confessed al-Qaeda member, in a 'statement of clarification' on a site run from London called, coincidentally, The Fortress. He said:

> Praise to Allah, the message of our sheikh and within it
> symbols for all Muslims or Mujahids have been received, in all
> corners of the globe, and in it are instructions that no one but
> members of this organisation can decipher.

'Patience,' he continued, 'relief will come soon, the next blow will
be hurtful, mighty, and in it a confirmation from Allah familiar only
to those that believe in jihad and Mujahids.'

It would have been too tempting to dismiss that as blatant
disinformation, were it not for the passages that followed. The
statement was trying to scotch a rumour that was rife in the ranks
about the nature of the next big target to be hit. It went on to refute
any suggestion that bin Laden had plans to nuke Mecca. The
rationale for this, according to the rumours, was that, assuming he
had access to warheads, Israel would be blamed and the resulting
outrage would result in an instant war with Arab states, and the al-
Qaeda leadership would emerge from the ashes as the new rulers of
the entire Middle East.

> Some cross bearers of the black house [derogatory reference to
> the Bush administration] have alluded that UBL will use WMD
> to destroy the land of the holy twin mosques and everyone on
> it. I swear by Allah, the al-Qaeda cells (the awake ones) in the
> holy lands are as far away as possible from them.

Orders had been given specifying that the 'spilling of Muslim blood'
must be avoided at all costs. He added: 'The holy lands are only part of
al-Qaeda's strategic planning . . . the blow will be, to any cross bearers,
a hurtful one, and it will be far away from pure Muslim blood.'

It reminded supporters that psychological warfare and the
avoidance of direct confrontation with the enemy are part of al-
Qaeda's modus operandi: 'And consequently we reveal the secret of
the delay to the second hit . . . the present quietness of al-Qaeda is
not an inability [to strike], as the enemy imagines or hopes for.'
Operatives were waiting for the start of US military action against
Iraq, which would be the trigger, it stated.

Nothing of great significance happened on sleeper-cell activation
day, 30 March 2003, though it did mark the point at which Saddam's
regime stated to collapse. The elite Republican Guard divisions
surrounding Baghdad were coming under heavy and sustained air
attack and there had been little resistance.

I did, however, try to keep an open mind on the issue of Web-based threat information, as a message on a discussion forum had seemed to portend the al-Qaeda attack on the Paradise Hotel in Mombasa, Kenya, on 28 November 2002. A car bomb driven by three suicide attackers killed fifteen people and injured forty others at the Israeli-owned hotel, and a near-simultaneous attack against an Israeli-chartered passenger jet with two surface-to-air missiles had narrowly failed. The apparent tip-off came in a jihad forum posting, in which someone called 'Aramco Boy' seemed to allude to the pending attacks three days before the event. It read:

> Today, at 6:20 hours, there will be a surprise program, one of the most beautiful I have ever seen over our Qatari channel. Anyone who knows what I mean must tell no one so as to keep the surprise whose content everyone will love. Only Allah knows what I mean. The program forced me to write these lines at great speed and I ask Allah to forgive me and reserve Paradise and not Hell for me. The zero hour has come.

It suggested that a breaking-news event would soon be covered by Al-Jazeera TV and the phrase 'reserve Paradise' looked like a direct reference to the target. Perhaps detracting from this, the actual attacks came three days later and two hours and ten minutes past the suggested time. On the other hand, perhaps there'd been a postponement. Extracting valuable information from the boiling cyber-ether is a tricky business. Prime Minister Tony Blair once illustrated the scale of the task the intelligence services face in this sphere by revealing that Britain sifts through some ten million items of electronic intelligence every day, though it seemed to me that even the latest supercomputers wouldn't have picked up on the Paradise message.

Giving evidence to Congress on 11 February 2003, the then CIA director George Tenet said that one of the indicators that had led to the orange-alert declaration was intercepted chatter about US targets in the region. Here, he may well have been talking about planning for a campaign of sabotage at US bases in the Middle East. It would have been difficult not to have noticed this, as a 2,000-word-long appeal, calling on all Muslims involved in maintaining and servicing these bases to do what they could to gather intelligence for the Mujahideen, had been broadcast across many pro-bin Laden sites. 'This is a demand to our brothers in the air bases who help with directing the airplanes of the crusader invaders to her targets and spreading murder and destruction on our Muslim brothers,' it said.

The appeal contained a long list of examples of how supporters might help, including reporting the locations of offices of American oil companies, the routes of fuel lines, maps of arms dumps, 'any information about concert times in places of entertainment' and details of drinking-water supplies. The statement also called for information on 'important personalities' and soldiers 'whose rank is not below general'. It also says that a team based in Qatar – where US Central Command was located – had been specifically tasked with monitoring the movements of 'the pig [US general] Tommy Franks', who was directing the war on Iraq.

I contacted a cyber-terrorism expert, Professor Vincent Parrillo, at William Paterson University in New Jersey, USA, for an impartial opinion on what I was seeing. I supplied all the offending material to him and he got back to me a day later. 'In my opinion, all of the site's content, both overt and implied, point to an al-Qaeda connection,' he said. 'The content of the message is virtually a call to arms, demanding that those working at or near airports or near airbases take action.'

He said his feeling was that intelligence agencies were struggling to keep up with terrorist activities on the Internet: 'Without intelligence-gathering that is way beyond our present capabilities, we can't be certain to what extent al-Qaeda uses the Internet. We would be foolish to underestimate their use of this means, however, as it is such an efficient, effective and economical means to communicate.'

Of the many potential threats I saw during this time, one in particular did strike me as being very significant. That's perhaps because there was no hair-raising rhetoric, just a technical exchange of information and brief comments about the aircraft carriers USS *Kitty Hawk* and HMS *Ark Royal*. The discussion centred on the best methods for attacking these ships.

Detailed technical plans of the layout of the *Kitty Hawk* and information on its capabilities had been posted, which had been procured by 'Osama's department', and there was a comment saying that similar information on the USS *Nimitz* would be forthcoming. One supporter suggested that it would be difficult to get close to enemy ships with small inflatable boats and that any attacks might have to be launched from a distance.

Taking an aircraft carrier out of action would be a huge

propaganda victory and a spectacular demonstration of the prowess of the network and its ability to disseminate information – too widely for the likings of some. A follow-up message urged silence on the subject and said that 'the sheikh' asks 'for a muzzling of the shrill mouths'.

It was the threat to the British ship, the *Ark Royal*, that was of most interest to me, as my main market involved UK-oriented news. One of the images on the site looked like a surveillance photograph of the vessel, with annotations in Arabic and English. It showed four dark-skinned men, one with a short beard, crouching down on the shoreline watching it sail towards them. An arrow was superimposed on the picture, pointing from a small boat moored near the shoreline towards the carrier, alongside a note saying '100 metres'. Above one of the men was written: 'The Prince'. The significance was immediately obvious: it was illustrating the same method of attack as that used to cripple the USS *Cole* in Aden, Yemen, on 12 October 2000 – a suicide bomb attack using a small inflatable boat packed with explosives. At the time, *Ark Royal*, with a crew of 800, was leading a British naval task-force of 15 ships and heading for the Gulf via the Suez Canal.

This looked serious. I tried to extract every scrap of information from that image, even to the extent of looking through many archive images of the vessel to see if I could figure out where the image was taken. The only clue was a landscape of low hills seen on the horizon and I was trying to see if I could match that up with a location. The four crouching men had their backs to the camera, so identification of the potential attackers wasn't possible.

I did find a very similar, recent image of the ship off the Scottish coast with low hills in the background, but it was difficult to be certain of a match as the website image had a brownish tint to it. It looked like a desert location, maybe the Suez Canal, though that may just have been down to the colour balance. It was also hard to be sure that it actually was the *Ark Royal*, as the ship is very similar in profile to HMS *Invincible* and HMS *Illustrious*. If the image had been taken in the UK, the implications were enormous, as it would suggest that a cell was conducting surveillance operations against military installations and reporting the findings to groups planning attacks in the Middle East.

The story was definitely sellable and I set about preparing some copy to go along with the picture, along the lines of 'Al-Qaeda plots Ark Royal suicide attack'.

I rang my newspaper contact the day after the story was published, which quoted a Ministry of Defence spokesman saying they were aware of the threat to the ships and were fully prepared. He had some hot news for me. They'd just taken a call from MoD officials and were now answering questions about the source material and its origins. We both knew what this meant and we didn't have to say it: the MoD didn't know about this specific threat, despite the impression they'd given, and they urgently wanted the details.

Two weeks later, Rear Admiral David Snelson, the chief of British naval operations in the region, told journalists at a press conference in Bahrain that the threat of small speedboats packed with explosives was 'uppermost in his mind'. Coalition ships had already fired warning shots at boats that had approached naval vessels at speed, he said. 'There are a lot of small high-speed boats operating in the region and it is one of the challenges to know whether they are a smuggler, a fishing boat or a high-speed boat with hostile intent.'

Six weeks after the original story was published, it was reported that two plots to attack Navy ships had been thwarted. Two tugboats, each loaded with 68 mines, were seized by Coalition troops in Iraq's Khor Abdallah estuary, near the southern port of Umm Qasr. The *Ark Royal* was anchored just out of sight, offshore of the port, though at the time its location was classified. It was also reported that Iranian gunboats had intercepted an Iraqi speedboat packed with half a tonne of explosives. Three other boats escaped during a confrontation in the mouth of the Shatt al-Arab river, which divides Iran and Iraq.

I returned to the website where I'd first picked up the story. The people there were absolutely furious and screaming dark promises of revenge, as it appeared that their best-laid plans to sink the flagship of the Royal Navy had been wasted.

The head of news at a Sunday newspaper phoned. I was sworn to secrecy before he'd spill the beans. They'd had a tip-off about the location of bin Laden and my help was wanted in confirming the story. After I promised that his secret would be safe with me, he confided. They'd had information indicating that bin Laden was cut off and surrounded by troops in a town in Pakistan. His capture was potentially imminent and this came from a trusted source. A wonderful scoop looked to be on the cards. My job was simply to find out as much about the town as possible and perhaps procure a satellite image of the place. I was a bit taken aback, especially when he gave me the precise map coordinates. 'The source must be good,' I thought.

The town was located in the Hindu Kush mountain range, in the remote north-west frontier province of Pakistan, on the border with Afghanistan. It was in one of the remotest places on the planet, at an altitude of 1,500 metres and inaccessible by road during winter. I knew that the mountains there, which reach heights that exceed 3,000 metres, had long been held up as ideal hideout territory for bin Laden.

If the information was correct, he'd slipped the net somehow, after being surrounded in Balochistan in the south, and had relocated to the northern end of the border, close to Kashmir. It occurred to me that he might have access to a helicopter, remembering that US defence secretary Donald Rumsfeld had hinted at that at the start of the war in Afghanistan.

As I was browsing through images of the target area and trying to get a handle on the geography, I was surprised to see that it was green and lush. It was on the route of the Silk Road out of China and it looked like a very calm and peaceful place: sweeping meadows traversed by glacial rivers and streams and overlooked by gigantic brownish mountain slopes – something of a high-altitude Eden. He'd certainly picked an ideal spot.

More than that, the appearance of the place looked very similar to the images of bin Laden in the latest video of him. That had shown him making his way down a rocky and grassy slope with the aid of a walking stick and with a blanket or shawl thrown over one shoulder. It looked as if it had been shot in a new location and in spring-like conditions. The general lushness of the vegetation and, in particular, a peculiar type of tree seen in the background made it look very much like the place I was concentrating on.

There had been little information prior to the tip-off to link al-Qaeda or its leaders to this place, beyond suggestions that he could be hiding in the mountain range that loomed over the town. To the north-east was Nanga Parbat, the ninth-highest mountain in the world, at 8,125 metres; to the north was the Pamir range, with peaks reaching 7,500 metres and home to abandoned Soviet inter-continental nuclear-missile silos.

Bin Laden would have been among his natural constituents in this location, as it was populated by the Pashtun people, who lived there semi-autonomously, as even the Pakistani government found it almost too remote for proper administration. Many members of the Taliban came from Pashtun stock and they operated a code of silence on the Taliban/al-Qaeda issue. I searched around to see if there was any jihadist chatter mentioning the place, but there was nothing. There was more talk about the place in the mountaineering community than anywhere else. Explorers now had to take unspecified security precautions, as there was the possibility of being kidnapped or killed should they accidentally stumble across bin Laden's entourage or those of other senior fugitives in the region.

The only thing that caught my eye was details of a disused railway line that seemed to wind its way up into the mountains. Maybe he was using that and sheltering in tunnels, I thought. I didn't have much luck on the satellite photos either; the company wouldn't budge from its five-working-days procurement estimate, as the town hadn't been catalogued, which was no good at all. Still, I packaged up what I could and pinged over some notes and images as my contribution.

The story was splashed on the front page, under the headline: 'BIN LADEN TRAPPED LIKE A RAT'. It quoted US intelligence sources as saying that they believed they had him surrounded and that elite SAS teams were involved in the operation. Bin Laden and 50 bodyguards were said to be 'boxed in'. He was believed to be with Taliban leader Mullah Omar and there was 'no chance of escape'.

The US National Security Agency had even positioned a geo-stationary spy satellite above the 'bin Laden box'. The story appeared to die a death after that, as I saw no follow-ups or chatter speculating on what was going on there. I wasn't involved in following developments, as it wasn't my story, though it turned out that bin Laden had managed to somehow teleport himself out of the danger area and regain his invisibility once again.

One account of where bin Laden may have gone appeared a couple of months later. A Pakistani newspaper reported that FBI agents operating in the country had 'got wind of' a planned meeting between bin Laden and the Afghan warlord Gulbuddin Hekmatyar, who'd recently formed an alliance with the remnants of the Taliban. They knew the general area where it was due to take place, though not the exact location. An FBI reconnaissance team, composed of one male and one female agent dressed in traditional garb, went into the target area looking for signs of activity. Despite touring the place for several days looking for signs of the venue, they found nothing.

It was said to be a US-led initiative and their Pakistani partners were sceptical but obliged to assist.

By then it was May 2003 and I was fielding requests for information on another great fugitive: Saddam Hussein. He'd decided to 'do a bin Laden' after one final public appearance as the president of Iraq as American troops were about to enter Baghdad. During the first Gulf War, he was constantly driven around the city in a battered old taxi to foil attempts to target him with cruise missiles. That wasn't an option this time and the best guess was that he'd been making his way cross-country towards his home town of Tikrit, to the north of the capital.

The comparison with bin Laden was apt, because he'd started releasing open letters to the Iraqi people and audiotapes calling for resistance against the Western aggressors. They were pretty clumsy and lacked the craftsmanship of bin Laden. He obviously wasn't accompanied by a speech writer so, being the author of several action-packed novels in which the noble dictator always heroically fends off the invading infidels, he let loose the writer in him and the results were cheesy and sometimes incoherent. His former publisher later made similar comments about the quality of his book manuscripts.

Even bin Laden was furious about the ease with which the country had been invaded. A 600-word letter was circulated among leading militant Islamic websites at the start of the previous month and it berated the people of Kuwait for allowing troops to pour over the border into Iraq unimpeded. It seems that the previous call for the provision of intelligence on Coalition operations and to conduct sabotage behind enemy lines had failed. There were no major incidents, just two minor blasts – one near the HQ of the US Fifth Fleet in Bahrain and another similar blast near US Central Command in Qatar, neither of which caused any injuries.

One jihadi message I had seen, in January 2003, named 73 specific military targets in the Gulf, including US and UK ports, airports and military bases, along with precise coordinates, maps and satellite photos. Ironically, most of the targeting information was freely available on American websites. There was one link to amazingly detailed 3D, zoom-able plans of the building in Bahrain which housed the commanders of the US Fifth Fleet.

A subsequent 1,800-word statement, which included tactical guidance from bin Laden's deputy Ayman al-Zawahiri, called for disruptive attacks using rockets, car bombs and suicide bombers. Bin Laden was outraged at the inaction:

> I am doing my best to choose the words of my message so that it is not misunderstood. They [Coalition troops] are not only killing the Iraqis, but also they are targeting our Islam which is their prominent enemy and their horrible nightmare. I and the Muslims beg you not to be a bridge for the criminals and killers; do not be a means through which your Muslim brothers get slaughtered; do not be a path for murdering Islam. They do not kill Saddam; they are killing your brothers, our brothers.

He added:

> Have you thought about the destiny of the Muslim nation if their criminal plan succeeds? Can you imagine what will happen to our Islamic and Arab identity if they achieve their goals? We beg you brothers – we call you in the name of Allah to preserve Islam; do not devastate this religion but be a fortress for Islam, and do not be a path for the enemies to destroy our religion.

The letter ended: 'Finally, do not forget to pray for your brothers in the wounded Iraq.' It was signed: 'Your brother, Osama bin Laden'.

One early rumour had it that Saddam and many leadership figures, including his two sons, had quit the country altogether and had assembled in a luxury resort hotel in Syria. Suspicions that they'd fled there were heightened when the SAS captured Saddam's half-brother, Watban Ibrahim al-Tikriti, close to the Syrian border. There were also reports of long queues of black armour-plated limousines at military airports in Syria waiting to spirit away Iraqi Baath Party officials.

The precise location of the hotel was the Cote d'Azur De Cham resort in the Mediterranean port town of Latakia, 250 km north-west of the Syrian capital Damascus. The unsourced speculation, which had surfaced in the Canadian press, claimed that the regime had pre-booked the entire development before the outbreak of hostilities and that security there had been beefed up by the recent arrival of Syrian army commando units.

I was asked to check it out. I thought I'd take the bull by the horns and telephone the hotel. The idea that Saddam was sunning himself in his favourite Hawaiian shirt and sipping pina coladas on the beach while US troops were running around pointlessly trying to find him in Iraq was an amusing mental image, if nothing else.

It was an establishment befitting a dictator, with 1,600 rooms and a private, 600 metre-long beach that was accessible via a tunnel that ran from the main building. The family villa of president Bashar al-Assad was a short walk away and it was a popular destination for wealthy Russian businessmen. Notable former residents of Latakia included one of bin Laden's wives, Nagwa, and his son Omar. They had left three weeks before the 9/11 attacks.

I found the number, called, and waited for an answer. Someone answered after a couple of rings and muttered something that I couldn't understand.

'Hello? Do you speak English?' I enquired.

'Yes, yes, how can I help you?' said a female voice.

'I'd like to be put through to President Hussein's suite, please.'

'Who?'

'Saddam Hussein, the leader of Iraq.'

There was a pause. 'There is no one here by that name,' she said.

'Are you sure? I was told that Saddam and his colleagues had booked rooms there.'

'No, it is not correct. They are not here.'

I was straining to try to detect any signs that she was lying or concealing something, but there weren't any. If she was, then she was well trained, because there was just a consistent bored tone to her voice. In fact, far from being booked out, it sounded like the place was half-empty, as she proceeded to try to sell me a room for $180 a night. I politely declined the offer and practically had to fend her off before I terminated the call.

'Well, that's the end of that one,' I thought, and relayed my findings back to the newspaper in an email titled 'Costa del Saddam'. There was nowhere else to go, really, and I just didn't get the feeling that it was a goer from the outset, anyway. There was much better information about Saddam Hussein on the jihad boards. There was little love between the Baathists and the global jihadists. The jihadis regarded Saddam with as much disdain as Westerners: as the father of all gangsters and mass murderer of a countless number of innocent Muslims. His belated rediscovery of Islam in the run-up to the invasion was met with derision, though criticism was slightly muted now, in acknowledgement of the fact that he was at least calling for resistance to occupation. Even so, he was regarded as yesterday's man and it was no skin off their noses if he got captured. He was usually talked of in an aloof manner with barely concealed distaste.

One frequent correspondent had been posting regular updates on Spook Central about Saddam's activities, and they were surprisingly detailed, to the point that it really did appear to me that they were based on observations from people on the ground. A 2,000-word summary published on 2 May 2003 reported that Saddam was still alive and he'd managed to assemble a militia of loyalists that comprised 40,000 men. They were said to be preparing for 'Vietnamese-style guerrilla warfare'.

The insurgents planned to start a jihad against the invaders on 17 July – to mark the 35th anniversary of the revolution that swept the Baath Party to power. Saddam and his two equally psychopathic sons, Qusay and Uday, were directing the 'new military command group' and moving between prepared hideouts dotted around the countryside. It even named three other senior regime figures who were travelling with them: Iraq's vice president Taha Yasin Ramadan; former defence minister Sultan Hashim Ahmad; and Latif Nusayyif Jasim, deputy chairman of the Baath Party Military Bureau.

The updates even included targeting information. The ousted regime leaders were said to be following the course of the Tigris river, moving between Tikrit and Mosul to the north of Baghdad. Another of the articles said:

> Saddam Hussein and his group represent a secret leadership . . . which is devoted to putting the final touches on a plan for a great encounter with British and American forces in Iraq. He controls secret caches that contain weapons, military equipment and foodstuffs – enough for a long and bitter conflict.

Saddam was reportedly extremely bitter about the surrender of his son-in-law Jamal Mustafa Abdallah Sultan al-Tikriti, his deputy chief of tribal affairs, whom he blamed for playing a key role in organising the capitulation of Iraqi forces.

The information did appear to have a whiff of truth about it, though there was no easy way of checking the claims at this stage. Soon after, I saw that British troops in Basra had uncovered a secret militia base stocked with weapons and ammunition. Saddam was plotting his comeback, though one of his first pronouncements from hiding was to deny involvement in a one-billion-dollar bank raid. The Iraqi Central Bank had been plundered as the government started to fold and the USA was pointing the finger at the now ex-president. He issued a handwritten letter in response, complete with numerous crossed-out mistakes, blaming 'criminal Americans and British' for the theft and claiming that 'Bush and Blair are thieves and killers': 'The invaders have created a state of insecurity in Iraq and the theft and murder and rape and plunder came with them. The shame will remain with them and will not escape the punishment of Allah.'

Perhaps his hotel booking had been cancelled at the last minute, because he branded the Syrian regime 'traitors' for cooperating with 'the CIA and Britain' and informing on leadership figures who had sought refuge there, before continuing on to rail against other governments in the region – Iran, Jordan, Kuwait, Saudi Arabia and Turkey – for aiding the invasion.

The letter, which was published first on the Internet, ended by claiming that it is now the 'religious duty' of Iraqi citizens to resist the occupying Coalition forces. 'We have fought with virility and honour and glory and dignity, and we will not be defeated as long as belief in Allah is in our souls; and the jihad remains our choice and resistance our answer,' he said.

He was certainly trying to ape the authoritative and statesman-like tone that was the hallmark of bin Laden, though Saddam was over-egging it and the end result sounded faintly ridiculous. One of his favourite books was reported to be Ernest Hemingway's *The Old Man and the Sea*, but his tendency towards grandiose long-windedness suggested that he hadn't actually studied it that closely.

Another decidedly un-regal letter emerged two days later, in which he said he'd 'promised to Allah that I will die a martyr'. Again, the handwritten, 1,300-word letter emerged first on the Web. Addressing 'the great nation of Iraq', he proffered a seven-step guide to preparing for the start of the jihad against the infidels. At the top of the list was a call to boycott any dealings with Americans, Britons or Israelis, or any organisations linked to those countries. He implored: 'Do not offer facilities to any of their individuals or corporations; to the extent of refusing to carry them in taxis or renting houses to them.'

He also elaborated on his condemnation of neighbouring governments that, he claimed, assisted with his downfall. He slammed Iran and Turkey for cooperating with 'the CIA, Mossad and British intelligence'. The few senior regime figures who'd been captured to date did not surrender but were betrayed by the leaders of Syria and Jordan, he insisted. Saddam also blamed Syria and Jordan for refusing to supply Iraq with new weapons and communications equipment prior to the conflict. Egypt featured for the first time and was criticised for refusing to act on a request to 'stop the passage of the weapons of the invaders through the Suez canal'. That, of course, made me wonder whether Egypt had played a role in thwarting planned attacks on Navy warships.

Saddam also alluded to living under less than plush conditions, although it could easily have been a calculated demonstration of his empathy with his people, as if they were all in the same boat. 'I write to you this evening . . . without electricity and writing is not an easy operation under the shadow of darkness.' He signed off with: 'I call on you to work under the flag of jihad.'

He wasn't the only fugitive who was upset at the lack of resistance to the occupation: another message from al-Qaeda's leadership concerning Iraq soon came. It seemed that relationships between al-Qaeda operatives in the country and Saddam's Fedayeen militia forces were far from cordial. The international jihadists were regarded distastefully as too bloodthirsty and fanatical. It had echoes of the war in Bosnia, where domestic Muslim militants gave the Afghan Mujahideen veterans a very wide berth, regarding them as barbaric.

A 3,300-word message was circulated among the usual core of half a dozen or so Spook Central-type jihad sites, and it rebuffed concerns that jihad fighters coming over the borders were 'lunatics' who had been 'deceived by their religion'. It asked: 'Why have you left the original unbelievers and directed your tongues on us? How has your conscience accepted that you direct your arrows to our backs?' It went on to forcefully defend the organisation against charges that it is an extremist fringe group: 'Our way is the jihad. That is the command of Allah. We promise and plan, we consult and we act.' Those who refuse to fight 'contribute to the humiliation, degradation and backwardness' of the Islamic nation. 'We hope that we see you inciting the nation to prepare and become ready. If you want glory without a jihad, then you are imagining things. We say to you: if you do not support us then you fight us.'

It is often hard for people to accept this, but al-Qaeda and its affiliate groups operate something akin to a freedom-of-information policy, as discussion of methods and tactics can be useful signposting material for potential new recruits. That's perhaps partially founded in the tradition of waiving individual copyright on material to be used for the propagation of Islam. It was generally assumed that the new jihad land of Iraq was providing al-Qaeda with a recruitment bonanza, and that had been hinted at in a statement a few weeks previously which announced the establishment of a women-only brigade of suicide bombers in Iraq.

It had come in the form of a claim of responsibility for an attack at a US checkpoint to the north-west of Baghdad, where two women suicide bombers detonated a car bomb, killing three American soldiers and two bystanders. The incident had a massive effect on the behaviour of Coalition troops, because anyone now approaching a checkpoint, regardless of their appearance, was a potential suicide bomber. Many innocent civilians were killed at checkpoints by stressed soldiers in the wake of the bombing. If it was just a move driven by propaganda needs, then it was devastatingly effective.

The leader of the women Mujahideen of al-Qaeda, called Um Osama (Mother of Osama), claimed that a multinational squad of female suicide bombers had been trained by the terror group and was now operating in Iraq. I was a bit sceptical about this, though I did find a Saudi newspaper article written in March that was based on an email interview with Um Osama. She said she took orders from Osama bin Laden and a senior lieutenant called Mullah Seif Edin and that the group's operations were overseen by the Saudi branch of al-Qaeda. Most of their communications took place over the Internet, she said.

In her latest statement, she called for the release of convicted and suspected al-Qaeda prisoners throughout the world, making particular reference to Ramzi Binalshibh. He was suspected of playing a pivotal role in the planning of the September 11 attacks and was captured by the USA in September 2002 after a gun battle in Karachi, Pakistan. It also contained – for the first time to my knowledge – apparent official confirmation of al-Qaeda's role in the October 2002 Moscow theatre siege.

Eighteen women were among the group of fifty Chechen guerrilla fighters who died when Russian troops stormed the building with the aid of sleeping gas. The rescue operation also left some 129 hostages dead. She praised the attackers, calling the siege a 'bold operation' and claiming that the terrorists were 'murdered'.

It was a busy month for all concerned. One militant group even published images of a training camp close to Baghdad, which was supposed to be putting new volunteers through an emergency jihad training programme. It was a specially designed course that aimed to cram the basics of a year's worth of military training into just two weeks. The pictures showed a motley group of men who looked like they were drawn from all four corners of the Middle East crawling in the dirt with weapons and climbing over part of an assault course in new, blue urban-warfare fatigues. There was one tubby guy with a moustache, who looked like he might be an ex-Iraqi army officer, puffing his way through his paces.

There was definitely a touch of *Dad's Army* about the scenes, though there was no way of telling where the pictures had been taken. The surroundings looked desert-like and it could have been Iraq but, as the people were shown without masks covering their faces to prevent positive identification by the foe, it suggested they'd become martyrs early on.

A letter written by one foreign volunteer described how he undertook a two-day trip into the country, entering from Jordan. He'd arrived on the eve of the war and simply reported for jihad duty at the Iraqi embassy in Amman. After some questioning about his motives, he was given a visa that was embossed on a separate slip of paper, rather than in his passport. He was told that this was to help him avoid suspicion when he returned home to Riyadh in Saudi Arabia.

The method of his onward journey to the camp outside Baghdad wasn't disclosed. He arrived to find 30 other volunteers there, who were housed in a two-storey building. They came from Saudi Arabia, Palestine, Egypt and Sudan and they were all enthusiastic supporters of Osama bin Laden. He described a typical day at the camp. They were woken up at 0400 by whistles and they assembled in ranks for roll call. Dawn prayers came next, which were led by a sergeant called Qahtan al-Zebeidi. The new recruit said he could hear gunfire in the distance during the ceremony. That was followed by an hour-long lesson on cleaning weapons.

Breakfast consisted of boiled eggs, which were well received, in preparation for an hour-long run in battledress at 0900, around the courtyard of the camp. Target practice followed, before a brief period of rest at 1145 prior to the call to noon prayers. Drill practice followed, then lunch at 1300, at which coffee and oranges were available. Activities resumed at 1400, with a lesson from a trainer called Ali on camouflage techniques, before afternoon prayers at

1500. Training resumed at 1600: this time it was unarmed combat and how to fight with knives. Evening prayers were at 1700, before Ali returned at 1800 with a lesson on how to sneak into buildings. That was followed by an hour-long exercise in how to crawl along the ground at night carrying a hand grenade and communicating with colleagues using animal noises. It was a technique to be used for silently approaching American soldiers and vehicles. Night prayers were at 2000 and that was followed by a power cut. A discussion about the latest news and events preceded bedtime.

Morale was 'very high' and the training was 'serious in the extreme'. They were given tours of Baghdad to prepare them for navigating around the streets and alleyways on their own initiative. 'Everyone welcomed and hugged us as if the protection of Iraq depended on us.' They were able to use Internet cafés during the Baghdad trips. A CNN correspondent encountered the group on one occasion. He asked if they were Saddam's Fedayeen, to which he received the reply: 'No, we are Islam's Fedayeen.'

The mention of the involvement in Iraq of al-Qaeda's Saudi group made sense in this respect, as its operatives were geographically best placed to fuel the jihad. Al-Qaeda in the Arabian Peninsula, to give it its official title, had only recently come to prominence. Since 9/11, the Saudi government had been fond of dismissing suggestions that the terror network might be active inside the country, citing the absence of any terrorist atrocities as proof that its policy of containing Islamic radicals was a successful one. Some sceptics have suggested that the lack of attacks was down to a covert agreement between the Saudi royal family and bin Laden, in which a blind eye was turned to the network's fund-raising activities in the country in return for a guarantee of security – a protection racket.

There had been some incidents of small explosive devices being placed under the cars of Westerners working in the country during the previous year, but it wasn't on a large scale. I'd noticed a growing trickle of propaganda and chatter emerging from Saudi over the past few months, which I assumed had its roots in the outrage caused in the region by the possibility of a US invasion of Iraq. There had also been a flurry of religious edicts and fatwas that appeared to emanate from radical Islamic scholars, but I can't say that I paid too much attention to them at the time.

These edicts were often in the 10,000-word region, and reading too many automatic Arabic-to-English translations of that length quickly made the brain ache. They were fine for gist purposes, but the limitations of the software became markedly apparent when discussion turned to the finer points of sharia law (Islamic canonical law) as it applied to jihad. Difficult concepts were made more so by the odd choice of words: al-Qaeda often came out as 'the rule', operations were 'certificates' and fighters were sometimes termed 'the jasmines'. One particularly baffling example was 'Alan's mother is two ibexes . . . a strange not this'.

Speculation about the terror network's presence in Saudi Arabia, however, ended when al-Qaeda came out of sleeper status there in the most spectacular circumstances on 12 May 2003. Three large car bombs exploded simultaneously inside Western housing compounds in the Saudi capital Riyadh, killing thirty-five people and injuring hundreds more. The Saudi government moved immediately to crack down on Islamic radicals, arresting some 600 terrorist suspects in the wake of the attacks and breaking up 'dozens' of cells. Crown Prince Abdullah bin Abdul Aziz al-Saud vowed to wipe out al-Qaeda and the government drew up a list of the 26 'most wanted' individuals who were now on the run.

The response was an al-Qaeda declaration of war against the 'apostate' Saudi royal family and a clear statement of its intention to overthrow the existing regime. It contained a lengthy analysis of the Prince's televised speech, made in reaction to the bombings, and a point-by-point refutation of his claims that the attacks were un-Islamic and the attackers misguided.

One group of Western anti-terrorism researchers that I was in contact with were incensed that the attacks weren't stopped. They had a habit of reading fatwas more closely than I and operated an impressive monitoring network, translating suspicious material at a rate of knots and on an industrial scale, covering a massive amount of ground between them. The upset was caused because they said they had detected information on militant Islamic websites in the previous few weeks that had suggested the approximate location and timings of the Riyadh attacks.

Signs of al-Qaeda activity in the country had been detected as long as 18 months ago, they said. They'd passed the leads on to the authorities via the proper channels and now they were very angry that their work as concerned citizens appeared to have been ignored. I reviewed the various source messages and there were some indications that something was being planned, but you'd have needed a forensic and obsessive interest in these types of communications to pick up the key signs.

A message published on a pro al-Qaeda website, dated 21 March, was 'an urgent request' to carry out a surveillance operation. 'I want the American and British housing complexes in Riyadh,' it said. Another message published on 28 March also mentioned Riyadh and said: '. . . the time for the hit has come'.

The researchers had also detected a series of assassination threats against US defence secretary Donald Rumsfeld, and a researcher made direct contact with the FBI's threat management unit to warn them, as Rumsfeld was due to make a visit to Baghdad. She was told by the FBI that she shouldn't have bothered to call and there was no need to pass on tips in the future, as they had all the bases covered. At the end of the visit, an unidentified gunman fired three shots at the bus that was taking Rumsfeld back to the airport. He escaped uninjured.

Another example they cited was a discussion about a plan to bomb a McDonald's restaurant, which had been passed on to the authorities in the usual way. Five weeks later, a bomb exploded inside a McDonald's on the outskirts of Beirut, in Lebanon, injuring three people. Disaster was averted only because a second bomb in a car, which was parked outside ready to catch fleeing customers, just partially detonated.

Law enforcement and government institutions tend to have turning circles that make oil tankers look nippy. I'd recently spoken to a contact who works on classified computer projects for intelligence agencies on both sides of the Atlantic and I was shocked to hear that nearly all computer systems at the FBI were incapable of displaying Arabic characters, or Chinese, or Korean. There were 'staggering omissions' in the technical capabilities of Western agencies.

FIFTH COLUMNS

BRITAIN WAS SPECIFICALLY IDENTIFIED AS A TARGET FOR A 9/11-STYLE operation in the wake of the Riyadh bombings. The jihadists were buoyed by their success and were indulging in a little sabre-rattling, though the chatter also revealed that the security situation in Jeddah had led to the cancellation of a similar follow-up operation there a couple of weeks later. London, Los Angeles and Washington DC were marked out as the next targets after al-Qaeda's 'successful ambush' of Westerners in Saudi Arabia. The main character in one conversation said: 'There remains Egypt, Jordan and Pakistan, and the overwhelming destruction in London and Washington.'

While a few months previously there had been a warning issued to Muslims to remove any investments they had in America, the informal al-Qaeda travel-advice service had now changed to advising American Muslims to start preparing to leave the country for their own safety. 'Coastal cities' in particular were dangerous now and the advice was to make for adjacent countries 'like Canada or Mexico'.

'I am certain that the coming days will be pregnant with shock and fear for America,' said the author. 'The next hit is coming and nothing will stop it, except Allah.'

Almost simultaneously, on 21 May 2003, America's terror-alert status was unexpectedly raised again to orange, signifying a high risk of an imminent terrorist attack, which sparked mild public panic in some quarters. Shops were thronged with buyers of duct tape, bottled water, weapons, ammunition, gas masks and parachutes; the media were full of talk about panic rooms and the true risk of contamination posed by dirty radiological bombs. Dollars were sold in favour of gold.

At the same time, in the UK . . . there wasn't a panic. Life continued in exactly the same way as the day before. The press suspected that there were political motives behind the move.

The question was: 'Why now?' There'd been no spectacular attack against a Western city in retaliation for Iraq and, at the start of the month, President Bush had announced that 'major combat operations' in Iraq were over. The US government was exuding confidence that it had Iraq under control and al-Qaeda on the run. The contradictory alert-change had the effect of suddenly pulling the rug from under people.

Many questions were asked about the reasons for the higher state of alert and the nature of the intelligence that had prompted it. The speculation wasn't helped by an initial reluctance to reveal the true reasons – national security, don't you know – though the Department of Homeland Security said part of the reason was the discovery of 'an email' that advised Muslims to leave US coastal cities. That was final confirmation for me that the sites I was looking at were taken seriously at the highest levels, though it also hinted at intelligence deficiencies. There may have been covert communications intercepts – wire taps – to back up this notion of a grave threat, but I suspected there weren't any.

The intelligence community obviously was a rabid consumer of content on the Spook Central jihad sites, as I'd been told. The alert upgrade seemed to be based directly on the words I'd had on my screen a few days previously. Maybe they couldn't bring themselves to say 'a message on a website discussion forum', because that would have sounded very lame to the uninitiated. My own personal suspicion was that this was a propaganda ploy by the jihadists to spread panic and the US government had fallen for it.

Maybe it was in retaliation when, towards the end of May, rumours swept the jihad community that bin Laden had been detained by the Americans. One version had it that he'd been in Iran and placed under house arrest to be used as a bargaining chip by the Iranian regime, looking to head off the possibility of a future US invasion aimed at curbing its nuclear ambitions. Speculation reached fever pitch when a picture emerged of a man who looked very much like bin Laden being escorted by a Pakistani soldier onto an aircraft, presumably in Afghanistan, under the watchful eye of an American officer.

It prompted the emergence of a suitably lengthy statement of denial which did the rounds on the main jihad sites. The speculation was denounced as a completely obvious propaganda ploy by the opposition to sap the morale of al-Qaeda supporters. The 'eternal sheikh' was well and untraceable. That also led to a long exposition on psychological warfare and how al-Qaeda too was very active on this front.

The essay looked like it had been penned by a senior leader, not bin Laden himself, and it explored the Western media's attitudes and the role of propaganda in al-Qaeda's strategy. It was a scholarly work and concluded, among many things, that the number of pro-jihad media outlets needed to be expanded if the imbalance was to be addressed.

It also explained, puzzlingly, that although people might think they know al-Qaeda operatives, their true identities are always hidden. It used an example: 'Abu Amr the Egyptian', who lives in Britain and heads al-Qaeda's recruitment activities from there. It pointed out – incredulously and with double exclamation marks – that his name is simply a deduction made by British intelligence and not his true identity. 'Our warrior brother' was the leader of 'the martyrs' convoys' heading for the 'brutal international battle between belief and disbelief'. He was an engineer by profession whose name was 'on some prisoners' tongues in Guantanamo'.

That appeared to be a reference to the person we know as Abu Hamza, the firebrand al-Qaeda-supporting cleric of Finsbury Park mosque notoriety. He was thought to be Egyptian, though even that wasn't certain, and he claimed to be a trained civil engineer. Attendees at Hamza's regular prayer meetings included the shoe-bomber Richard Reid and the '20th hijacker' Zacarias Moussaoui, among many others. He was also known to have links with some of the British detainees being held by the USA at Guantanamo Bay in Cuba, notably Feroz Abbasi.

For Hamza, and other militants in the UK, Iraq was great material to work with. His website had recently been taken offline, after it was revealed in the press that the site was carrying a statement that called for Coalition troops captured in Iraq to be executed or exchanged for prisoners held at Guantanamo (I wonder where that tip came from?). Similarly, the Web presence of Hamza's colleague, the leader of the extremist group al-Muhajiroun, was interrupted after lawyers acting for the hosting company concluded, when it was pointed out to them, that statements on the site could be deemed as 'advocating racial violence'. Omar Bakri, sometimes and very inaccurately known as the Tottenham Ayatollah, was invited by the company to remove his site after a flurry of complaints was received. Most were prompted by the graphic close-up images of dead British soldiers that had been published there, the effects of which were compounded by claims that UK troops had been committing atrocities against civilians in Iraq.

Syrian-born Bakri made no secret of his support for al-Qaeda and claimed to be the spokesman for the International Islamic Front for Jihad against Jews and Crusaders, which was established by bin Laden in 1996. He was fond of referring to his al-Muhajiroun organisation as 'the mouth, eyes and ears' of bin Laden and regarded the 9/11 hijackers as martyrs. If Hamza's charisma lay in gravitas and certainty, Bakri was marked out by his gregarious zeal and fast-talking. There was that certain twinkle in his eye that said he was thoroughly enjoying his job, which largely consisted of touring the country to inform the Muslim youth about the necessity of fighting jihad in Afghanistan, Kashmir, Chechnya and Iraq. His group was an international network and his message spread far and wide. A memo written by FBI agent Kenneth Williams just prior to 9/11 – the infamous Phoenix Memo that could have prevented the attacks had any notice been taken of it – noted a connection between Bakri and several suspects attending US flight-training schools, including one that was used by 9/11 hijacker Hani Hanjour, who guided flight 77 into the Pentagon.

Al-Muhajiroun's latest press release in the UK called on Muslims to wage jihad against Coalition troops in Iraq, and it was a message that was reiterated on its Pakistan-registered website. A statement attributed to an al-Muhajiroun member called Hassan Butt called for volunteers to step into the breach and defend Iraq. Butt, from Manchester, had been arrested under anti-terrorism laws six months previously but released without charge, following an interview on BBC Radio 4's *Today* programme, during which he claimed that he'd recruited 200 Britons to fight with the Taliban in Afghanistan.

Soon after, in February, Bakri had made headlines by claiming that suicide bombers were poised to strike at government buildings and financial institutions in the UK, in retaliation for the country's involvement in Iraq. Like Hamza, he was keenly aware that jihad could also be fought successfully over the airwaves: terrorise them by all means possible.

He generated much coverage after admitting to teaching the two British suicide bombers who'd been sent on a Hamas mission to bomb a beachfront bar in Tel Aviv called Mike's Place. Three people were killed and fifty-five were left injured after Asif Hanif, 21, from Hounslow in west London, a Finsbury Park mosque regular, blew himself up. Omar Khan Sharif, 27, from Derby, was later found dead on a beach – presumed drowned – after he'd fled the scene when his device failed to detonate.

Bakri was said to be a computer wizard and a heavy user of Internet discussion forums and instant messaging, I discovered. That's now simply a fact of life, as the technology can hardly be uninvented; blaming the Internet for all the wrong-doing in the world is as mad as blaming telephone wires.

Bakri was in good company, as it emerged that Khalid Sheikh Mohammed, regarded as one of the chief architects of the 9/11 operation, had personally run a well-known Pakistan-based Internet discussion forum. Even the '20th hijacker' Zacarius Moussaoui had filed a court motion complaining that he'd been waiting for six months to get an Internet connection to his cell, so he could prepare his defence, which rested on his insistence that he was the victim of an FBI cover-up over 9/11 and that the Bureau deliberately allowed the attacks to take place. Hamza's website re-emerged around this time – ironically on servers based in George W. Bush's home state of Texas.

One of al-Qaeda's major problems with its own natural constituency was that it did not seek a prior fatwa that authorised the 9/11 attacks. This omission left it open to criticism from moderate Muslim scholars that it was an un-Islamic act because it had not been properly sanctioned. Bin Laden's moral high ground was being eroded by the accusations, and the Saudi government was helping this along by running a 're-education programme' for the country's clerics. The issue became a thorn in the side of the lion of Islam and bin Laden set about trying to rectify the situation.

The solution to the problem came a few days after the death of one of al-Qaeda's spiritual leaders in a shoot-out with security forces on 31 May. Yousuf Saleh Fahd al-Ayyiri was fatally shot after fleeing from a checkpoint in the north of the country. He was hurling hand grenades into the path of his pursuers during his attempted getaway, which resulted in the deaths of two Saudi security troops, before he was taken out. He was wanted on suspicion of involvement in the May Riyadh bombings of Western housing compounds and was thought to have reported directly to the number three at al-Qaeda central, Saif al-Adel, and was regarded as the leader of al-Qaeda in Saudi Arabia.

The announcement of his death was accompanied by the news

that a six-month-old handwritten letter from bin Laden was found in his possession. A belt of explosives was also strapped around him: he'd apparently taken to wearing it whilst sleeping. The blood-soaked piece of paper was simply a note expressing deep gratitude for everything he'd done to forward al-Qaeda's cause, referring to 'the achievements of the cells'. On its own, that wasn't too significant, as both men had known each other since the Soviet–Afghan war.

Al-Ayyiri had accompanied bin Laden when he moved to Sudan in 1989 and he had later fought against US troops in Somalia. It also transpired that he had been the administrator of al-Qaeda's official home on the Net, a site called al-Neda (The Call), and had run two training camps in a remote part of Saudi Arabia. He was also suspected of being a key figure in arranging entry to Iraq for incoming foreign fighters.

His death was marked in a way to bring cheer to bin Laden's heart and may explain the leader's written praise for him: a fatwa was published that provided the religious justification for the use of weapons of mass destruction by al-Qaeda against innocent civilians in the West. It was posted on the Internet a few days after he was gunned down, seemingly to honour his leadership and threaten the West at the same time.

A huge amount of work had obviously been put into producing the 11,500-word document, which addressed the question of whether al-Qaeda was within its rights, under Islamic sharia law, and it did so, delving into extraordinary detail. It was called a 'religious verdict' and it certainly had the look of a judge's summing-up. It was titled 'Judgement on the use of Weapons of Mass Destruction against the Unbelievers'.

My mental news-o-meter started to flutter when I saw the title, so I first skipped through the body of the text to try to find the final conclusion. It provided exactly what bin Laden had been looking for. It said that the West was responsible for the deaths of ten million Muslims, directly and indirectly, over the past few decades, so al-Qaeda, in an eye-for-an-eye fashion, was justified in trying to even the score.

It claimed that the Koran allows the use of chemical, biological and nuclear weapons to inflict mass casualties on the enemy. It was a fatwa that pre-approved the use of unconventional weapons in the network's next big strike against the West and the deaths of up to ten million people.

In many ways, it could be regarded as a go-ahead for a grand solution to deal with the West once and for all. And it was published just before the director general of MI5, Eliza Manningham-Buller, said in a newspaper interview that an attack against a Western city by terrorists using WMD was 'inevitable'. Perhaps she'd already seen the fatwa.

It was split into four parts and twenty different sections, which examined each aspect of the issue, and presented the views of six other scholars who had been consulted. Section six was the key passage, as it was titled: 'Proof that the Use of Weapons of Mass Destruction is Permissible'. The final three sections dealt with key arguments against the use of WMD: the deaths of innocent women and children, killing Muslims, and long-term contamination of the environment.

The document started by defining what was meant by the term 'weapon of mass destruction', before asking the question: why should Muslims tolerate the imbalance of firepower in this area? Those who objected to escalating the war against the West by using such devices had forgotten that Britain had used chemical weapons to quell a rebellion in Iraq in 1920 (on the advice of Sir Winston Churchill) and America had dropped nuclear weapons on Japan in the Second World War. 'The Jewish arsenal is full of these weapons!' it said.

The answer lay in the Koran, which taught that when killing became necessary in conflicts, victims should be dispatched as efficiently as possible. It cited the tradition of beheading captured enemy fighters as an example. The use of WMD adhered to this principle, it was claimed – it was just efficient killing on a mass scale. 'The [holy] texts indicate the permissibility of such weapons, if the Mujahideen saw an advantage in their use,' the document concluded.

It was also stated that efforts should be made to avoid the deaths of women and children but, if they are unbelievers, then their deaths are excusable. Similarly, the killing of innocent Muslims should be minimised by careful targeting, though it noted that extreme care should be taken with the use of poison or nerve gases, as a change in wind direction might endanger adjacent Muslim population centres. It was a concern that was repeated twice later in the text.

The bulk of the wordage was taken up with voluminous quotations from the Koran and other religious texts, Hadiths (accounts of the sayings of Muhammad) and the Sunna (accounts of his daily practices), to back up the judgements. Several pages of the collected sayings of prominent scholars from down the ages followed, and all of the passages referred to the acceptability of wreaking widespread destruction on the lands of an enemy. Under Islamic sharia law, it claimed that 'there is no harm in poisoning their [non-Muslims'] waters or destroying their houses'. Jihad warriors were also absolved of responsibility for birth defects in children caused by radiation after a nuclear attack.

It was a disturbing read, mainly because it wasn't about the permissibility of killing non-Muslims in the West: that was taken as read. This was about murder on an industrial scale and there were obvious and troubling Nazi-like overtones. It's not often that you come across a treatise on the mechanics of mass killing and I can't remember ever seeing anything comparable to this. It would have been too easy to brush this off as just some kind of propaganda effort, but that would have been wrong. This smelled very different.

A friend and I shortly afterwards had a spirited discussion over whether bin Ladenism could be equated with fascism. He insisted that the word couldn't be applied to al-Qaeda's philosophy, as it was inaccurate and too soft. The organisation's philosophy could accurately be described as Nazism, however, he thought. This latest finding certainly demonstrated all the hallmarks of Nazism. My friend was normally a cool customer but he became surprisingly impassioned on the subject of the fatwa. 'These are hard-core Nazis,' he said. 'There's no other word for it. That's a plan for a holocaust.'

In militant Islamic circles, Hitler was despised for his occultist beliefs but admired for his 'work on the Jews'. Abu Hamza has suggested that the Holocaust was Allah-ordained and that a similar Muslim-inspired event was in the offing. To Hamza, Hitler and bin Laden are two examples of leaders ordered by God to sort out the Jewish question. Others, too, saw the connection. Britain's top Nazi, David Myatt, had appreciated the synergy many years ago and converted to Islam, and he's since written extensively on jihad.

I was somewhat taken aback when, a few days after 9/11, a close friend confided in me to say that she thought that bin Laden might be the returned Jesus Christ. He had many of the same attributes, she suspected. That might have seemed like madness, except it wasn't. A tradition of a second coming exists in Islam. It forecasts the coming of a saviour figure called the al-Mahdi (the right-guided one), who will lead Muslims in a time of great tribulation and re-establish a Muslim empire. Prior to his return, he will meet Jesus and Jesus will pray behind him. There's some dispute over whether he'll emerge from a long sleep in a cave that's protected by genies.

Al-Qaeda wouldn't be as impertinent as to directly advocate bin Laden as the candidate, but he was certainly in the ball park. He must have been very pleased, as the WMD document really gave him absolute carte blanche to do as he pleased, militarily. He wouldn't be caught short next time. The leadership had also been addressing the scholarly objections after 9/11 that insufficient warning had been given. I suspect bin Laden would refer questioners to his 1996 declaration of war against America, and her allies, as being ample warning of his intentions.

I didn't know at the time that the WMD document was considered classified material by the CIA. It wasn't until 2004, in an interview with former CIA analyst Michael Scheuer, that it emerged that the same words I had been squinting at on my dirty screen were being taken just as seriously at the top. He suggested that news of the fatwa was withheld from the public to avoid causing alarm.

The steady trickle of statements and pronouncements from bin Laden and al-Zawahiri after 9/11 contained a common theme, as there were often references to the attacks being a warning to America to back off; then warnings that the warning must be heeded to avoid worse attacks in future; then warnings that the warning was not being heeded; then warnings that time was running out and the lesson of 9/11 still hadn't been learnt; then warnings that America appeared to be incapable of learning.

The progression seemed to be building up to: 'Time for the second strike.' Al-Qaeda statements have always stressed that a second round of attacks on America would be much bigger than 9/11 and would be aimed at finishing the nation off. There would be no second warning.

One late version of the 9/11 plan was to plough most of the hijacked planes into nuclear power plants, though that was changed, as even the al-Qaeda leadership agreed that it was going too far at that early stage. I already knew that it would have been relatively easy to acquire radioactive materials to construct 'dirty bombs' and I'd seen some recent messages that referred to 'explosive nuclear belts', which appeared to relate to explosives strapped to suicide bombers, only pepped-up with radioactive shrapnel for added misery.

Working nuclear warheads were, I knew, more problematic, as they were not only difficult to obtain but had added problems of maintenance and transportation; however, many in the intelligence community wouldn't rule them out. One contact said he had solid information that al-Qaeda had bought nine small 'suitcase nukes' on the black market, though substantial technical knowledge would be needed to make them operational. On biological materials, it was even murkier, though one phial pilfered from an insecure laboratory would go a very long way. Chemical weapons were the easiest option, as all the materials needed are commonly available in DIY stores and garden centres.

News of al-Ayyiri's death produced wails of disbelief and furious vows of bloody revenge and reprisal attacks on the jihad boards. I wasn't overly familiar with him, but it was clear that he was held in the very highest regard among grass roots supporters: genuine grief was being expressed in all quarters. That seemed to be especially felt among the younger ones, who, after a security crackdown in which hundreds of people were arrested and dozens of suspects captured and killed, realised one of al-Ayyiri's pet projects as a permanent memorial to him.

That came five months later with the launch of an online bi-monthly magazine 'dealing with Jihad and the Mujahideen in the Arabian Peninsula', called *Sawt Al-Jihad* (The Voice of Jihad). It was a radical new departure and a very adventurous move, in publishing terms. It was packaged together as a traditional-looking magazine in a format that meant it could be read on-screen on the Web or printed out for studying at leisure. It amounted to a comprehensive self-analysis of the mindset of the organisation.

It was packed with doctrinal information and contained the first of a two-part biography of al-Ayyiri's life. He had served as a bodyguard to bin Laden in Afghanistan before he was arrested on his return from Sudan to Saudi Arabia. After being released from prison, he became heavily involved in raising funds from wealthy Saudi supporters to fund the jihad in Chechnya. He wrote several essays for a website run by the rebels and the titles included 'A Guide to the Perplexed on the Captives', 'Martyrdom Operations: Suicide or Shahada?' and 'The Moscow Theatre Operation and its Benefits for the Mujahideen'.

The editorial on the opening page of The Voice of Jihad asked the question: 'Why is jihad necessary in Saudi Arabia?' The answer:

One of the greatest places in which jihad is a commandment applying to each Muslim individually is the land of the two holy places [the Arabian Peninsula]. In this land there is the occupying Crusader enemy who steals the land's treasures, determines its policy, and sets out from it to make war on the Muslims.

It also has an apostate agent government, and it implements the plans of colonialism, supports the infidels, and rules by a law that is not the law of Allah . . . Its prisons hold the oppressed who are subjected to insufferable tortures, and in it there are aggression and curses against Allah, insult to the religion, and contempt for the believers, [and all this] under the protection and patronage of the family of Saud, whose members simultaneously silence the reformists [those demanding a more fundamentalist state] as well as those who call for virtue, and jail those who call on them to impose the law of Allah.

Another article, by Sheikh Nasser al-Najdi, urged readers in a headline to 'Kill Americans Whose Blood is Like the Blood of a Dog'. He said: 'Bush, the son of Bush, is a dog and the son of a dog; his blood is the blood of a dog; his bark is the bark of a dog; and he has all the traits of a dog except for loyalty. Thus, he is a hyena.'

There was a rousing call to arms and a review of Mujahideen activities worldwide, which signed off with the line 'See you in Paradise', and the text of a *New Yorker* article about the US National Security Agency, which I suppose was there to remind readers that walls can have ears. There were also quotes from Sheikh Nasser al-Fahd, a cleric who was arrested after expressing support for the May Riyadh bombings. A review of the late Sheikh Abdullah Azzam's book *The Virtues of Jihad Granted to the Slaves of Allah* preceded the reproduction of an entire chapter from a book written by bin Laden's deputy Ayman al-Zawahiri, called *Knights Under the Prophet's Banner*.

An article by al-Ayyiri's replacement as leader in Saudi Arabia, Abdul Aziz al-Muqrin, writing under one of his aliases, described how he was originally recruited into the network. He had gone to Afghanistan to fight jihad 13 years previously. Afterwards, he was posted to Algeria for a few months and joined a logistics cell which was overseeing the smuggling of weapons from Europe into Algeria, via Morocco. After fighting in Bosnia, he went on to Somalia:

Today, Allah be praised, I am [in Saudi Arabia] at the front that
we sought to purify and liberate from the defilement of the
treacherous rulers and, even before them, from the defilement
of the American Crusaders and their allies . . . [contrary to
rumours] I did not go to Iraq. I swore to purify the Arabian
Peninsula from the polytheists.

After a bizarre article about 'Jihad and Sorcery', which was basically
a guide to protecting yourself from Satan and his messengers, was a
final rousing call to arms. It asked readers not to wait for the next
issue, but to get out there and fulfil their obligation of jihad.

A second magazine venture was soon launched to accompany
this, which focused on military training. It was called *Mu'askar Al-
Battar* (The Al-Battar Military Camp). Again, it was in honour of al-
Ayyiri, as it was named after the training camp he ran in the Saudi
desert which also became his nickname, Al-Battar meaning
'cutting edge' or 'swift sword'. It was even more radical than its
predecessor, because it was dedicated to training recruits for jihad
by distance learning. No longer did you have to risk raising
suspicion by physically attending an al-Qaeda jihad camp – you
could organise your own training to suit your lifestyle. Much of the
training could be done unobtrusively at a gym or a shooting club
or just in your own backyard. It was the start of the phenomenon
of 'DIY jihad training' and, in effect, marked the relocation of
basic-training camps onto the Internet. It was an ingenious and
innovative concept, I thought, as it was clearly designed to spread
the culture of jihad among young Muslims at Net speeds like a
virus.

The magazine was described as being produced by the 'military
committee of the al-Qaeda organisation in the Saudi peninsula'. The
very basics were covered in the first issue, with a lengthy review of
the AK-47 Kalashnikov rifle. Al-Ayyiri also made an appearance,
credited with an examination of the importance of sport in the
preparation of Mujahideen fighters. Two articles on the reasons for
starting a guerrilla war came before a piece by al-Qaeda's number
three, Saif al-Adel, which focused on security and intelligence. He
told readers that they must take care to avoid being exposed as
members of al-Qaeda. It ended with this:

Oh Mujahid brother, in order to join the great training camps
you don't have to travel to other lands. Alone, in your home

69

> or with a group of your brothers, you too can begin to execute
> the training program. You can all join the Al-Battar Training
> Camp.

The second anniversary of the 9/11 attacks was fast approaching. It
was a few months off yet, though I could tell that a pyroclastic surge
of media coverage was coming and there'd be a news white-out for
a week or so. Extraordinary events demand extraordinary coverage,
admittedly, though having to wade through more of those emotive
'tears of the children' or 'out of the blue sky' pieces, or variants
thereof, made me shudder.

I should have been more optimistic this time around, as it was my
specialist subject coming up. Features schedules were being drawn
up well in advance and plans were being formulated for special
issues. I'd had a few emails asking for suggestions, but I didn't make
any. I'd been working on the story constantly for the past two years,
full-time, and I was somewhat jaded. It would be a struggle to come
up with a major new angle on the story, as I'd already covered all the
bases, I thought.

There were, however, plans being made to hold a celebration of
the attacks in London. Ostensibly, it was meant to be a conference
held by al-Muhajiroun to discuss the issues surrounding the 'blessed
hijackings'. There were celebrations outside Finsbury Park mosque
on the day itself, so it was no surprise to hear that Omar Bakri's and
Hamza's groups were getting together for a shindig. They'd done the
same thing on the first anniversary, by holding a conference titled
'A Towering Day in History'.

Bakri's attitude towards victims of terrorism was made crystal clear
on his website, before the plug was pulled. A 'news story' on the site
about the Moscow Theatre Siege said:

> The current Russian hostage crisis being faced by the murderer
> [Russian president Vladimir] Putin is totally justified and even
> an Islamic duty as far as Muslims in Chechnya are concerned.
> Having been subjected to years of bombardment,
> displacement, murder and occupation . . .

Ironically, there was an additional complaint that the Russians had
played dirty by using sleeping gas to end the siege. There was also
news that 40 US soldiers had disappeared during a covert operation
in Afghanistan and notice of a demonstration to be held outside 10

Downing Street to protest against the continuing detention of Abu Qatada, widely regarded as the leader of al-Qaeda in Europe. A press release about the Iraq war said:

> It is an obligation upon Muslims worldwide to defend their fellow brothers and sisters. Those who are capable and in the region must do so physically and those outside according to their capability. This could be verbal, financial and creating public opinion and awareness about the barbarism and oppression of the USA and UK and for Jihad.
>
> Ironically, by bombing Muslims, the USA and UK are making themselves more of a target for the Mujahideen everywhere, who quite rightly see this as a Christian fundamentalist crusade against them, judging by this anti-Muslim rhetoric which has accompanied the propaganda campaign for war post 9/11.

The vision of Bakri and his supporters in the UK was to speed along the rise of the Islamic Republic of Britain. A synopsis of their primary objectives read:

> THE REASONS FOR THE ESTABLISHMENT OF AL-MUHAJIROUN:
> Al-Muhajiroun was established in response to the saying of Allah, 'Let there rise from among you group(s) calling society to Islam, commanding society to do what Allah orders and to refrain from what He forbids and these (group(s)) are the ones who are successful.'
>
> Its purpose was to revive the Islamic Ummah from the severe decline that it had reached, and to liberate it from the thoughts, systems and laws of kufr [non-Muslims] as well as the domination and influence of the kufr states. It also aims to restore the Islamic State (Khilafah) so that the ruling by what Allah revealed returns.
>
> THE DEVELOPMENT OF THE AL-MUHAJIROUN MOVEMENT:
> 1. Al-Muhajiroun started as an Islamic thought which sparked in the mind of the founder.
> 2. The founder digested the Islamic thought and became a live cell with it.
> 3. The motion of the cell started to develop and deliver multiple cells, i.e. followers.

4. The cells (followers) formulated the first study circle (Halaqah) around the thought.

5. The study circle (Halaqah) became a unit (Kutlah).

6. The unit became a group (Jama'ah) or collective body.

7. The group transferred into a party (Hizb) with a particular task and duties in society.

8. The party continued and within three years it became a mass movement (Harakah).

9. The movement will (Insha'Allah) formulate a fifth column (Tabour Khaamiss) in society.

10. The fifth column will (Insha'Allah) be in a position to get support from the people of power, i.e. Muslim forces (Al-Ansaar) or to lead the Islamic revolution (Al-Thaworah Al-Islamiyyah) in order to establish the task, i.e. Al-Khilafah (The Islamic State) to dominate the world by Islam.

The group's website had resurfaced and it now appeared to contain an overt threat of terrorist attacks against government targets. It was in the form of a poster advertising a forthcoming rally to be held in Trafalgar Square. Much of it was taken up by a large image of a masked man with an RPG launcher posing outside 10 Downing Street. Above him was a black Islamic flag flying from the top of the clock tower above Parliament. It was accompanied by a press release that claimed that the government had embarked on a campaign to disrupt al-Muhajiroun's activities. It alleged that a recent meeting had to be cancelled after the venue booking was cancelled – at the behest of the government, they claimed. 'There is no doubt that Islam is the only alternative to the corruption and oppression of man made law and it is therefore only a matter of time before we see the Islamic flag flying over 10 Downing Street,' it concluded.

When I saw this, I thought that Bakri was now very much on the warpath. Coupled with his previous warning about suicide bombers being poised to attack institutional targets in the UK, it could easily be construed as being a direct threat against the prime minister and parliament. Sure enough, a few days later on 31 July, anti-terrorism police officers launched a series of dawn raids which targeted al-Muhajiroun's headquarters in north-east London, Bakri's home, plus the house of the group's 'UK leader', Anjem Choudary. Bakri was taken into custody and questioned under the Terrorism Act and the properties were thoroughly searched. A van-load of material was taken away from Choudary's place.

Bakri was no stranger to visits from the police. He was arrested in 1991 after claiming that the prime minister, John Major, would be a legitimate target for assassination, because of the UK's involvement in the Gulf War. Five al-Muhajiroun members were arrested in 2000 for distributing leaflets calling for the murder of Jews, but no charges were brought. In October 2001, Scotland Yard said it was investigating comments made by a Pakistan-based al-Muhajiroun spokesman who'd claimed that Tony Blair was a legitimate terrorist target. Some 16 senior members of the organisation had been arrested by police in all since 1998, though only one person was convicted over activities directly relating to al-Muhajiroun.

A statement was promptly issued, denying that al-Muhajiroun was involved in recruiting jihad fighters. In a typically threatening way, it concluded:

> For the moment, Muslims in the UK have a covenant of security which prevents them from attacking the lives and wealth of anyone here; however Muslims are also obliged to defend their life, honour and wealth when it is attacked and violated. With the worst housing, the highest unemployment, the largest number of race murders in Europe, a whole range of draconian laws tailored to intimidate the Muslim community, the Blair regime is today sitting on a box of dynamite and have only themselves to blame if after attacking the Islamic Movements and the Islamic scholars, it all blows up in their face!

The big question about Bakri centred on his credibility. Was he the real deal, or was it purely propaganda? I got in touch with an intelligence contact to sound him out on this. He was surprised that I needed to ask. He told me: 'Sure, they [al-Muhajiroun] are a major recruiter for terrorists; they are not a front in the UK to preach the gospel. It is common knowledge among counter-terrorism operatives and agents that they are a front for bin Laden.

'I can confirm that there are clear Chechen al-Qaeda ties by way of religious, criminal and foreign Arab Mujahideen links. For example, the most violent rebel group in Chechnya, the Islamic International Brigade (IIB), utilises some 200 to 300 foreign Mujahideen alone.' He thought it was mostly likely that recruits were sent into the country along secure routes used by heroin traffickers.

73

Russia was in no doubt that Bakri and al-Muhajiroun were in the jihad business. President Putin's spokesman on Chechnya, Sergei Yastrzhembsky, had claimed that the group was one of a number of extremist organisations in the UK who'd sent 'several dozen' fighters to Chechnya. To prove the point, he gave a newspaper a recruitment video that appeared to show a teacher from Manchester sitting cross-legged with an AK-47 in his lap. The man, who called himself Assadullah, delivered a plea to Muslims worldwide to join the forces of jihad in the struggle against Russia. Yastrzhembsky said Russia had called on Britain to close down al-Muhajiroun, after seizing hundreds of similar cassettes during raids in the conflict-torn regions. I spoke to the press office in the embassy in London and a spokesman confirmed that that was the view of the Russian government. He said they'd recently been lobbying the UK to include measures to restrict the circulation of recruitment and propaganda material by militant Islamic groups in forthcoming anti-terrorism legislation, but to no avail. I detected frustration over the continuing lack of action in stopping British citizens killing Russian soldiers, though there were obvious free-speech implications in taking the steps they were advocating.

Bakri was eventually released without charge and there was no word on the reasons behind the raids, though a source told me at the time that they were part of an investigation into possible links between al-Muhajiroun and the Palestinian terror group Hamas. That wasn't so surprising, as Bakri had publicly stated on several occasions that the group provides physical and financial support for Hamas. And, of course, he'd also admitted that he'd taught the two British suicide bombers who'd undertaken the mission to destroy Mike's Place three months earlier in the name of Hamas.

Why the raids took place when they did is still a mystery. Maybe the combined diplomatic pressure from the Russians and the Israelis was being noted and perhaps the 10 Downing Street poster caused a fit of anger somewhere in government and finally tipped the balance. Reading the runes, that seemed to be a fair assumption. There was even a rumour that Israel had had enough and had sent a 19-strong Mossad death squad to the UK to set about 'disabling' 50 prominent members of al-Muhajiroun. The country was said to be working with the knowledge of MI5 and was allegedly also targeting the operators of the London-based Islamic charity Interpal, which Israel maintained was a prime source of funding for Hamas, though it had been cleared of any wrongdoing by a Charity Commission probe in 1996. Suspicions weren't helped by the name of the main contact at Interpal, which some were sure was a joke; it was 'Mr Jihad Qundil'.

I suspected that these rumours were a bit over-dramatic, until I stumbled across an al-Muhajiroun statement titled 'Suspicious Deaths of Muslim Activists in the UK'. It detailed the circumstances of the death of 'a key member of al-Muhajiroun's publications team', Sulayman Zein ul-Aabideen, whose body had been found floating in the Thames in London on 5 February 2003. It was estimated that he'd been in the water for three to five days. He was a black convert who was a regular at al-Muhajiroun meetings, and he often filmed the events and helped to edit videotapes of proceedings. The statement suggested that he was far from contemplating suicide and that he'd been murdered by police officers. It said:

> His professional audio and videoing skills were well known and his sudden death, claimed to be suicide by the police, is therefore being treated with great suspicion especially considering that [he] had often complained about being harassed by the police and in light of the intimidation and oppression currently being suffered by the Muslim community generally at the hands of the British government through their police . . .

Undeterred, al-Muhajiroun continued working on plans to mark the second 9/11 anniversary. The result was a conference called 'The Magnificent 19'. The flyer for the event was bordered top and bottom with pictures of the faces of all the hijackers, most of them taken from an al-Qaeda-released video which contained new footage of them training in Afghanistan. The central image was of the burning World Trade Center twin towers next to an enormous image of a smiling bin Laden. It would have been difficult to make it more inflammatory.

News of the event circulated on the Net before reaching the traditional media and caused widespread outrage. The group responded by claiming that the event was not a celebration and the headlines were part of the Western media's 'onslaught against Islam and Muslims'. Still, there was also a reminder that participating in the commemorative one minute's silence on the day was forbidden under Islam.

Even the time of the press conference planned for the day was provocative – 1109. If I remember correctly, it turned into a shambles; the event had been switched to a secret venue, certain newspapers were barred from entering, and Bakri didn't show up.

The subsequent conference declaration stated: 'It has become clear that there can never be any peace with the US government and their allies'; that jihad is a divine obligation on all Muslims; that Muslim soldiers with the British Army in Iraq deserved death; and that Muslims are obliged to do what they can to spring Muslim prisoners from Western jails, 'whether that be in Guantanamo Bay, in Belmarsh Prison or elsewhere'.

> The Magnificent 19 conference this year is not a celebration but an insight into the lives of 19 brave warriors who made the ultimate sacrifice for the sake of Allah. Seeing the oppression and corruption perpetrated against Muslims worldwide for generations, they decided to take the war to the enemy's home. There is no doubt that they shook the world with the operations on the 11th of September 2001 and that they revived the obligation of Jihad worldwide . . .

There was pretty widespread public bemusement over why al-Muhajiroun were allowed to continue to operate, though there was acute concern in government about being seen to be trampling on the right to free speech and being open to accusations of persecuting Muslims. Public patience was wearing thin at this point. The reaction of the head of the Commission for Racial Equality, Trevor Phillips, a champion of the rights of minorities, was to call for Bakri's 'immediate' deportation. The trouble was he couldn't be deported, as he'd been granted indefinite leave to stay in the country in 1993.

One possible explanation for the inaction of the authorities that had been floated was that Bakri was working for MI5 and he was the honey in the trap. It was a fair point to raise, as his colleague Abu Qatada had revealed in an interview that the Security Service had tried and failed to gain his cooperation. I'd heard lots of anecdotes from fellow journalists and contacts in the field about various people being 'tapped-up' and it seemed to be a policy.

The most damning allegation of possible collusion had been made a few years previously and from Bakri's own natural constituency. In November 2001, Azzam Publications published a very curious notice that appeared to warn visitors to steer clear of Bakri and al-Muhajiroun. It said: 'Warning Regarding British Muslims Going for

Jihad in Afghanistan – "In the land of the blind, the one-eyed man is king."'

It admonished a British Muslim group that it said it wouldn't name, but it was al-Muhajiroun, for revealing the personal details of four British Muslims who'd been killed in a US air strike on a house in Kabul the previous month. The news prompted a warning from defence secretary Geoff Hoon that anyone returning to the UK after fighting with the Taliban risked being tried for treason. Bakri retaliated with a warning that there would be 'a war within Britain' if anyone stood trial.

Azzam Publications had correctly predicted:

> As part of a plan to reinforce the 'sincerity' of the leader of this organisation in the eyes of British Muslims, we expect the British authorities to arrest him in the near future, but for him to be subsequently released.

INVISIBLE BOMBS

I'D ANTICIPATED WATCHING THE 9/11 ANNIVERSARY FROM THE sidelines, though I ended up writing a front-page story about it by mistake. The thought of competing in a cat fight with the purveyors of cliché-ridden comment pieces revolted me. I was mulling over whether we had a true phenomenon in the global jihad movement and trying to take a bird's-eye view of the entire subject.

It's not an easy thing to sum up, as related events on a typical day represented by dots on a world map would look like they had been randomly scattered across it. I felt that there had been an explosion in propaganda since the invasion of Iraq started to look imminent, though scientifically quantifying the effects of that in terms of the resultant numbers of new jihad recruits was going to be near impossible. I suspected that these thoughts were also high in the minds of our leaders, as gauging the fallout could tell us whether Iraq had produced a whole new generation of Mujahideen to fight the long-range war that al-Qaeda wanted.

The expansion in the number of pro-al-Qaeda websites certainly seemed to be in line with bin Laden's expressed wishes from the early days of the Afghanistan war. Public opinion polls showed that the al-Qaeda leader enjoyed approval ratings of around 70 per cent or more in many parts of Asia. Far from being a motley collection of volunteers drawn from the dregs of society, a recent academic study based on interviews with detained terrorist suspects found that some 70 per cent held a university degree and concluded that, on the whole, they were highly intelligent.

The most impressive response to bin Laden's call was from al-Qaeda's Saudi Arabia branch; its recruitment material was reaching all corners of the Net. The online magazines in particular became required reading for experts in the West. There had also been a flurry of new material published in the fortnight leading up to 11 September 2003, and chief among these was a new al-Qaeda publication called 'The 39 Steps to Jihad', or 'The 39 Principles of Jihad'. It was basically a crib sheet, produced by the Saudi branch, for reminding potential recruits of what was expected of them. It was the usual stuff to start with – jihad was an obligation; there must be a desire to achieve martyrdom; financing the jihad with donations was vital, as was supporting the fighters and their families. Step 14 was about avoiding publishing information that could endanger the safety of the Mujahideen, and here they took the opportunity to denounce a newspaper editor. Something published in the London Arabic daily *Al-Sharq Al-Awsat* had been a cause of upset, as the editor was branded part of 'a Crusader-Jewish scheme to spread false information about the network'. I'm not sure what it was, but they were incandescent about it. Graphics also appeared on the Net which featured a mugshot of the editor crossed through in red. Step 21 described how the network wanted jihad to be ingrained into the culture of all Muslim populations, using all available modern methods:

> 21. Publishing the Mujahideens' activities in order to arouse the notion of solidarity and strengthen pride and hope among the believers, to praise the ideal of self sacrifice for the sake of Allah and to break the media siege imposed by the enemy. There are varied ways recommended for distributing information praising Jihad including Internet websites and forums, distribution lists, circulating publications in public places (for instance mosques, schools), sending SMS, etc.
>
> . . .
>
> 34. Performing electronic Jihad – Al-Salem attributes paramount importance to the Internet as a component for Jihad. He calls believers to join the Jihad by participating in Internet forums to defend the Islam and Mujahideen, to preach Jihad and to encourage Muslims to learn more about this sacred duty. The Internet provides an opportunity to reach vast, target audiences and respond swiftly to false allegations. Computer experts are asked to use their skills and experience in destroying American, Jewish and secular websites as well as morally corrupt websites.

Advice on physical fitness, firearms training, horse riding and first aid followed. I read it and it struck me that I had accumulated quite a body of evidence from the previous few months that would back up the notion that a recruitment drive was under way to capitalise on the siege mentality caused by the Iraq war. I set about putting together a story along those lines, even though there was no obvious market for it, as it lacked a domestic angle. It was, however, simply waiting to be written and there was an opportunity here to get out the seminal piece on terrorist groups recruiting online, as no one had done it yet.

The transnational nature of the subject often made it difficult to know which country to pitch my findings to first. In the UK, for example, there was little interest in publishing news of the emergence of al-Qaeda's new third-in-command, as there was no obvious British angle, even though he posed a threat to the country. It felt like I was patrolling the news equivalent of the *Twilight Zone* sometimes. I decided to turn to the *Washington Times*, just because I had an inkling that they would like the end result. They had expressed an interest in looking at terrorist recruitment when we were chatting in the past. I called to explain what I'd got and I was invited to send the copy over. The response was immediate and positive, and my piece was slated for inclusion in the 11 September anniversary issue.

There was a last-minute change to be made. Two audiotapes by bin Laden and Ayman al-Zawahiri were released on 10 September, and Al-Jazeera had broadcast a new video of the two of them on the move in an unknown, mountainous location. I got a call from the *Times* asking me if I'd amend the story to take this into account, which I did. Bin Laden praised the 9/11 hijackers and al-Zawahiri urged Muslims to 'devour the Americans as lions do and bury them in the graveyard of Iraq'.

It made for a busy afternoon, though the hard work paid off. It was published as the lead story on the front page of the anniversary issue and it carried my byline. The headline was 'Al-Qaeda uses websites to draw recruits, spread propaganda'. It was a summary of the latest militant Islamic propaganda developments, highlighting how Iraq was being used as a recruitment tool by a wide variety of groups. I used al-Ayyiri's words to illustrate the point, which contained an admission that al-Qaeda was operating in Iraq. In one of his final articles, about the triple Riyadh bombings, he said:

The number [of those who carried out the bombings] reported by the press is inaccurate. Some of them who were not predestined for martyrdom continue to cause losses to the enemies of Allah, the Americans, in Iraq, and carried out acts of heroism there . . .

Although the al-Qaeda organisation fights to defend the [Islamic] nation, it does not fight on the nation's behalf; therefore, anyone who cannot join al-Qaeda is not exempt from the obligation of jihad [until] he has done everything possible to search for jihad and did not succeed in joining any of its fronts . . .

I also identified the group Hizb ut-Tahrir (Party of Liberation) – which was founded in the UK by Bakri before he left in 1996 over unspecified disputes over policy and formed al-Muhajiroun – as a prime example of a group that was capitalising on the situation in Iraq. Like al-Muhajiroun, it operated all over the world, in forty countries, and it was using a series of six primary websites based in the United States, Britain, Germany, the Netherlands and Pakistan to urge people to go and fight jihad in Iraq. The group shared al-Qaeda's ultimate goal of establishing a global Islamic dictatorship, a caliphate, and it claimed to have set up shop in Iraq three months previously.

I got a phone call from the *Washington Times* about a week later, to tell me there'd been a complaint. They'd had a letter from a leader of Hizb in the UK, a Dr Waheed, who was strongly objecting to my article. To cut a long letter short, there was a problem over just about everything I said about his outfit. It was the juxtaposition with al-Qaeda that appeared to be at the root of his organisation's problems. I was asked if I could prepare a response to the allegations for consideration by the *Times*'s management.

There was a brief period of worry, and a quick re-read of the story to check it for errors, though it was a very brief read. Dealing with complaints is part of the job, and I'd been in this position before, though infrequently. They usually come from litigious individuals and corporations who try to make a technical case for publishing a retraction from a damaging story, using a solicitor's notepaper to try to hammer a wedge into a small crack – unless a genuine mistake has been made, of course. The crack can be something as minor as a not totally accurate description of a person's job title, though causing general feelings of anger in someone is not a prosecutable offence.

I've lost count of the number of people who've insisted that they'd win hands-down in court if I quoted them without their prior approval. Their objections are mostly down to a natural fear reflex caused by just speaking to a journalist, because doing so must surely mean trouble. Dealing with reporters is an admittedly tricky business, as I think many people would be surprised to know that 'off the record' means nothing, legally. It's a confidentiality assurance between a journalist and a source, and upholding it is a matter of honour.

Solicitors will do anything for money, and in many instances it appears that the strength of the client's case barely matters. There is even a regular and ancient ritual performed on these occasions, as there is a standard wording for these types of complaints. Claims of grievous harm are always followed by a demand that an apology/clarification be published with the same prominence that was given to the original article. The prominence claim is always rejected out of hand, as that would mean according editorial control of the publication to an aggrieved third party. The solicitor always backs down and the publication seizes the opportunity to bury any clarification as far back in the paper as possible.

The letter denied that Hizb ut-Tahrir was involved in recruiting jihad volunteers or was connected with violence in any way. As I was drawing up my defence document, it didn't escape my attention that the group operated a deliberate policy of complaining about media coverage, come what may. It's a tactic that's been used very successfully by Christian cults and sects in the past to escape serious examination by the media. By being known as being litigious and prone to complaining about everything, the hope is that journalists and editors will be deterred.

I noticed the text of a Hizb complaint about a BBC *Newsnight* report a few weeks earlier. It was titled 'BBC NEWSNIGHT ATTEMPTS TO MALIGN HIZB UT-TAHRIR AND SILENCE MUSLIMS IN BRITAIN'. It then went on to accuse the programme of being sensationalist and the reporter of lying and cheating, and claimed that one of the people interviewed had since withdrawn his remarks. The report had focused on the text of a statement published on one of Hizb's websites that called for the killing of Jews. I'd watched that particular programme. It was followed by an interview with Waheed in the studio and he consistently refused to address the question of advocating Jew-murdering and instead used the opportunity to repeatedly and virulently accuse the BBC of biased reporting.

There were also similar complaints about a recent *Daily Star* story headlined 'Boot out these bin Laden nuts', and another from the *Daily Express* headed 'Britain lets in the bin Laden maniacs'. Then I saw a 2,000-word complaint about my piece on the same website – before I'd had the opportunity to pen my defence! Talk about getting your retaliation in early. It was so swift, in fact, that Waheed couldn't even get the date of the story right, which he said was 10 September, so it really was a pre-emptive strike, which must have relied on reading my mind at the time. It concluded:

> We therefore consider that all of these allegations are false, incorrect, unsubstantiated and wrong. In view of this we would ask you to remedy this situation by printing a prominent written retraction and apology at the earliest opportunity that points out that the allegations made by your newspaper were in fact incorrect and unfounded.

After I'd read that, I stretched my fingers, cracked my knuckles and thought, 'Goodnight, Irene,' and started tapping out my defence document.

It was very simple to cut him off at the knees right from the start, by quoting from a document I discovered on a Hizb website. I expressed no opinion: just pure fact. It was a statement titled 'Annihilate the Fourth Crusade':

> In view of the fact that America is in an active state of war, the Muslims must adopt a state of war as the basis for relations with America . . . It is a Shariah obligation that the Muslim armies [should] mobilise and break the chains and fetters that the rulers use to restrain them from assisting their brothers in Iraq, just as they restrain them from helping their brothers in Palestine and Afghanistan . . . Is it not a great shame that the armies of America and Britain are mobilised to commit aggression upon Muslim countries, one after another, whilst the armies of the Muslims lie dormant in their barracks, watching the shedding of Muslim blood? . . . Your previous generations, O Muslims, triumphed in the opening of lands and spread justice worldwide . . . should you not go forth like them, following their footsteps, and annihilate the new crusaders? . . . Let the armies move to help the Muslims in Iraq for they seek your help.

Another call to arms said:

> Has not the time come, O Muslims, after all of this, that you
> take matters into your own hands . . . With the Khilafah you
> shall go forth to fight your enemy . . . O Muslims: Hizb ut-
> Tahrir calls you to rise up with it and support it. The word and
> deed has become incumbent upon you, so will you not
> respond?

That they were seeking to attract recruits for a jihad in Iraq is a
logical conclusion that would be drawn by any reasonable person
reading the material above, I argued, before citing another recent
statement, 'The true meaning of Jihad':

> Whichever style it takes, it is clear that there is a concerted
> effort made by the Kuffar to destroy the true meaning of Jihad.
> All in all this line of discussion is a red herring, placed there by
> the Western governments in order to divert the Islamic agenda
> of discussion. Let's face it, war is an inevitability in life.

The cuttings showed that Hizb ut-Tahrir had a history of violence, as
it was blamed for mounting an attempted coup against the Egyptian
government in 1974. Its preferred means of establishing a Caliphate,
as expressed in its own literature, was by way of violent revolution,
as it had tried to do in Egypt. It was Hizb's core reason for existence.
Bin Laden's aim and method were identical. 'It's undeniable that
both groups share the same goal,' I summarised in my response.

Twenty-five people were on trial in Egypt for trying to resurrect
the group there, including three British Hizb ut-Tahrir members.
Some 55 Hizb members were arrested in an FSB raid in Moscow,
Russia, in June 2003. Hand grenades, 500 grams of plastic explosive
and extremist literature was seized during the operation. 'These are
terrorists who want to overthrow the existing regime by military
means,' FSB spokesman Sergei Ignatchenko told NTV television.

Some 500 Hizb activists had been detained in Syria and 15 in
India. It was a banned organisation in Russia and was outlawed in
Germany under anti-terrorism legislation at the start of the year. The
German authorities launched raids targeting 80 buildings across the
country a few months later. Interior minister Otto Schily said: 'This
organisation wishes to sow hatred and violence.' Governments
across the world viewed the group in similar terms.

In Denmark, in the previous year, a Hizb ut-Tahrir spokesman had been convicted of distributing racist leaflets that called for the killing of Jews. The organisation was also causing problems for former Soviet republics across central Asia and it was branded in a Heritage Foundation report as an 'emerging threat to US interests'. It was free to operate in the UK.

My response concluded with the words:

> There is a big gap between rhetoric and reality when it comes to Hizb ut-Tahrir. He should not be allowed to get away with this. His attack on my abilities as a journalist is serious, especially as his letter of complaint . . . is now being circulated on websites.

According to a *Sunday Telegraph* report, one of the British Tel Aviv suicide bombers was a member of Hizb ut-Tahrir as well as being a student of Bakri's. Hizb ut-Tahrir had also put out a statement calling for US and British troops to be treated as 'unlawful combatants' by the Iraqi Army, which was a view almost identical to that expressed by Abu Hamza's Supporters of Sharia group. As explained in my previous book, I'd even obtained a Hamza video that appeared to show the two Mike's Place bombers undergoing training in Bosnia.

One common thread in the letters was repeated denials that the party had any association with Bakri or al-Muhajiroun, which was extremely fishy. Al-Muhajiroun's own mission statement said that one of Bakri's early ideas was to found a political party as a cover for establishing a militant Islamic fifth column in the UK. Perhaps this was why some in intelligence circles were starting to whisper about 'the second Battle of Britain'.

One site that I'd started to monitor on a regular basis was an online betting operation. It was a good provider of indicators about how strong certain rumours were of the whereabouts of Saddam or bin Laden, as you could place bets on when they'd be taken out of action, or rather 'neutralised'. Until I stumbled upon it, I'd never have believed that quality terrorism information could be found in a betting shop. Gambling on terrorism-related events does sound, superficially, like a sick pastime, but it could also be a new and hugely innovative counter-terrorism tool.

The reasons why I landed there escape me, but when I saw that bets like that were on, I had to look further. As well as betting on if or when Saddam or bin Laden would be captured, you could also speculate on when it would be announced that WMD had been discovered in Iraq, or even when a Palestinian state would be established. The site, Intrade.com, based in Dublin in the Republic of Ireland, was seeing heavy betting on Saddam; punters were sensing that the net was closing in on him following the deaths of his two sons, Uday and Qusay. They had been killed in a shoot-out with US troops in July 2003, after being betrayed by a relative for a $30 million reward. The musty scent of cash was in the air.

The way it operated was pretty simple. The bets were time-limited 'contracts' that could have a value of anything between $0 and $100. The contract could be traded at any time during its lifetime, like a futures market. If you bought a contract at $10 and the prevailing price had risen to $50, then you might be tempted to sell and happily trouser the $40 profit. Or you could hold on to it in the hope of a resolution on the contract, in which case the payout would be $100 and a $90 profit. If there was no successful resolution – Saddam hadn't been captured by the end of the month, for example – then the value dropped to $0 and the contract expired. The prices could also be read as percentages, so the value of a contract could be interpreted as being a measure of confidence: if a price was very high, that would indicate a high degree of certainty that an event would come to pass. It was August 2003 and the price on Saddam being neutralised by the end of September had risen from $20 in June to $80 in July, after the death of his sons, and it had now settled down to $55. The market was estimating that there was something like a 55 per cent likelihood that he would be captured before the following month was out. An alternative, longer-term contract on his death/capture before the end of December, then priced at $68, would have proved to have been a wise investment, as that turned out to be a winner.

One factor that might have been keeping prices volatile was chatter on the jihad boards that Saddam had had the audacity to come out of hiding to visit Baghdad on a walkabout. One intercept said that he'd grown a beard and sported white hair as a disguise. He made a detour into Baghdad whilst in transit to a new hideout on 26 July and stayed for 'a few days' with hard-line supporters there. The deposed dictator even toured the streets and went unrecognised; six US military patrols were said to have passed by him. It also said that the relative who betrayed the locations of his sons did so after 'growing tired of their autocratic demands'. Uday in particular 'acted as if he owned the house', in Mosul, and threatened to kill their protector on several occasions.

It claimed that Saddam intended to announce his return to power on 25 September 2003 and he'd sent letters to Baath party officials and ex-regional governors asking for situation reports and ordering them to make preparations. He also gave them a hit list of 65 former army commanders and regime officials whom he blamed for his downfall. The report seemed to have reached the ears of US Central Command, as it had just issued a new set of images showing what a white-haired, bearded Saddam might look like.

I got in touch with Intrade.com and arranged an interview with managing director John Delaney. I was interested in finding out whether there were plans for expanding this market in betting on the news. There were fascinating possibilities, because prices were moved by rumours, speculation and inside knowledge. The price on Saddam, in theory, should roughly reflect the distance that Coalition troops were away from him.

These were early days, but 11,000 Saddam contracts had been traded since they were first listed and they'd proved to be surprisingly popular. Delaney was pretty matter-of-fact about it all, really, and I suppose it was just the free market in action and no big deal to him. The business was centred on traditional sports events, but you could also bet on currency changes, the outcome of major court cases, elections and even the weather. I asked him why they didn't trade contracts speculating on where terrorist attacks might happen next, and he said there were problems in clearly defining those kinds of contracts and judging when they'd reached a resolution. He did point out that they were taking bets on if or when the discovery of WMD in Iraq would occur, as that was a near equivalent to what I was talking about. I looked at the numbers and, as would be expected, confidence abounded prior to the invasion. The price had soared to $80 in March, but it had slumped to $22 since, as it started to become clear that there might not be anything to find.

There were also contracts out on bin Laden. The probability of his death or capture by the end of September had stood at 69 per cent in March, when he was believed to be cornered in the Balochistan province of Pakistan. That had since collapsed to just 14 per cent, and the likelihood of the USA getting to him by the end of 2003 was little better at 24 per cent. It was the nearest you could get to a scientific measurement of the heat of the trail.

At this time, details emerged of a surprisingly frank report by Italy's military intelligence agency prepared for the Italian parliament's national security committee. It said that bin Laden left Afghanistan a few days before the 9/11 attacks. It also claimed that he'd met with seven top al-Qaeda leaders and chaired a strategy meeting in the Iranian capital Tehran at the start of May. The purpose of the meeting was to finalise plans for attacks in a number of European and Asian countries, and the report named two al-Qaeda suspects – Khalid Amin and Musa Jabir – who were using Iranian passports to carry out surveillance missions in Europe. The meeting followed a 'reunion' of leaders of the network in Jeddah, Saudi Arabia, home to bin Laden's mother. No date was mentioned, but I guessed this could have been in January, when his son Hamza was married in Mecca. Father and son exchanged poems to mark the event.

Saudi Arabia was the source of the next technological innovation: the first documented, overt al-Qaeda cyber strike. There was growing resentment in the online jihad community about a site called Internet Haganah, which was dedicated to pursuing terrorism-supporting websites and getting them taken off the air. Run by Aaron Weisburd from the USA, it was also a showcase of the worst kind of content that these sites were carrying. A message attributed to bin Laden the previous year had urged supporters to, in effect, 'get him'. His time had now come, it seemed.

Weisburd was of the school of thought that argued that decisive action must be taken against sites spewing out hatred, while others thought they should all be quietly harvested for intelligence leads. Aaron's site was proudly claiming credit for the takedown of numerous jihad sites and each success was notched up on the site with a little blue AK-47 graphic. There were 65 so far and it was causing discontent among jihadis, to the extent that various groups started to talk about cooperating to return the favour and bring down his site.

He had, of course, picked up on the stirrings and responded by publishing a regularly updated list of online groups who'd responded to the call for a cyber war by declaring, one by one, 'count us in'. I watched as the list grew, though I doubted whether it was serious because I'd seen plenty of threats like this in the past and nothing had come of them, and it would be a major undertaking anyway.

The first indication that I was wrong came when I tried and failed to connect to his site. That carried on for a few hours and I was even moved to email Aaron and ask if everything was OK, but there was no response. He eventually surfaced a couple of days later with the news that his site had been wrecked by a massive cyber assault called a Distributed Denial of Service attack. This is when a computer server is 'bombed' with floods of useless data from all angles and overwhelmed, causing it to shut down. It's a method favoured by organised crime, and there have been numerous publicised incidents of hackers threatening to take down gambling sites using this method unless, for example, a ransom is paid.

Participating attack groups were directed to two websites: one carrying the software required and a second that detailed how it should be used. The software enabled participants to hijack the computers of innocent users to join in on the attack, creating an army of 'zombie boxes', or a 'bot net' comprising hundreds of thousands of boxes. There were undoubtedly many innocent users who took part, as it's not easy to detect if your machine has been press-ganged in this way. It did happen to me once. My hard drive had started clicking when it was supposed to be idle and the performance had slowed a little, so I took a look to see what was happening. I found that a 'covert channel' had been opened and my machine was being used regularly from an address in Pakistan to route who knows what on to an unknown destination.

The target was identified, the proposed method of attack was known, only the timing of the strike was uncertain. The first of three attacks came on 16 October 2003 and lasted for five hours. It briefly disrupted services for hundreds of thousands of people unconnected with Haganah as the networks clogged up. Most of the suspected attackers operated sites registered in Saudi Arabia, though some sites were hosted in places like Malaysia, where complaints tended to fall on deaf ears.

Aaron suspected that it was retaliation for managing a rare success in the country. He told me: 'Supporters of a number of al-Qaeda-affiliated forums registered to Saudi Arabia and running in Malaysia basically declared an online jihad against Haganah after eight such sites lost their . . . service a couple of weeks ago. These guys take their websites very seriously, since the sites are an important part of their communications infrastructure.'

I got in touch with Internet Traffic Report, which monitors the performance of the Internet, to see if there were any indicators of the scale of the attack, and a spokesman confirmed that it was serious. 'There was a massive spike in response time and data loss, so it's probably safe to say it had a substantial effect for at least a few hours. That spike is well beyond anything that would normally occur.'

He estimated that hundreds of thousands of people were caught in the fallout, although millions would have suffered if the attacks had taken place during office hours. 'If it affected the overall numbers that dramatically, then it certainly wasn't isolated to just a few networks,' he added.

Substantial damage had been done and it cost him several thousand dollars to get Internet Haganah back on its feet and ensure that he wouldn't be in that situation ever again. His solution was to set up a dozen 'mirror' sites – exact copies of the main site – on servers spread around the world. It would require massive firepower to bring down all of them at once. He launched a fund-raising drive to finance the plan and supporters rallied round.

The losses could have been hundreds of thousands of dollars, millions perhaps, if this had happened to a major gambling site or financial institution. Some innovative new software has now come on the market, currently available only to the richest of corporations, that can not only defend against attacks, but will attack back as well. It's like having a team of a thousand of the world's best hackers in a box and working at light speed on the premise that you have the right to strike back. It's an untested legal area at the moment, but it enables you to respond with overwhelming force and take your tormentors out of action. They would be automatically outsmarted by the software at every step.

That made me wonder: what would happen if that technology proliferated? Robot-hacker pitched against robot-hacker sounded like the introduction of weapons into cyberspace and a nightmarish, *Terminator*-like outlook for the future. It's long been predicted that the computer-dependent West is wide open to Net-borne terrorist attacks and that a cyber version of the attack on Pearl Harbor will inevitably happen at some point. The Haganah attack was a case in point and perhaps even a rehearsal for a more powerful al-Qaeda spectacular.

There had been several isolated but suspicious incidents involving hospitals, and some blamed hackers for the electricity blackouts that hit New York and other major cities on the east coast in August 2003, followed by London later in the month, then Canada and Italy. Terrorism was ruled out as the cause, though suspicions remained because there was no way that it was going to be officially admitted if it was. That didn't stop Bakri and al-Muhajiroun from stoking the speculation by putting out a triumphant press release claiming that the New York blackout was a fulfilment of 'the threat of al-Qaeda when they promised to attack the US power grids supplying the USA with electricity'.

Electricity grids have long been identified as a prime target for electronic attack, especially in the States, where many substations are controlled remotely by computers via the Net. I'd read an interview with the head of Norway's power grid, Tor Inge Akselsen, who revealed that the country's network was under constant 'aggressive' attack from unknown hackers, though no one had yet managed to get through. One theoretical case study outlined a scenario in which hackers destroyed Australia's and New Zealand's electricity grids by gaining access to computers and simply upping the voltage in the cables until they melted. Grave physical damage could be caused in a virtual instant.

I also talked to a senior IT security consultant about the situation and he said Net-borne attacks by militant Islamic groups were currently on the rise. Cyber-terrorism had become more organised over the past 18 months and groups from different countries were working together. Most of the activity seemed to revolve around Saudi Arabia, Morocco and Malaysia. 'There's been a broad realisation that the soft underbelly of the West is not government targets but business targets,' he said. 'Now, the big thing is to attack businesses. In the past, the protests came in the form of website defacements, protesting about Iraq, Chechnya, Kashmir and Afghanistan, but that has now moved towards attacking the wheels of the capitalist system.'

Haganah-type attacks are the most serious, taking corporations a day and a half to recover on average, he said. These were now frequently driven by ideology: 'We find that if Osama bin Laden names Norway as a target, for example, then Norwegian oil companies start being attacked. All this is taking place because they are motivated by speeches on Al-Jazeera. The more reporting there is of political events and of taped messages released by militant groups, the more sympathetic hacker attacks and radical insurgence occur.'

His greater concern was that terrorist groups and their supporters were currently 'pillaging' credit-card numbers from websites in vast quantities. Not only were they a source of funding, they could also be used to obtain false identification for terrorists entering the UK.

Economic sanctions and crackdowns on traditional funding routes, notably via Islamic charities, had become difficult, so credit-card fraud was an easy alternative. 'The current problem for any would-be terrorist is to be able to find a way to pay for the things he requires. For example, chemicals can be bought by credit card. We're talking about a serious number of credit-card numbers going astray: five to ten per cent of incidents involving between 1,000 and 50,000 cards.'

The thefts were usually carried out by elite hackers exploiting security loopholes in e-commerce sites. A hacker contact told me that you could even use Google to acquire credit cards. It happens when someone places a list of credit-card details in a non-secure area, perhaps by mistake or to transfer it from one machine to another, not realising that it's liable to be indexed by Google and other search engines. A lot of sensitive data like that was available, providing you knew what you were looking for. Credit-card lists tend to have a common phrase in the title of the document and are usually contained in Excel spreadsheets. Knowing this, it's possible to zero in on the mistakes.

'That's the reason why credit-card companies are moving towards PIN numbers,' said the security specialist. 'If one had to be perfectly honest, an Islamic terrorist would be a pretty terrible terrorist if he couldn't find credit cards to buy materials. The amount of effort that is going into demonstrating a semblance of normality is extraordinary. Behind closed doors, the amount of activity going on to apprehend these people is enormous. It's several orders of magnitude bigger than with the IRA.'

Fears over the UK's vulnerabilities were heightened in March 2005, when the former chair of the Metropolitan Police Authority, Lord Toby Harris, warned that a cyber-terrorist attack could bring Britain to its knees. He said that computer-literate al-Qaeda terrorists could target banking and financial systems, government, public services, communication networks and police. I was a bit mystified as to why this had suddenly come from out of the blue, but it seemed that something was in the wind. The interior ministers of the UK, France, Germany, Spain and Italy had just met to agree on closer cooperation in closing down extremist websites. More worrying were indications that just such an attack was already in the making. Cybernetic terrorism was starting to become a reality.

A day after Lord Harris's warning, and in an unusual break with the protocol on not commenting on current security threats, the government's anti-terrorism coordinator revealed that al-Qaeda-linked terrorists were actually in training for a major cybernetic attack against the UK. Sir David Omand, the former head of GCHQ, made the revelation at a conference of business leaders and security experts. Many terrorist suspects already in custody were highly computer literate, he noted. He said he was reluctant to speak publicly about the matter, out of fear of causing panic, though he quoted from an MI5 assessment of the situation that pointed out: 'Britain is four meals away from anarchy.'

The UK did seem to be in the cross hairs towards the end of 2003. The first signs of movement in Britain came during the summer, with the emergence of a fairly sophisticated Internet movie. I was interested because it was the flavour of the moment on the jihad boards and the originator appeared to be a guy operating the website of a seemingly ordinary and legitimate computer shop in London.

The film didn't appear on the shop's website; it was secreted on the server and didn't show up on the home page. Hiding material beneath an innocuous-looking site in this way was, I knew, a semi-covert method favoured by jihadist groups. It's a smart way to operate, except when prying eyes are watching.

The shop was effectively broadcasting a pro-al-Qaeda film that included a call for the assassination of the prime minister. It branded him a criminal, a godless oppressor and a 'spiteful Christian' and called on all Muslims to pray for his death. It wasn't the sort of thing you would expect from a computer hardware store in east London, but it was now a blinking red dot on the map, especially as its website was hosted by a British Internet company that was favoured by extremist groups.

US president George W. Bush and secretary of state Colin Powell also featured in the film and were accused of being 'perpetrators of debauchery'. 'Oh Allah, send upon them a hand from the truth . . . and destroy our enemy with it,' said the soundtrack. 'And for whom You have willed no guidance . . . make misery his destiny and disaster his path.'

It was titled 'The Destruction of the Unbelievers and Freedom of the Muslims' and went on to show images of the burning World Trade Center twin towers. It hinted that similar attacks were planned for the near future: 'Oh Allah, direct your forces against America . . . send upon them that which descends from the skies . . . make hurricanes a constant for them.'

There was no indication of which group may have produced the video; the only clues were the messages and the personalities who were featured. Osama bin Laden and Ayman al-Zawahiri were praised as 'the hardworking scholars'. It asked for Allah to ensure 'victory for the Mujahideen'. The style of the film was consistent with al-Qaeda's practice of attributing attacks to the will of Allah and avoiding taking any personal credit – that wasn't the done thing. Tellingly, it featured Abu Qatada, the detained radical cleric and presumed spiritual leader of al-Qaeda in Europe. He was a guru for Bakri and Hamza and their followers, so the finger pointed vaguely in their direction.

It amounted to a very powerful eight-minute package, and the overall message of the video was that new 9/11-style attacks were coming, thereby reassuring al-Qaeda supporters that the network was still functional. The addition of English subtitles to the soundtrack, which I was told was a recording of a sermon given by a radical Saudi cleric in Mecca wholeheartedly backing al-Qaeda two months after the 9/11 attacks, indicated that it might have been produced in the UK.

Sheikh Muhammad al-Mohaisany was arrested by the Saudi authorities immediately after he'd finished delivering the speech. He was held in high regard by al-Qaeda members and supporters because of this. Al-Mohaisany spoke with the greatest of passion, perhaps because he could see the police waiting in the wings, and he even broke down in tears halfway through; he was giving it all he could muster. Some 30 seconds of the soundtrack consisted of just highly amplified sobbing. His final words were about the pursuers of bin Laden: 'O Allah, convert his health to disease, And his strength into sickness, And his wealth into poverty, And his power into weakness.'

Complaints flowed once the existence of the site was publicised and the film promptly disappeared. I didn't follow up on it and try to find out what the deal was with the shop, as I got diverted onto other, more urgent, stories. It could have been a front company, or an overzealous employee, or maybe the site had simply fallen victim to militant Islamic hackers. I also figured the cops must already be onto it, so why tread on their toes?

The use of video on the Net was taken to an entirely new level of sophistication in October 2003 by al-Qaeda in Saudi Arabia, with the release of the Riyadh Martyrdom Tapes. I found the 45-minute-long video on a link that had been posted to a jihad forum and soon found out that it contained the last wills of four of the suicide attackers in the bombings of the Western housing compounds.

I had few clues about what it was all about initially, because it was in Arabic, but when it came to a man addressing the camera with an AK-47 propped up behind him, it was obvious that he was delivering a statement of some sort. As I was listening and puzzling over what he might be saying, I got a shock. He paused, and then started speaking in English.

This was the first time that an al-Qaeda operative had spoken in English on such a video. Normally, they stick to Arabic and avoid using English at all – even when they know the language – as it's the tongue of the infidels. There were only two minutes of English on the tape, but I was entranced by it. Wearing a red and white turban and a handlebar moustache, the speaker had Indian or Pakistani features. It became apparent that he was one of the suicide bombers who participated in the May 2003 attacks in Riyadh. Here he was, locking eyes with me from beyond the grave. 'For the American soldiers, we say you have to know that your government has become a big evil, killing innocent people, destroying homes, stealing our money and holding our sons in jail,' he said. 'We promise that we will not let you live safely and you will not see from us anything else, just bombs, fire, destroying homes, cutting your heads. Our Mujahideen is coming to you very soon, to let you see what you didn't see before.'

His eyes opened so wide at the end, they looked like those of a madman trying furiously to control his rage; he leaned in towards the camera and held the evil stare for a few seconds before it faded to another scene. He was followed by another man, who, after speaking at length in Arabic, also gave a brief address in English. He was of a more slender build and looked like he might be from one of the Gulf states. He said:

> I invite you to accept Islam by saying ['there is only one God and Muhammad is His Prophet'] and I will be your brother in Islam. And it doesn't matter what is your nationality or your colour. After you accept Islam, if any enemy attacked you, I will do everything, even if it cost my life, to save you.
>
> We want from all Christian and Jewish to go out from our Islamic countries and release our brothers from jails and stop killing Muslims, or we will kill you as you are killing Muslims.

We will continue in our fighting until we get what we want. The real Muslims, they mean what they say: very soon, all the world will see what we do. You will not enjoy in your life forever.

They were doing with the Riyadh attackers what they'd done with the 9/11 hijackers: making sure they lived on forever and continued to serve the cause as digital recruiting sergeants. A report later named the first English-speaking attacker as Hazam bin Mohammed al-Kashmiri. The second was identified as Mohammed bin Abd al-Wahab.

The production quality of the tape was worthy of an established international broadcaster. There were other surprises. One long section featured long-distance footage of the attacks filmed by al-Qaeda as they were taking place. The soundtrack at this point changed to what seemed to be a recording from a mobile phone that had been left on by one of the attackers. There were lots of shouts of 'Allah-u-Akbar!' and sounds of explosions and bursts of automatic weapons fire.

Bin Laden was shown briefly at the end. It was brand-new footage, though it wasn't covered in the mainstream media to any great extent, probably because there was some initial uncertainty over whether it was unique. It was close-up, overexposed film of a smiling and cheerful bin Laden, dressed in camouflage fatigues and wagging his finger as he apparently dispensed words of advice to a group of followers. There were no clues about the location or possible date, though he was dressed in the same manner as seen in his first video statement after 9/11, when he was probably in the Paktia province of Afghanistan.

As I was chasing various leads connected to the emergence of the Saudi videos, I soon came across another powerful example of the connection between virtual and physical terrorism. One site that had showed up on the radar was a UK-based jihad discussion forum and I was just browsing through the threads, looking for anything suspicious, when I came across a link to a document full of Arabic and odd diagrams. My suspicions were heightened when I looked at the home page of the site, because it didn't have one: there was just a message from the hosting provider, which said the owner hadn't yet uploaded the main index page.

That suggested the site was being used for some covert purpose, as I recognised this as a signature of such sites: no home page, yet files on the server. It was worth a closer look, I thought, and fired up some specialist software that's designed to interrogate Web servers and find out exactly what's stored on them. Using this, I can 'see' what's underneath a blank home page and look into the inner structure of a site in a way that's not possible with a standard browser program. The results were utterly spectacular. There were literally thousands of files lurking there.

It would have taken me days to download all of the material, so I set about selecting the most interesting stuff. There were video clips, audio recordings of sermons in Arabic, handbooks, Word documents, weapons guides . . . it went on and on and I set about sampling the materials. There was an operating guide for Stinger surface-to-air missiles. Some of the warfare and weapons manuals carried an email address that was mentioned in the *Mujahideen Poisons Handbook*, which had emerged the year before and contained instructions on manufacturing ricin. It has been associated with the al-Qaeda-linked Algerian Armed Islamic Group (GIA).

The site was being used as a central 'data warehouse' and other sites were drawing on the lake of content there. I took to referring to it as The Repository. It was an extensive library of technical terrorism know-how. There was little doubt in my mind that it was al-Qaeda connected, as it was hosted by the same company that was keeping the network's official, but rarely updated, home page online. Some of the documents there also sported al-Qaeda's logo: a silhouette of a man on a rearing thoroughbred horse holding a rifle aloft in mid-war cry. Detractors preferred to describe the steed as a donkey.

Even after distilling the content down to the most obvious candidates worthy of further examination, there was a vast amount of information to cope with. Some of the documents clearly related to bomb-making, as their names contained abbreviations such as TNT, C4 and PETN, which is an explosive that's usually used in detonators. One file was a 143-page-long eulogy to Yahya Ayyash, Hamas's former chief bomb-maker, alias 'The Engineer'. He was assassinated in December 1995 by the Israelis with an exploding mobile phone.

There were also more mysterious documents showing strange-looking black machines and some sort of guide to handling small cylinders of liquid. Some of the files were computer programs. I checked one out with an expert who disassembled the code to see what made it tick, and he said it was a Trojan Horse program. These are used by hackers to secretly take over someone else's machine and turn it into a zombie box to be used in Denial of Service attacks against websites, like the one directed at Aaron's Internet Haganah site.

Aside from anything else, I found it fascinating that instructions on physical and cybernetic weaponry were listed side by side. It spoke volumes about al-Qaeda's keenness on exploiting information technology, and it seemed that bin Laden's past statement about the importance of the Internet as a new land of jihad had been heeded. It also looked like a menu for just the kind of asymmetrical warfare (where a weaker force attacks a stronger one by unconventional and opportunistic means) that had long been warned about. Using the material on the site, you could, for example, carry out massive bomb attacks against a city and then maximise the casualties by knocking out computers at electricity stations, hospitals and law-enforcement agencies to hamper the rescue effort.

I started to ponder on the legalities of actually possessing this material and all the other documents that I'd collected over the years. I was certainly in breach of anti-terrorism laws by possessing documents likely to be of use to a terrorist. I could even be charged for planning terrorist attacks, as I had technical plans for aircraft carriers, buildings and even the by now classified details of the internal layout of Air Force One. I had everything I needed to start my own international terrorist group.

All I required was an anonymous Net connection and Google to fetch some credit-card details and I'd be able to tap into a substantial line of funding within minutes. I could then hit the chat rooms to find the recruiters, maybe undertake an interview over the Net via a webcam and put forward my attack plan and request back-up. With the assistance of like-minded individuals, I could then start discreetly putting together some massive nerve gas bombs, using the credit cards to order the components, and start casing the targets. I might even be able to do much of that remotely, by simply monitoring traffic-cams on the Web. Al-Qaeda's best-practice guidelines on setting up safe houses and avoiding detection by law-enforcement agencies was to hand, so avoiding making basic mistakes was just a quick read away.

Members of the attack team would spread around the country and we'd communicate in couched terms via the guest book of a website devoted to flower arranging. Number 10 Downing Street would be referred to as red tulips, the Ministry of Defence building in Whitehall as yellow roses and Buckingham Palace as white lilies. We'd swap links to satellite images of the targets via Hotmail accounts to plan the timing of the attacks. A network of hackers in the Middle East would be on standby to disable London's traffic lights and Underground system and flood computer networks with viruses to enhance the effectiveness of the strike. I wouldn't say it would be easy, but it was all very possible, and everything I needed was sitting on my hard drive.

The more mysterious documents in The Repository interested me most, because I hadn't seen them before and they were obviously construction guides, though I didn't know what for. I needed the advice of an expert and I sent some notes and a link to the site to a prime counter-terrorism contact to see what he made of them.

On several of the documents was a mention of another website address and I checked it. It carried copies of all the documents in the al-Qaeda repository and they were also hidden beneath a conventional-looking site. Even more intriguingly, I traced the operators of the site to London. They were supporters of an al-Qaeda suspect called Abu Musab al-Zarqawi (they had named one of their websites after his spiritual mentor, Sheikh Abu Mohammed al-Maqdisi), who would soon emerge as the leader of al-Qaeda in Iraq.

There was a solid UK angle to the story now, so I thought it was time to contact a newspaper. I got in touch with a friend on the *Sunday Times* and explained what I had and emailed over my ever-lengthening file of notes. There was a little scepticism at first and it's always awkward, as a journalist, to be on the receiving end like that. He was quickly satisfied that something was up after he'd looked through the documents, though he thought that the London address I'd come up with was bound to be bogus.

It was and it wasn't: the postcode was nonsensical, but the house number and street existed and it was close to Heathrow airport. Maybe it was a slip-up, as they'd already failed to ensure that the documents weren't visible to outsiders. Security obviously wasn't their strong point and they needed to re-read their own material. 'Maybe they've just made another mistake,' I suggested to the reporter. He agreed that it was possible, but he wanted to immediately answer the question by casing out the house. He said he was going to drive there to take a look and he'd call me when he arrived at the target.

A couple of hours later, he phoned. He had the house in sight and he was whispering. 'You could be right,' he said. 'This looks dodgy. I mean really dodgy.'

He explained that the street was a smart one – two rows of well-kept, desirable suburban properties – except for the house he was looking at. It stuck out like a sore thumb, he said. 'It looks like the kind of place where people doss down on the floor for the night.'

This prompted me to have a look on the Net for more information. I struck lucky right away and came up with floor plans for the house. I relayed information about the internal layout to the reporter and he was flabbergasted. It was like I was providing him with X-ray vision.

'How could you possibly know that?' he said.

I explained that the owner of the house had recently filed for planning permission for alterations to the property and the application was available via the local authority website, complete with architect's plans. The owner wanted to extend the house at the back and add more bedrooms. It looked like nine or more individuals could be housed there and it could have been student accommodation. Indeed, I'd tentative evidence to suggest that one of the individuals involved with the site might be a student at a local college, or was using facilities there.

'This just looks really dodgy,' he said again, explaining that there was a van outside a large garage at the side of the house. There were bright lights on inside and he could see from the gap under the doors that several people were moving about in there. They were working on something. It dawned on us both at the same time that we might have actually tracked down a terrorist cell at work in London.

The reporter decided to withdraw to make further enquiries, out of fear of interfering with any surveillance operation. This was just days after news had leaked that MI5 had recently briefed Britain's emergency planners that there was 'a real and serious' threat of north African al-Qaeda supporters carrying out a huge bomb attack. The Foreign Office had just issued a warning to Britons not to travel to Saudi Arabia.

The following day, the reporter called to say that an expert he'd contacted had identified the purposes of some of the diagrams of strange-looking machinery in one of the repository documents. One looked so odd that we took to calling it 'the Doomsday device'. It wasn't that bad a guess, as the specialist said it was a machine for producing nitrates which were used in the bulk manufacture of explosives.

With the deadline for that week's issue fast approaching, my counter-terrorism contact came back to me with his results. The peculiar diagrams of fluid-filled containers and tubing were in fact instructions on how to build a bomb that would escape detection by airport screening equipment. A liquid explosive could be detonated using electricity-conducting fluids rather than wires. He thought it was ingenious: it was an 'invisible' bomb. He said: 'It's pretty clear they are looking for mechanisms to get past detection devices, from X-ray to thermal neutral analysis to search by a human. The device suggested is a major first step, since it could be componentised and designed in such a way that it passed *all* detection mechanisms.'

That was the headline for the subsequent story: 'Al-Qaeda "invisible" bomb plan found'. It seemed that there were grave concerns about this turn of events behind the gilded doors of officialdom. The article noted that 'Terrorism experts confirmed the site was genuine and the technical information accurate' and added that 'The *Sunday Times* has been asked not to name the site . . .'.

There was also an alternative bomb design there that was so fiendishly simple and unobtrusive that I appreciated, after my expert contact had explained what it was, that I shouldn't describe how it works. It would be capable of bringing down an airliner and would leave no trace of explosive.

He added that he was going to re-examine the forensic evidence gathered in the investigation of the mysterious crash of an airliner in New York City on 12 November 2001. Flight 587 was bound for the Dominican Republic when it nosedived into the Rockaway Beach residential area of the borough of Queens four minutes after taking off from JFK airport. Around 274 people were killed in the incident, which added to the trauma that had already been caused to the residents of the city and stoked mild panic about a second wave of al-Qaeda attacks.

It was initially suspected that one of the aircraft's engines had fallen off, though the subsequent investigation decided that the cause of the crash may have been due to the tail-fin becoming detached, perhaps due to turbulence caused by the take-off of the previous departing aircraft. That was greeted with scepticism and claims that the US government was covering up something because it didn't want people to avoid flying, but no trace of explosives had been found. If, however, this invisible bomb had been deployed that day, then just such confusion could be expected.

Everything I'd uncovered, said my contact, would be considered highly classified if it had been discovered by an intelligence agency. I needed to be careful about revealing too much, he advised me. And I have been, I think.

HOLD TIGHT, LONDON

BRITISH INTERESTS IN TURKEY WERE ATTACKED THREE WEEKS LATER IN a double bombing that targeted the British consulate in Istanbul and the headquarters of HSBC bank. Consul-General Roger Short was among at least 14 people killed in the attack. In all, some 27 people died and 400 were left wounded. The bombings had followed attacks against two synagogues the previous week, which killed around twenty-five people.

I contacted a security consultant to see if he'd picked up any cybernetic signals that could have given advance warning of the attacks. He said the best he could do was to point out that there had been an increase in 'politically motivated hacking activity' in Turkey prior to the event. He worked for major banks, so he may have had some insight into the situation at HSBC.

He'd done a study to see if there were any correlations between cybernetic attacks and physical terrorist attacks, and there were some. There was an increase in malevolent hacking activity in Saudi Arabia and Turkey at a time when war in Iraq was starting to look inevitable. Since 9/11, he said, there had been a steady rise in assaults on targets that were primarily located in the UK, the USA, Australia, Germany and Italy. The main centres of hacking activity were in Pakistan, Morocco, Egypt, Kuwait, Indonesia, Turkey and Saudi Arabia. There had been a rise in cyber attacks on British and Australian targets just prior to the Bali bombing in October 2002, which killed over 200 people, and the same went for the Morocco attacks and the Riyadh bombings.

The hottest jihadi chatter was a story claiming that bin Laden had paid a flying visit to Iraq. I wasn't sure if it was to be taken seriously, as it seemed too risky a proposition for someone who took no risks at all in evading his pursuers. There was much joyous praising of the leader, who'd apparently moved into the country under the cover of darkness and had paid a pre-dawn visit to a training camp there. The purpose was said to be to 'oversee the transfer of the battle from Afghanistan to Iraq'.

Bin Laden had apparently toured a number of training camps, though no further details were given. At the same time, more credible chatter pinpointed Saddam as hiding out on a farm to the south of Baghdad. There was a big upswing in attacks on Coalition troops around this time, including a failed attempt to assassinate US deputy defence secretary Paul Wolfowitz in a rocket attack on his Baghdad hotel. I sensed that al-Qaeda were on the rise in Iraq, though it was difficult to gauge which faction, incoming jihad fighters or Saddam's militia, was responsible for the most chaos.

Saddam seemed to be under far more pressure than bin Laden, judging by the betting on when they'd be dealt with. The price was high on Saddam and low on bin Laden. The flurry of letters and audiotapes from Saddam had dried up, and he hadn't been heard from for two months now, since August. Many of his former colleagues had surrendered or been captured or killed, as US forces worked their way through the famous deck of cards of most-wanted regime figures.

Saddam was said to be accompanied by three close aides and was moving from one safe house to another each night. A sighting in mid-November placed him in the city of Ramadi, where he met with 15 commanders of the Republican Guard. He apparently was sporting a long beard and wearing traditional Arabic dress. No one recognised him at first. A new audiotape emerged soon after the reported meeting, urging all Iraqis to join in a jihad to oust the occupying forces.

At this point, little was known about the leaders of the Mujahideen, or how many there were in the country. Some sceptics suggested that, like WMD, there weren't any. I knew from the chatter that they were operating in Iraq. Any doubts about this, however, started to evaporate in November with the emergence of a brand new phenomenon that was probably the last word in reality television: Terrorism TV.

It started with the release of three short videos on a variety of militant Islamic forums. The first showed a shaky, long-distance view of a busy road intersection in a city – Baghdad, I presumed. I could just about make out what looked like a woman, or someone dressed as a woman, approaching a police officer standing at the junction. A brief conversation ensued, before the woman turned away from him and ran. Seconds later, the policeman disappeared in a cloud of smoke as a bomb exploded close to him, the blast-wave rocking the cameraman's car.

The second, 15-second-long, video was shot from inside a car moving in busy traffic. The shoulder of the driver was briefly visible, as was the silhouette of someone sitting in the rear nearside passenger seat, when the cameraman swung around to get a view of the rear window. Momentarily, an orange fireball was visible as a roadside bomb exploded on the opposite carriageway.

The third clip was footage, with sound this time, of a firefight with US troops. The target was a US Humvee armoured vehicle that had stopped at a road junction and the attackers were blasting away at it from inside a wrecked shop, while a call to prayers from a nearby mosque wailed above the cacophony of gunfire. The Humvee was peppered by small clouds of dust as the attackers' rounds impacted on the ground around it.

It looked like the jihadists had adopted a media strategy that was pioneered by the al-Qaeda-linked Islamic rebels in Chechnya, where a camera operator was an essential component of any attack team. The difference in Iraq was that the videos were being released on the Net as soon as possible and getting close to real-time.

The rest of the media didn't share my sense of wonder, initially, as the clips were low resolution and unsuitable for transmission. They'd first emerged on the website of a Saudi cleric who was known to be a friend and spiritual adviser to bin Laden. Sheikh Salman al-Oudah was released from prison in 1998 after serving a five-year sentence for speaking out against the Saudi royal family. In 2002, he was forcibly deported by a dozen Jordanian intelligence agents one hour before he was due to deliver a speech titled 'The Islam of Jihad or Terrorism?' at a conference in Amman. He had been forbidden from giving sermons in mosques and so he was using his website, islamtoday.net, as an alternative public-speaking platform.

He had built up a huge worldwide following, and two other major websites that were devoted to distributing his messages were operated out of the UK, from south London. A couple of weeks after the Iraq videos, a new film came from al-Qaeda in Saudi Arabia, which showed a terrorist cell in training, apparently inside the country. Black-clad recruits were shown practising the storming of a building and handling weapons and missile launchers. The only identifiable figure in the film was an al-Qaeda operative called Abdel al-Otaibe, who was shot dead by Saudi security forces days before the Riyadh bombings in May. His message from Paradise was a familiar one: 'I strongly encourage young Muslims to join the jihad for Allah's sake, to protect our land and to drive Christians and Jews out of Muslim countries.'

Al-Qaeda's propaganda and recruitment machine was clearly expanding at breathtaking speed and had already become much bigger than I'd anticipated in the summer. It seemed that I was right to suspect that it was taking control of the insurgency in Iraq, as Saddam's influence on events seemed to me to be waning markedly, with the USA hot on his trail. Perhaps I should have expressed my feelings by buying up some Saddam contracts on the betting markets, as those in the know reportedly made a killing in the hours before it was announced, on 13 December 2003, that he'd been captured alive.

There had been a window of an hour or so between the rumour first surfacing and being widely propagated when the winning contract could have been bought at a price in the high 60s. Those few who traded in that hour were looking at very easy and handsome profits, as they bought up all the contracts they could get their hands on, knowing they were worth the maximum $100 apiece. Some of them crowed about their prowess in a discussion forum afterwards. There were suspicions that some of the buyers might have had military connections and inside information. I was kicking myself that I'd spent that hour searching around the Net for more news, rather than getting in on the betting feeding-frenzy.

When he was famously hauled out of his spider hole, Saddam was indeed sporting a beard and big bushy hair, giving him the appearance of a mad flasher who'd been caught red-handed. He'd obviously had little time recently for keeping up personal appearances. He had been finally tracked down to a farm near his home town of Tikrit, very close to the spot where he took his annual televised swim in the Tigris. The most poignant symbol of his fall from tyranny, for me, came when his shack-like living quarters were examined. They were located on the opposite bank of the river from one of his most lavish palaces. There wasn't a tin of his favoured Quality Street chocolates in sight; just a few Mars bars and a box of fun-sized Bounty bars.

Saddam's capture did nothing to halt the rise in public anxiety about mega-terror attacks. The jitters had spread as far as Japan, where a recent opinion poll had shown that 63 per cent of the population said they were afraid of terrorist incidents at home and 80 per cent thought that the chances of an attack were increasing. This anxiety was intensified when bin Laden and al-Zawahiri released new audiotapes warning of fresh attacks in the USA and calling for a jihad in Iraq to oust the Americans.

Japan had been named by bin Laden as a particular target for al-Qaeda in his previous audiotape in October, along with Britain, Australia, Poland, Italy and Spain. I guessed that the worries in Japan weren't helped by memories of the sarin nerve gas attack on Tokyo's subway system, which was perpetrated by the Aum religious cult in 1995. Twelve people were killed and five and a half thousand injured as the gas, released from glass jars on three trains, spread through the network. The country's inclusion on al-Qaeda's hit list was due to the participation of Japanese troops in the occupation of Iraq, despite this deployment being highly controversial amongst the Japanese people, as it required the passing of new legislation which was at odds with the country's post-Second World War pacifist constitution. Concerns were also expressed in the country that the move would be viewed as part of a policy of Japanese expansionism.

In the latest tape, bin Laden claimed that the US takeover of Iraq was simply the start of a full-blown invasion of the entire region. He referred to the capture of Saddam, which indicated that the tape had been made within the last three weeks. The leaders of surrounding states were warned that 'their turn is coming', following 'the capture of their former comrade in betrayal and treason and puppetry to America'..

The tapes, as always, received saturation media coverage. They also reinforced the public impression that the USA chose the wrong target in Iraq. No WMD had been found and here were the al-Qaeda leaders, clearly alive and in ebullient mood, threatening to wreak more unprecedented havoc on the world. It added power to the arguments of those who maintained that the USA should have fully dealt with bin Laden before Saddam. I, despite having spent several years researching this area, still cannot understand what exactly made invading Iraq such a high priority for the American administration after 9/11.

Officials were claiming that three-quarters of the al-Qaeda leadership had been taken out of action since 9/11 and that alone proved that they hadn't taken their eye off the ball, yet the tapes and the WMD no-show made people, including me, wonder how truthful that might be. I thought the time was ripe for looking into how damaged the network was and what role the 'situation' in Iraq, i.e. the growing jihad, was playing in generating new recruits. And I soon found part of the answer in Italy.

It came in the form of leaked police transcripts of a bugged telephone conversation between two alleged al-Qaeda members discussing how to recruit and train new brigades of terrorists in Europe. The documents formed part of a court case in Milan, but they were leaked to a Milanese newspaper, *Il Nuovo*, which had quoted at length from them. I stumbled on the story by accident really, because foreign-language exclusives don't travel well and they are not automatically picked up by UK and US newspapers. This major insight might have slipped by quietly in the night, if it hadn't caught my eye.

Italian isn't one of my strong points and I could see that there were yards of it – some 5,000 words – and most of it was a verbatim transcript of the phone conversation. It was fairly easy to get a translation of the material and I'm glad I did, because it cast new light on exactly how al-Qaeda was regrouping post-9/11. It also revealed that London was considered 'the nerve centre' for the command and control of al-Qaeda's operations in Europe. In June 2002, operatives could be smuggled in and out of the UK on false passports with apparent ease, though by March 2003 it appeared that the authorities were cracking down and the capital had 'become a dangerous place'.

The transcripts were part of the results of an 18-month-long investigation into the activities of the al-Qaeda-linked Ansar al-Islam group in Italy. The group had established a foothold in northern Iraq and ran a number of training camps there. They were at the top of the list of targets for the Americans in the run-up to the invasion of Iraq. The leader of Ansar al-Islam was a radical Islamic cleric called Mullah Fatah Krekar, who had studied under Sheikh Abdullah Azzam in Pakistan and claimed to have met bin Laden in Peshawar in 1990. He'd fled from Iraq to Norway in the early 1990s and sought refugee status there, though it's since transpired that he'd been making regular trips back and forth to oversee the group's activities in Iraq. He is currently facing expulsion from the country to face terrorism charges levelled by the new Iraqi government.

The Italian case had also highlighted close links between Ansar and another network called al-Tawhid wal Jihad, which was headed by Abu Musab al-Zarqawi. He was the one pulling the strings and it was the second time I'd come across that name. It had first cropped up during the previous *Sunday Times* investigation into the suspected terrorist cell in London, so I read on with great interest. Maybe there was scope here for a follow-up, I thought, as he was suspected of involvement in the bombings of British interests in Turkey.

The bugged phone conversation involved a radical Egyptian cleric called Nasr Usama Mustafa, also known as Abu Umar. He has since vanished without trace and it has been suggested that he was captured by a Western intelligence agency and secretly whisked to a friendly Middle Eastern country where torture is legal, for interrogation, in a process called 'extraordinary rendition'. It is known to be a method favoured by the CIA and is a hugely controversial practice.

The conversation took place on 15 June 2002 inside the offices of an Islamic organisation in Milan. Abu Umar was speaking to an unknown 'Arab from Germany'. Parts of the conversation are reproduced below. The document was officially known as Transcript No. 13,596.

After an exchange of pleasantries, the man from Germany said there had been a meeting with 'the Sheikhs' in Poland on 16 May 2002 and 'the final decision was to completely change the Hizb ut-Tahrir front'. That appeared to confirm that Hizb ut-Tahrir, with which I'd had a run-in after the second 9/11 anniversary, was an al-Qaeda front organisation, though it's an allegation that the group strenuously denies.

The German refers to new groups that have been established in Europe by al-Qaeda number three Saif al-Adel and a Sheikh Abd al-Wahab, composed of operatives who'd undergone jihad training in camps in Chechnya. He also refers to an Abu Serrah, who is planning to set up a 'battalion of 25 to 26 units', and talks of the need for intelligent and highly educated people for 'our project', which will require careful planning. The master-planner for the project, which is never outlined, was said to be based in Saudi Arabia and 'of the blood of bin Laden', called Abu Salman (or Abu Suleyman).

The overarching aim of al-Qaeda in Europe was to build an Islamic army, which had the codename Force 9. The network was avoiding operating out of mosques, because they were under surveillance and it was now too risky. Instead, it was in the process of buying nine multi-storey office buildings to use as alternative bases. Very intriguing insights into the scale and methods used in establishing cells in Europe followed:

> [Abu Umar] How are things going in Germany?
>
> [Man] I cannot complain. There are ten of us; we are taking an interest in Belgium, Spain, the Netherlands, Turkey and Egypt, Italy and France, but the nerve centre is still London . . . Sheikh Adlen has given a great deal of money; as I told you this plan has no need of any further comments or words.
>
> [Abu Umar] I hope that this will cause our youth to shine.
>
> [Man] That is our objective; each of us has a task, for instance if one has ten operatives available, he becomes their leader and then it is up to him to decide whether to organise them into smaller groups or to keep them like that. The important thing is to use one's intelligence.
>
> [Abu Umar] Even if they are not Arabs?
>
> [Man] That is not important. We need also foreigners; we have Albanians, Swiss, British . . . It is enough that they be of a high cultural level. In Germany we have interpreters and interpreters that translate books; we have also in telecommunications, also in Austria; the important thing is that their faith in Islam be sincere.
>
> [Abu Umar] We have never had any problems with them; on the contrary, we have noticed that they are very enthusiastic and they participate.
>
> [Man] Besides, neither you nor I are the ones who decide whether to take them or not; those who make the decision are the people with Hizb al-Tawid.
>
> [Abu Umar] I am very enthusiastic about this plan.
>
> [Man] Never worry about money, because Saudi Arabia's money is your money; the important thing is not to rush ahead, because it is all new; there are old things too, but the training is completely new. The man who wanted to set up the plan is close to Emir Abdullah [Osama bin Laden] and we are grateful to Emir Abdullah. Get prepared.
>
> [Abu Umar] I am ready.
>
> [Man] We are also awaiting the sheikh from Iraq . . .
>
> [Abu Umar] [interrupting] Is he not the one from Algeria?
>
> [Man] The one who used to be in London.

After a brief discussion about a rumour about an al-Qaeda figure that was circulating on the Internet, the man in Germany revealed more:

> [Man] Beware of the Internet, it is frightening. These are the initial indications from Sheikh Adlen; we must ignore the Internet. If you communicate via the Internet, use a different language . . . The main point is that each group protects the next group without mutually destroying each other, and each group must be distant from the next. Chechnya takes care of training the youngsters, while another group takes care of information. And yet another takes care of the air that we breathe. There is only one condition. One or two people from the group take part in every meeting, where they discuss their situation and they listen to the others. The important thing is that these people be of the same rank as the others . . . and they must all be aware of everything. We are all one and one is God.
>
> [Abu Umar] We fight for the word of freedom, even via paper.
>
> [Man] Yes, this too is part of our plans. There is a certain amount of information that I cannot provide now until we see each other next, God willing . . .
>
> [Man] There is need of merchants, of professors, of engineers, of medics, of trainers, but on one point . . . There is money for this cause but money needs to bring in more money, as I told you earlier I am not the one making the decisions. Those who err pay in the name of the Sharia and there are tests to pass. I take care of my city in Germany. The other guy takes care of his city in Algeria. Each city has its pupils. And he . . . is the one who chooses them. The responsibility is totally his; if a person errs, then the [leader] answers for that. But, dear Abu Umar, it is not quantity but quality; even if they number only ten, that is sufficient. Because you can study them, you can understand them psychologically. You do like at school: there is kindergarten, there is elementary school, high school and college. At each stage, there is an exam. But the most important things are security, prudence, intelligence, order and communications, which must be conducted via other people [messengers] or else one speaks in a different language, so it is necessary to carefully study that point because each group refers to its own region. I will give you a small example: Italy is part of Austria, Germany is part of the Netherlands,

the Netherlands is part of London. This is only an example, though; for this, too, lessons are required because prudence is the thing that saves you. Take for instance the case of Ismail who has been in the Netherlands since 1979 and no one knows who he is . . . I repeat, the organisation must be unimpeachable where confidentiality is concerned . . .

[Abu Umar] What do I busy myself with?

[Man] You sell, you buy, you print, you record, after which the person involved will come to you and speak with you personally; it is sufficient for things not to get mixed up with one another, and it is sufficient to avoid easy arrests; we know perfectly well that I, you and the others are all under surveillance. I know that I am being followed by the police but I take them for a ride; the important thing is to find a way of getting a message to someone else. Dear Abu Umar, technology is needed to fight God's enemies.

They must have been under the misguided impression that the phone line was very secure, as the Germany guy was being very candid and breaking all of his own rules. He then briefly talked about Abu Qatada, and how other people are now running his group in the UK in his absence, and how a network of cells inside a country is actually managed by leaders in another, adjacent country. He explained to an incredulous Umar that each group sends messages and shifts money around Europe inside books.

The Polish network, called the Katilea Group, communicated with others by simply posting books with dollars 'and other things' concealed inside them. It was simple and he suggested that their efforts were eased by the cooperation of corrupt officials. He explained that lack of surveillance and rampant corruption in eastern European countries that were not yet members of the European Union, notably Poland and Bulgaria, made it 'easy' to operate.

The most favoured country was Austria, where 'a great deal of money is circulating'. 'If you are on the wanted list, you have two options. Either you hide there [in Austria] or in the mountains,' he explained. An operative known as Abu Othman had spent a long time in Austria before he was 'transferred' to Saudi Arabia, where he wrote several communiqués in support of bin Laden. Key al-Qaeda figures were currently on the move in Algeria, Morocco and Bosnia.

There was a second transcript, this time between two other members of Abu Umar's group, who appeared to be of a lower rank. The conversation between the two took place in a bugged, high-security cell in Milan's police headquarters after the two had been captured during raids against the group in March 2003. During the conversation, one of the suspects wonders why they're being held together, as he expected them to be isolated from one another. I thought that it must have been a deliberate ploy by their captors and halfway through they appear to suspect that something's up and start singing jihad anthems and reciting from the Koran.

What shone through from the conversation was the determination and fanaticism of the two, tinged with disappointment, in that they might be denied the chance to achieve martyrdom. The two are identified as Mera'i, otherwise known as Radi al-Ayashi, and 'Mohammed the Somali', alias Ciise Maxamed Cabdullah. After introductions and some chat about why they were being held, they soon got down to talking about getting their stories straight.

> [Mohammed] We do not know each other.
> [Mera'i] You do not even need to say it. They have already asked me if I knew you and I answered that I met you at the mosque.
> [Mohammed] Fine, let us stick to that version, because they have nothing on me. When they asked me how come I was here, I answered that I came to look for my cousin, a member of the family whom I have been desperately seeking high and low. But quite honestly here in your place there is something wrong. I am astonished by the business of the bag. How could they know that it was there? How could they have brought me the bag? Why are they asking me where the training camps in Syria are? I am speechless.
> [Mera'i] You know, they try to get you to speak; they try to make you believe that they know everything, but they know nothing. I have very many brothers in jail who have been sentenced to serve from five to fifteen years, in Italy, in Bosnia, in the whole world.
> [Mohammed] So there is a link. So you are under surveillance.
> [Mera'i] Listen, brother, if I had been discovered I certainly would not be here. I would already be serving my sentence. You have to know that spies sometimes come to the mosque; a few spies come. These guys want to know who a

person is and where he comes from when they see new movement . . . They try to gather information and then they go tell them.

[Mohammed] I will tell you that I saw them from the very first day, even when we were arrested and they put me into the car and pointed a pistol at me. They told me that they will conduct enquiries concerning me and that they will ask the Americans too. I told them that they are enemies of God, to take their hands off me; after that, they asked me what my true nationality was.

[Mera'i] Take them for a ride; tell them that you are Egyptian. Let us thank God that they did not find our passports. I have few things at home; I have only money, but the others are hidden, but . . . I have only a few euros at home . . .

[Mohammed] They do not frighten me; one must always have faith in God.

[Mera'i] I have been reciting the Koran all night.

[Mohammed] So have I.

[Mera'i] They are just waiting for a word, for us to say that we are Mujahideen, and they will be happy; since they have nothing, let us take them for a ride . . .

His colleague then expressed concern that the police had found the false Moroccan passports that had just been made for them. Mera'i told him that he gave them to another member of the group called Brahim and he didn't have them on him when he was arrested. Brahim knew where all the passports, money and hideouts were located, but he could be trusted not to talk.

Mohammed said that as soon as he was released, he would head for Romania, where he knew that other wanted terrorist figures were hiding. He suspected that he was where he was because his phone had been tapped. He then named three people who he said were on most-wanted lists and were waiting for him: Abderrazak, Abu Zaied and Abd al-Karim.

Mera'i was sure that he wasn't the reason for them getting busted, as he knew when he was under surveillance because he often recognised the people following him and he knew who the informants were at the mosque. He also constantly changed phone cards to evade detection, but Mohammed wasn't convinced. He said he'd been questioned about Lagha Lotfi, who was apparently incarcerated in Guantanamo Bay, and a suspect called Bouyahia

Hammadi, who was already in the custody of the Carabinieri's Special Branch. Someone called Amin was also mentioned and he thought that the ultimate target of the police investigation was a Mullah Fouad, a 32-year-old Iraqi al-Ansar leader who was suspected of recruiting suicide bombers and getting them into Iraq via Syria.

Mohammed indicated that he'd recently been to London and said: 'I am not worried for myself, I am worried for the others, for the brothers over there who are waiting for me. I will not set foot in London again because at this juncture I am on the files.'

They then both rail against their captors, calling them 'enemies of God', 'sons of dogs' and 'devils', and discuss ways of frustrating them by refusing to answer questions and quoting from the Koran. Before they both join in reciting verses from the Koran, Mera'i says: 'Enemies of God. They will undoubtedly ask you about the people who were in Afghanistan; they want the leader. They like life. I want to be a martyr; I live for the jihad. There is nothing in this life; life is afterward. Above all, brother, the indescribable feeling is that of dying a martyr. God, help me to be your martyr.'

I passed the material on to the *Sunday Times*, and they made further enquiries into the case. The story was published on 4 January 2004, headlined: 'Al-Qaeda London network exposed'. Investigators in Italy estimated the Force 9 European army numbered about 200 people and British officials said that, despite the 500 terrorism-related arrests since 9/11, al-Qaeda was still operating from London, though it was under close scrutiny.

Bin Laden's latest statement claiming that the USA was preparing an all-out invasion of the Middle East might have been a scare story, but such fears weren't without foundation. A declassified British government document had been made public on 1 January 2004 which revealed that the USA had seriously considered using military force to seize control of the major oil fields in the Middle East in 1973. The once top-secret memo showed that the US administration was prepared to go in during the Arab oil embargo to end it, or if war broke out between Israel and surrounding Arab states.

The embargo was imposed by the OPEC oil cartel as a way of bringing pressure to bear on Israel to withdraw from land it had occupied following a three-week war with Syria and Egypt. The sanctions created an energy crisis in the West, causing power cuts and the introduction of the 50 mph speed limit on roads in America, although it gradually petered out over the following three months. At the time, though, the Nixon administration was starting to believe it was near the point where intervention was the only way to break the deadlock and the military planners had started work on a contingency plan.

The US defence secretary James R. Schlesinger told the British ambassador in Washington, Lord Cromer, that 'it was no longer obvious to him that the United States could not use force'. If this 'dark scenario' had been played out, the USA would have used airborne troops to occupy oil fields in Saudi Arabia, Kuwait and Abu Dhabi. The memo, sent to Prime Minister Edward Heath by the head of the Joint Intelligence Committee, Percy Cradock, assessed that two brigades of troops would be needed for Saudi Arabia, one each for the others. It warned that the UK might be asked to assist in Abu Dhabi and that the occupations might have to last ten years or more.

It all sounded familiar, and this was emphasised by a line that said that Iraq might use the opportunity to invade Kuwait, with the backing of the Soviet Union. A direct confrontation between the two superpowers was judged to be unlikely, though it didn't rule out the possibility of pre-emptive US strikes against Arab states in the future, should they decide to use 'the oil weapon' to issue greater demands. Discontent among Western allies was also foreseen as being a consequence of taking action: 'Since the United States would probably claim to be acting for the benefit of the West as a whole and would expect the full support of allies, deep US–European rifts could ensue.'

Another related report expresses prime-ministerial anger about the failure of the USA to inform the UK that its military had gone on to a nuclear-war footing at the outbreak of hostilities between Israel, Syria and Egypt. When Israeli troops crossed the Suez Canal, the Soviets warned that enough was enough and it would send troops in unless the Israelis withdrew. A nuclear superpower stand-off reminiscent of the Cuban Missile Crisis 11 years previously ensued, until the US seemingly backed down when Israel pulled back.

This was the time when the USA first started to seriously ponder a policy of preventative, pre-emptive military action to deal with troublesome Arab states. For me, this took some of the sting out of the shrill arguments against George W. Bush's policy of pre-emptive military action and the warnings of doom about wandering into uncharted territory. It wasn't such a new departure; it had its roots in the Nixon era, as the government looked for ways to ensure it was never held to ransom by less-developed countries again. I'm no foreign-policy wonk, but the only real difference, to my mind, was that 'non-state actors' and Islamic terrorist networks had since been added to the list.

Dealing with an al-Qaeda ideological mind-virus wasn't envisioned in the early 1970s, and no one could have guessed then that many of the USA's future enemies would be found on the soil of its main ally. London cropped up constantly as a hotbed of jihad activity during the early part of 2004, despite waves of police anti-terrorism raids and new legislation.

These people were persistent innovators, and a case in point came when a contact alerted me to the latest claimed outrage: a children's computer game where the player takes on the role of a Hezbollah fighter in battles against Israeli soldiers. I wasn't initially that interested, as it had been launched in 2003, but then I was told that distribution of the game had just started in Europe and it was being shipped out to buyers from an address in south London. My contact asked if I could check out the address, seeing as I was in the UK and he wasn't. The game had produced wails of disgust from Jewish quarters when it was announced, as would be expected, but there was a counter-argument. If it's acceptable for people in the West to play shoot-'em-up games in the role of soldiers killing Arabs, then why not the other way around?

The game was called *Special Force* and the scenarios were based on real Hezbollah operations mounted against Israeli troops during the occupation of Lebanon. As well as being a sophisticated and action-packed game, the group was quite open about it also doubling up as a training and recruitment tool to school young Muslim minds in the ways of jihad. Demand for the game had proved extremely strong and the group had decided to bring it to a wider audience. It would take the US Army a year or more to catch up and bring out its own equivalent product.

The importance placed on winning over minds was probably best illustrated when Hezbollah went global in mid-2004 and launched a multinational satellite television station. Individuals may have been concerned about supporting Hezbollah, but Western corporations were seemingly not at all bothered. It was broadcast using satellites operated by several Western companies, and major advertisers were falling over themselves to buy up advertising space. Activists on the Net first raised the question of whether those companies were in breach of anti-terrorism legislation by providing funding to a proscribed group and government bans soon followed.

I looked at the main *Special Force* website for the Middle East and browsed through some screenshots. The rendering of the graphics wasn't top notch, but there was nothing at all to suggest that this was a home-made, amateur effort. A Western gamer would be quite at home with this, I thought, because it all looked very familiar: they could blaze away for many a long hour and, at £5 a copy, it was a bargain.

A product of the Hezbollah Central Internet Bureau, the slogan on the box said: 'Be a partner in the victory. Fight, resist and destroy your enemy in the game of force.' It said that playing the game 'will render you a partner of the resistance'. There was also a special mode for fine-tuning your shooting skills, and the targets included a variety of Israeli politicians, including the prime minister Ariel Sharon.

None of that was of much concern to me; it was the London angle that had my attention. I wasn't entirely sure that it was legal to sell it in the UK, as I didn't know what the latest case precedents were. It would at least be regarded as distasteful by many people, though anything beyond that was unknown territory. Australia's government had addressed the issue and its attorney general had said the game couldn't be banned using anti-terrorism legislation.

Hezbollah has always been a tricky issue and a source of division in the West, as the USA and Israel regard it as a terrorist organisation, although it wasn't proscribed in the EU because many nation states preferred to recognise its important social role in Lebanon. Hezbollah fighters are archetypal heroes in the country, due to their success in repelling US and Israeli troops.

A little basic investigative work soon suggested that there was more to this than just a game. The website of the London distributor looked fairly innocuous, in that it was selling a wide range of Islamic bric-a-brac, and the *Special Force* link stood out as a result. The site was owned by a seemingly ordinary electrical business, which made it even more curious, and it was hosted by a British company that had entertained terrorism-supporting customers in the past.

It looked promising, so far. As I focused in, I analysed one document on the site and found that it had been created using software owned by a well-known London merchant bank. The writer might have been a current or former employee, or perhaps stolen software was used. It was one of 13 sites hosted on the same server and they were under the control of the same group or individual.

One of the other sites was distributing books and, now knowing that this is a favoured method of communication, I took an even closer look. According to the records, the bookshop site was registered to a London-based money-transfer business, which was listed. An email address led me to a second money-transfer company operating out of the same postal address. The real knockout finding was that another business based there, which had apparently been dissolved in 2002, was a subsidiary of a Congolese air-freight company. That was startling, because I'd recently read several articles about al-Qaeda and Hezbollah raising funds by illegally trading 'blood diamonds' (diamonds that have been illicitly mined or purchased in a war zone) from Congo.

Congo wasn't just a source of diamonds; there was also trading in gold and uranium. One report from 2001 quoted a European investigator into terrorism finances as saying that Hezbollah and al-Qaeda used the same infrastructure and their operations were often seen to overlap. Failed states such as Congo, Liberia and Sierra Leone had become free-trade areas for terrorist and more traditional organised-crime networks. Diamonds were bought for a fraction of their market value, from middlemen or often directly from corrupt mining-company employees, and then smuggled out of the country. Most were sold in emerging markets, such as India and the United Arab Emirates, though the best-quality stones were sold at the world's biggest market, in Belgium.

Regulations had been tightened, though not nearly enough, according to lobby groups. A new international agreement aimed at curbing the trade wasn't backed up by a mandatory inspection system. Associates of President Robert Mugabe of Zimbabwe were said to be major buyers, as was the UNITA movement in Angola and the RUF rebels in Sierra Leone, so it was fuelling the arms trade in the region as well.

I backed away from probing into the accounts because, having done this many times before, I knew that it would take a lot of time and work. And it might be all for nothing if money was being routed through trust funds in tax havens, for example. There'd be little untoward in the accounts, if they'd done their homework. A further indication that I was on the right track was the discovery that all the sites appeared to be controlled by a company based in a Gulf state. Its main areas of operation were drilling and mining, though it had fingers in many other pies, so it fitted the mould.

I had done enough to at least sound out a newspaper about the story, I reckoned. Aside from anything else, researching this story was a prime example of just how much ground could be covered with a Net connection and some lateral thinking. I'd followed the blood-diamond trading route from London to Congo and back, with a few detours on the way, in the space of a couple of hours.

I pitched the story to a national newspaper contact and he was enthusiastic about it. He asked me to send over some notes with Web links and contact information so he could have a look and make some further enquiries. I already had that packaged together and I sent him the full report as we were talking on the phone.

He asked me to hold off from delving into company accounts for the time being, and I was glad of that. We both appreciated the scale and expense of the task at hand. As a former business reporter, I was perfectly comfortable with doing this and I knew how to read balance sheets; he just wanted to satisfy himself that we were on the right track. He had recently cultivated some new high-ranking contacts in the field of cyber-crime and he wanted to see what they thought of it first.

I gave it a week or so and called again to see what progress there had been. The lack of information in the response spoke volumes. He mumbled something to the effect of it being very interesting and that it was 'still being looked at'. We probably needed to give it a few weeks, he suggested. And we left it there. I recognised these as signals that someone in authority might have asked the paper to hold off from publishing, because an investigation was under way.

I did check the *Special Force* website a few months later and something had certainly happened in the meantime. It had moved out of the UK and was now hosted by a US company that was known to be favoured by militant Islamic groups. More tellingly, the operator of the website had signified his displeasure at whatever had happened in a typically innovative way. The pages where *Special Force* was previously being sold had changed and they now automatically redirected visitors to the home page of an American white supremacist group.

THE SILENT SCREAMERS

ANOTHER STORY ALSO FAILED TO MAKE THE PAPERS AROUND THIS time, though it wasn't for law-enforcement reasons. This time, editors found it too revolting to publish. That doesn't happen very often and I suppose I should have seen it coming. I was pretty angered by it myself, though I think the balance was tipped by a prevailing professional wariness about aiding the spread of extremist propaganda.

The story was most probably a misjudgement on the part of its authors, but it was also a telling reminder of how al-Qaeda supporters in the UK view their own fellow countrymen. Pure viciousness and contempt dripped off the page. Perhaps I'm helping to propagate those views by printing them here . . .

It was a collection of lengthy essays, from a jihadi point of view, on the state of British society. What revolted hard-bitten Fleet Street journalists was that the writers were using the tragic case of the murder of James Bulger in Liverpool in 1993 as part of their justification for using violence to advance Islam.

The three year old was abducted from a shopping centre by two ten-year-old boys, who took him to a nearby railway line and beat him to death, then placed him on the tracks to be run over by the next passing train. The crime shocked the nation and provoked a great debate on the state of society and whether children were capable of evil, and the meaning of evil, even. There was some inconclusive evidence to suggest that James may have been sexually assaulted as well and, though the police decided to withhold specific details about his injuries at the time, there was general incomprehension over why the two older boys were moved to do what they did. They, Robert Thompson and Jon Venables, have never revealed, to my knowledge, what drove them to it. The lack of information was and is a torment for the infant's parents and that's why the case is still perused by the media to this day – that and its genuine uniqueness.

The jihadis were, however, presenting this as typifying the increasingly misguided behaviour of the nation's youth. That's what people couldn't stomach. And that wasn't all. In the articles, all British non-Muslims were dismissed as 'pigs', women were referred to as 'prostitutes', freedom was branded 'a corrupt concept' and Western society in general was 'deadly and poisonous'. The site openly supported terrorism and one page featured an animated bomb with the timer counting down to zero and displaying the slogan 'The West is Dead'. One statement said: 'Al-Intashar fully supports the late Bali bombings that killed over 100 "people".' A caption below an image of tourists weeping after the event said: 'Then cry fools! This is the price of having your fun on our Islamic Land. Take your hooves off our land!'

They also had the usual accoutrements: many pictures of masked gunmen brandishing weapons, jihad poems and videos of terrorist operations. They made heavy use of quotations by Abdullah Azzam. They were all in English, and one of the links on the site pointed to the website of Supporters of Sharia, which was headed by Abu Hamza, though the site's true operators couldn't be readily identified.

The site claimed that it was supported by Hizb ut-Tahrir, and I wished I'd had this to hand when I was defending myself against the allegations they'd levelled against me months earlier. Some of the authors were clearly identified as Hizb ut-Tahrir members. In a section called 'The Criminal Offspring', the author, who was identified as 'Nizam Khan, Hizb ut-Tahrir', claimed:

> Committing crimes seems to be becoming the norm for an ever-younger set of the British populace . . . Over the last decade there has been a spate of crimes committed by children, as young as ten, which have shocked the nation. Everyone will recall the murder of Jamie Bulger as a particularly horrific incident; however there have been regular reports of drug abuse, muggings and even rapes committed by young children. The concept of 'freedom' has truly run riot and it is the impressionable who are the first to mimic others.

What followed was a comprehensive trashing of every aspect of modern Western life. It was disingenuous in every way – and often contradictory. According to Al-Intashar, the majority of people used mobile phones not primarily as a means of communication, but rather as pornographic-video players. It said: 'To simply look at an advertisement for a Siemens S55 phone – a phone, which can be used for good communication, is turned into a pornographic-type video by the West. It involves sexual content and sexual content in the West brings money. It does not matter if it will make a whole generation of pig-like women, it makes money. The West invents a beautiful phone that can take pictures yet turns it into (as it does with all it's [sic] creations) utter trash . . .'

Having just worked on the Hezbollah *Special Force* story, I was almost amused to see the Western penchant for computer games criticised for training young minds to enjoy violence. Gone were the days when children used to be taught manners and etiquette by their parents; this important stage in their lives was now supposedly taken care of by rap music: 'Social skills are formed by listening to the lyrics of rappers like "Eminem", which gives [sic] the young the impression that it is OK to treat women like objects and threaten others with serious violence.'

These were strange words for a site that was otherwise devoted to celebrating killing. It was obviously intended to play on many people's distaste for the excesses of the consumer society, but the site's authors were certainly overdoing it here. There was no finesse at all in their arguments and it was backward-looking. Some speculated that the site may have had something to do with the south-east Asian al-Qaeda-linked terror group Jemaah Islamiah, which carried out the 2002 Bali bombing, due to the statement that supported the attack. The fact that it was written in English, the UK focus and the pro-Taliban sentiments expressed on the site made me wonder otherwise. Maybe it was a joint operation of some sort, at best.

The tone certainly did evoke images of gleeful writers with menacing half-grins on their faces and those telltale determined gleams in their eyes. I called it the 'terrorist stare', because you could almost feel intense beams of hatred firing out of the eyeballs and it was an expression that was often seen in images of detained terrorist suspects.

I talked to a crime correspondent friend who had just returned from a court hearing in a terrorism case. I asked him about what he made of the suspect. He paused to review his thoughts and said: 'Hmmm . . . he had that stare – that look on his face. Do you know what I mean?' This could or would never be submitted as evidence of anything in a court of law, of course, but I did know what he meant. The same attitude, for instance, seemed to shine from the suspects who'd been arrested for involvement in the Bali plot, as seen from their interviews in prison, like those conducted by the BBC's Peter Taylor.

'Hence, with these concepts of "freedom" combined with an atmosphere glorifying violence and corruption, is it any wonder that more and more children are becoming out of control and committing crimes?' the section concluded. The magic wand for solving all the ills of society was, of course, claimed to be Islam.

Not only that, Islam was an immediate cure for gonorrhoea, according to the next part. Epidemics of sexually transmitted diseases in the West would soon cease to exist after the switch to Islam, due to sexual relations being strictly confined to wedlock. It continued:

> This precludes the ability of any sexual disease from becoming an epidemic, and shields the society from many of the other Western social ills. Western nations will never be able to deliver such effective solutions, but instead will fight a losing battle to contain the ever-growing list of social ills that affect them. This is because they refuse to give up the corrupt concepts they hold about this life, such as freedom.

These were not the brightest bulbs in the pack, for sure. They were even upset by the way the American flag was treated by celebrities (a 'disgrace'), especially the way the Stars and Stripes was used as underwear in videos shown on MTV. Jennifer Lopez was singled out as a prime offender and the film *American Pie* was described as 'the most immoral and sinful film in the history of mankind'. In Lopez's case, I trust it was TV images of her that he was referring to, as the Internet was flooded with fake images of her in positions that I'm sure she wouldn't have agreed to adopt.

The writer had clearly studied this subject very carefully. Beautiful women gyrating suggestively in tiny panties and revealing bras with the Stars and Stripes pattern on them deserved death, he said. Not only was he closely watching MTV and Western romantic films, he'd also been buying up magazines to gather further

124

evidence. Yes, all those hours spent leafing through all those pictures of peachy bottoms, skimpy knickers and perky breasts and selecting the most sexually provocative poses were just too much to take. Maybe he'd cut out pictures of the prime offenders to make up a 'mood board' to illustrate his case to his colleagues. He exploded with frustration:

> If I were to send you the *Sports Illustrated* swimsuit magazines where prostitute pigs, who pass off as women, have the American flag in between their buttocks (thongs) and on their breasts. Or the gay parades where the American flag is flown alongside the gay flag. The examples would kill you and it will then again be very clear to you, as it is to every Jew, Christian and Westerner who has gone corrupt, that you are amongst the losers.

The nature of friendship in the West was even explored, and the conclusion was that there were no true friendships: they were all universally based on deriving benefits from relationships. It was another over-generalisation, at the very least, and this section came replete with quotes from the Koran to illustrate how Islam operates on the basis of mutual trust. Close relationships with non-Muslims should thus be avoided, it advised.

It wasn't difficult to let this one die on the vine. It was full of mealy-mouthed, nasty diatribes and I began to think that perhaps my colleagues were right to judge that this just went too far over the line. It was one of many signs that there was something brewing in those kinds of circles.

The latest one came when I was alerted to a new website – UK registered – that had just cropped up. All that was there was a diagram with notations in Arabic of how to wire something up to a mobile phone. It looked like a plan for a bomb and, sure enough, that's what it turned out to be: one that was triggered by a mobile-phone call. It was completely blatant, and fairly simple to recognise, but there were no indications of who had produced the document, or what the intended targets might be.

It was enormously frustrating, because the site had all the characteristics of a 'dead-letter drop' – an agreed place where covert information is placed for collection – though there was no way of telling who the recipients might be. As it stood, there was no story, just evidence of a curious new innovation in bomb-making. Eleven days after the document had emerged on the Net, its significance became starkly apparent.

The Madrid train bombings happened on 11 March 2004, killing nearly 200 people and injuring thousands of others. Ten bombs, placed in backpacks and activated by mobile phones, had exploded in quick succession on commuter trains during the morning rush hour. The attacks came on the eve of voting in the general election there, and the Spanish conservative government was ousted from power, after it initially blamed the Basque separatist group ETA for the outrage in an effort to win votes. Opponents claimed that Aznar's government was trying to obscure links to Islamic terrorism in order to prevent the attacks being seen as retribution for Spanish participation in the US-led coalition in Iraq, and the public agreed.

I was completely mystified when it was announced that the blame was being pinned on ETA. I even stuck out my neck and emailed a few friends and contacts to say I was sure a militant Islamic group was responsible, as the operation demonstrated a sophistication that was way beyond anything that had been attempted by ETA in the past. Plus, I'd seen the plans for the type of bomb that was used. It was a prime and depressing example of the lengths to which politicians will go in order to cling to the reins of power and privilege. I was as disgusted as anyone else was with the Spanish government's claim – well, probably more than most, actually. First Iraq and WMD, and now politicians actually scrambling over the warm corpses of their fellow citizens in order to secure an electoral advantage. How low can they stoop? Remember Madrid when you hear a politician blaming the media for all of his troubles in an interview. The Spanish government was a key ally of Prime Minister Blair, so remember also that the foreign secretary, Jack Straw, held a press conference to back up their view and claim that the British intelligence services had evidence to suggest that ETA was behind the attack.

Maybe I was on the right lines in suspecting a UK link to the mobile-phone bomb plan. A year later, in March 2005, a key suspect in the Madrid bombings, Moutaz Almallah Dabas, was arrested in Slough, Berkshire, to face extradition.

Spring 2004 had been pretty quiet otherwise. That's not to say that there were no significant events during this period, however. The spiritual leader of Hamas, Sheikh Ahmed Yassin, was killed in a missile strike in late March, causing worldwide condemnation of Israel's policy of 'targeted killings'; Ayman al-Zawahiri issued an audiotape calling for the downfall of President Pervez Musharraf and his government in Pakistan; and an issue of the Saudi al-Qaeda *Al-Battar* training magazine carried an article on how to attack targets within Western cities.

There was a growing campaign aimed at securing the release of British detainees at Guantanamo Bay in Cuba, and this caught my eye. I think the worthy part of me thought I should explore their plight to keep me on the path of objectivity.

One group, called the Muslim Programmers and Designers Community, was operating an impressive operation from a site called cageprisoners.com. It was a good-looking site and the people there were well organised. They had even roped in schoolchildren to participate in a letter-writing campaign to 'bring a smile to a Muslim prisoner'.

There was growing incredulity at the possibility that the Guantanamo detainees might face execution after secret US military tribunal hearings. Despite the US government's iron-fist terror rhetoric, protests were being made to the American administration behind closed doors. Setting up a poorly disguised, semi-secret televised torture centre to act as a deterrent for all the wrongdoers in the world must count as one the biggest PR failures in history, if not the biggest. It handed the opposition the biggest propaganda win imaginable and rocket-fuelled anti-American sentiments worldwide.

I couldn't have been the only person in the world who jumped up and started shouting at the TV in outrage when the first images were shown of orange-suited prisoners on their backs strapped and shackled to wheelbarrows, being pushed between interrogation sessions in full view of the world's press. They are images that will burn in many minds for generations.

The campaign site displayed a gallery of over eighty greetings cards that children aged between eight and ten had sent to prisoners at Guantanamo Bay. One, addressed to Shafiq Rasul, 160 Camp X-Ray, Washington DC 2053, USA, said: 'Dear Shafiq Rasul (British), Inshallah [if Allah wills it], Allah will give you Jannah [Paradise]. He will always be with you, whatever happens.'

Writing to Feroz Abbasi, little Abdullah Ahmed expressed similar sentiments: 'May Allah give you Jannah. We will pray that Allah protects you.' Funnily enough, the same message was sent to Moazzam Begg from another kiddie: 'Dear Moazzam Begg from British. May Allah give you Jannah.'

The greetings cards were all scrawled in big, crayoned, child-like writing and most of them were adorned with drawings made with colouring pencils. The site said they'd been made by children at an unnamed London mosque and it seemed that they'd had a production line going. The similarity in the messages was suspicious, and I admit the thought that some enterprising group of adults was producing these by imitating children, probably by writing left-handed, did cross my mind. If they were made by kids, however – and they did look convincing enough – they were almost certainly acting under orders, and you had to wonder if they really knew what they were doing.

In an exclusive interview on the website, the brother of Shafiq Rasul praised it as 'an excellent source of information'. He condemned the government for its alleged inaction on the issue. He said: 'On occasions, talking to the Foreign Office was like talking to a brick wall. It took nearly a year before the Foreign Office bothered to arrange any sort of meeting, and that itself was a total waste of time.'

These complaints were all fair enough, you'd have thought, unless you clicked on the link to the group's promotional video. It was called 'The Forgotten Ones', and the producer was credited as Azzam Publications. I had a look. The film praised the detainees as innocent heroes of crusader oppression and displayed a long list of names before it started to get interesting.

The viewer was then urged to pray for the release of the '20th hijacker' and self-confessed al-Qaeda operative, Zacarias Moussaoui, and Richard Reid, the convicted shoe-bomber. Many other convicted terrorists were also portrayed as innocent victims, including Sheikh Omar Abdul Rahman. Also featured were the main planners of the 9/11 attacks: Khalid Sheikh Mohammed and Ramzi Binalshibh.

The person who had put this together had access to a database of mugshots of al-Qaeda operatives. Many of the names of those who had been detained and killed were accompanied by photos that looked like they'd been taken by the group involved before they'd set out to undertake an operation. Finding the source of those images would be very revealing, as it would be a virtual membership list, and it looked like someone in the UK had access to a covert online repository or had kept his own database.

At the end of March, the general terror quietness was broken by the news that hundreds of police officers had carried out a series of dawn raids across the country. Dozens of properties were searched and arrests were made, though the finer details can't be discussed

A leader of al-Qaeda in Saudi Arabia threatens the US in a video.

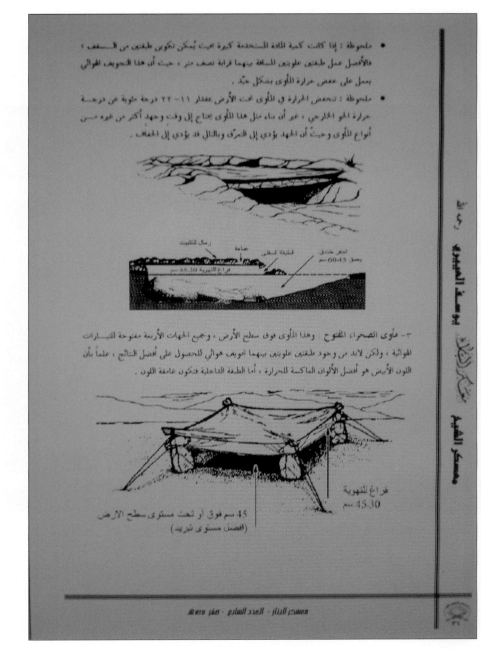

A page from the first issue of al-Qaeda's
Al-Battar military training magazine.

A scene from the video showing Ken Bigley being beheaded.

A suicide bomber reads his final will to the camera
before embarking on his mission in Iraq.

An image of the mini-WMD from the construction manual
(annotations removed).

أمام السفارة الأمريكية ٢٠٠٥/٠٥/٢٠   محمد المسري / عبدالمنعم مصطفى / أنمار المسعري / عمر بكري / محمد المسعري   التجديد

The now-exiled leader of al-Muhajiroun, Omar Bakri Mohammed
(second left) with Muhammad al-Massari (far left).

Demonstrators hold a burning cross aloft during the demonstration
outside the US embassy in London in May 2005.

Bakri speaking at the demonstration.

Fire breaks out after Bakri has warned the
West against playing with fire.

The suspected Madrid-bombings mastermind Mustafa Setmarian Nasar in a scene from one of the virtual-jihad-camp videos.

Screenshot from the first video celebrating the 7/7 London bombings.

Young jihad volunteers seen in the al-Qaeda in Iraq recruitment video that was released just before the London bombings.

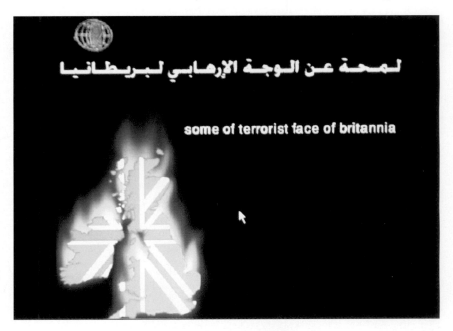

Post-7/7 al-Qaeda propaganda video threatening more attacks in the UK.

here, as there are court cases in the pipeline. Just after Madrid, Metropolitan Police commissioner Sir John Stevens had warned that a spectacular terrorist strike on London was 'inevitable' and that pubs, clubs and shopping centres could be targets.

Raids were taking place at all sorts of unlikely locations across the nation, and it has been suggested that, in the confusion caused by pre-emptive action designed to disrupt the operations of suspected cells and conflicting media reports of plots that were allegedly being worked on, Britain's appointment with 9/11-style catastrophe may have been postponed.

Soon, an extraordinary twist in the struggle with al-Qaeda meant that the quiet period could go on for a few more months yet. On 15 April, Al-Jazeera broadcast an audiotape from bin Laden in which he offered Europe a truce if a timetable could be agreed for the withdrawal of Western troops from Islamic countries. He said a three-month window was now open for talks and suggested that it could be extended, if needed. The USA was excluded. According to the voice on the tape, which was quickly verified as bin Laden's by the CIA, 'What happened on 11 September and 11 March are your goods returned to you, so that you know security is a necessity for all. Stop spilling our blood so we can stop spilling your blood.'

The truce offer was greeted with general dismay and Western leaders queued up to gleefully mock the suggestion and wheel out the old line about never negotiating with terrorists. Politicians *do* talk to terrorists, so hearing that line brings out the cynical side of me, because the underlying truth behind statements like these is often very different. The public impression of politicians as being insubstantial, lying gas-bags has been well earned. It's the only job where you can lie your teeth off and never face prosecution, unlike ordinary folk, and they exploit that advantage to the hilt and beyond.

Margaret Thatcher was the most prominent user of that line, but even as she was regaling the House of Commons with tub-thumping defiance and declaring her intention to deny the terrorists 'the oxygen of publicity', the deputy prime minister was holding secret talks in London with, er, the leadership of the IRA. Her madcap plan to ban Sinn Fein leaders from speaking to the media backfired when images of Gerry Adams and Martin McGuinness continued to appear on the TV news – more often than ever – with actors speaking their words.

During the 1990s, leaders of the notorious Tamil Tigers, who used suicide bombing as a way of advancing their struggle for independence in Sri Lanka, were regular guests in parliament. Sympathetic MPs took tea with the Tigers. More recently, the USA has been quietly trying to start talks with the Taliban in Afghanistan to persuade them to call a halt to their hit-and-run attacks. A delegation of religious leaders travelled from Pakistan to try to persuade Mullah Omar to see sense, but he refused to meet them. Those are just a few incidents that spring to mind.

The al-Qaeda truce offer came at a time when people were wondering why it had taken so long for the network to organise a major attack in Europe and why there hadn't been more of them. Bin Laden, who appeared to be slowly morphing himself from a guerrilla leader into a world statesman, judging by the content of his recent speeches, was no different to Western politicians in this manoeuvre. His hidden agenda was to try to force a split between the USA and Europe, to exploit the marked difference in attitudes towards the Middle East. A prime example of that was Hezbollah and Hamas being designated terrorist organisations in the USA but not in Europe.

More suspicious minds might have thought that bin Laden's statement was an excuse for failure. Several hundred terrorist suspects had been detained in Europe and many plots were claimed to have been thwarted, most notably in the UK and Italy. It would be a neat and probably irresistible propaganda ploy to appear statesman-like by granting mercy on Europe, even if that was far from the truth. There were no signs that a stand-down order had been issued to operatives – far from it.

During al-Qaeda's three-month European truce period, the heat was on in the Middle East, and perhaps this was a demonstration of what we could face if the overture was rejected. I thought it was more likely that it was business as usual and that the offer served more esoteric purposes. Bin Laden faced clerical criticism after 9/11 for failing to give a required warning to the enemy before launching a mass casualty attack so, as he was now armed with a religious judgement in favour of using unconventional weapons, the offer could be seen as a move to issue adequate prior warning and pave the way for future attacks.

The Middle East wasn't off the hook and, on 21 April, al-Qaeda suicide bombers attacked a government building with a car bomb in Riyadh, Saudi Arabia. The administration had quietly ditched its policy of denying that it had a problem with terrorism, mainly because it was just too obvious now that it did. And the latest bombing seemed to prove that, despite all the security activity since the bombings of the Western housing compounds, the terror network clearly had spare capacity inside the country.

Activity was also on the rise in neighbouring Iraq, and the name Abu Musab al-Zarqawi was starting to become a regular fixture on the news. Soon after the Saudi bombing, for the first time, he issued a statement claiming responsibility for an attack in Iraq. It was for a series of suicide boat attacks that put Iraq's two key oil terminals in Basra out of action. One American was killed and four others were wounded during the assault, though production was soon resumed. Nevertheless, the flow of an estimated one million barrels of oil was interrupted, costing some $28 million.

The USA named al-Zarqawi as one of the suspected leaders of the increasingly violent insurgency against coalition troops in Iraq. There was some initial cynicism about why the USA was suddenly offering him up as a major bogeyman figure; very little was known about him and that's still pretty much the case today. Mystery surrounded him because, although he'd been named as a leader of the militant Islamic Ansar al-Islam group, which was formerly based in a conclave in northern Iraq, he'd not been known to have pledged allegiance to bin Laden.

That made alleging links between al-Qaeda and Ansar difficult for the West, and that looked to be a deliberate strategy. The Americans claimed that the group had been conducting experiments involving chemical weapons in camps in the north and they took a pounding from air strikes long before the ground action started in earnest. But, it seemed, nobody was home at the time.

Members of the network now looked to be spread out across the centre of the country and were leading the charge against the Americans. The group's shadowy, 37-year-old Jordanian leader had connections far and wide, and he was soon forced to issue a statement denying plans to attack the Jordanian capital Amman with a chemical weapon.

The precise target in Amman was the headquarters of the General Intelligence Directorate. Days earlier, Jordanian television had broadcast confessions from captured militants who'd admitted that they planned to demolish the building by detonating a bomb containing cyanide. The authorities said that 80,000 people could have been killed by the poison gas mega-bomb, had they not intervened.

Al-Zarqawi's statement admitted that he was behind the plot, calling the building 'the source of all evils in our home'. He denied the claims that a chemical attack was being planned, but he said it was a good idea. 'God knows, if we did possess [a chemical bomb], we wouldn't hesitate one second to use it to hit Israeli cities such as Eilat and Tel Aviv,' he said in the audiotape message.

In recognition of his growing importance, the USA increased the existing $5 million bounty on his head, which was levied in October 2003 after he was suspected of involvement in the bombing of the Jordanian embassy in Baghdad, to $10 million in February, and then raised it yet again four months later to $25 million. That was the same price being offered for information on the whereabouts of bin Laden himself, yet the nature of the links between the two, if there were any, was still unclear.

Both bin Laden and al-Zarqawi had risen to prominence as leaders of the Arab Afghans during the war with the Soviets, after which a radicalised al-Zarqawi, formerly a petty street criminal, returned home to Jordan. The network he'd built up over the intervening period was seen as at least an autonomous component of the al-Qaeda network, or maybe even a rival network. The lack of a pledge of allegiance to bin Laden was the blocker, though that hadn't stopped US defence secretary Donald Rumsfeld from claiming the supposed relationship to be solid fact and one of the prime pieces of evidence that justified military intervention in Iraq.

The Iraqi resistance leader had spent seven years in jail in Jordan for plotting to overthrow the government regime and establish an Islamic caliphate. Al-Zarqawi then fled to Europe after his release and a cell of German militants subsequently uncovered by police there was said to be under his command. A Jordanian court had sentenced him to death *in absentia* for planning to kill Western and Israeli tourists. From Europe, he returned to Afghanistan to establish a training camp near Herat, which specialised in teaching methods of manufacturing poison gases.

Some speculate that he entered the al-Qaeda fold at this time, before he went on to Iraq to establish links with the Kurdish Islamic militants of Ansar al-Islam. It's presumed that he might have been acting as an emissary of bin Laden, and the USA had accused him of transferring his poison-gas knowledge to Iraq by setting up camps in the mountainous north, though he was forced to flee from Afghanistan after losing a leg in a US air strike in 2001. He was now the governor of the Iraqi resistance movement.

The news focus shifted back and forth between Iraq and Saudi Arabia during May and June 2004. There had been a wave of shootings and kidnappings of foreign workers inside Saudi Arabia. It all started after bin Laden had issued an audiotape offering large payments in gold for anyone killing civilian and military personnel belonging to Western countries involved in the occupation of Iraq. Among those who were caught up in the violence in Saudi Arabia was the BBC's security correspondent Frank Gardiner, who narrowly escaped death after being gunned down in a Riyadh street in broad daylight.

A very ominous sign of a turn for the worse came from Iraq with the release on the Internet of a video of an American hostage in Iraq, Nick Berg, being beheaded by al-Zarqawi's group. It showed him sitting, in an orange-coloured jumpsuit that was reminiscent of those worn by detainees at Guantanamo Bay, in front of five masked men. After reading a statement to the camera, the leader of the group produced a large knife. The four others jumped on Mr Berg and held him down while the man with the knife sawed through his neck and held his head aloft. It was then placed on the back of the victim's prostrate body. The titles indicated that al-Zarqawi himself may have been wielding the knife.

The barbaric nature of Berg's death was deeply shocking and there must have been some delight in the perpetrators' ranks at the sheer scale of the media coverage. It was even more astonishing because the mainstream media were bypassed and the Internet was used instead to parade a prisoner, and then his body. This was a new departure and the message to Westerners inside the country couldn't have been clearer. The method of his execution was in accordance with the arguments outlined in the WMD fatwa about killing the enemy in the most efficient way possible.

The depth of the impact on the public mind was measurable. The visitor statistics for my website went right off the scale as people, en masse, went searching for more information about Berg's murder. I wondered what had happened at first when I saw those incredible figures – traffic was 100 times above normal levels – until I checked the newswires. Judging from the emails I got, there was great outrage at what had happened but there was also a contradictory thirst to see the video, and I was bombarded by requests for the link.

The world's full of ghouls, and sites featuring pictures of people who have been killed in traffic accidents and so on are some of the most popular on the Net. There was certainly an element of voyeuristic curiosity here, though I'm sure many people simply wanted to judge for themselves whether this was some kind of Iraq-like ruse to get the public behind the war on terrorism, perhaps perpetrated by an intelligence agency.

Being asked for the images put me on the spot, morality-wise. Was it right that I should post the material on my website? Should I be catering for sickos? Would it be disrespectful to the victim? And would I be helping the al-Qaeda propaganda drive by doing so? It was a particularly tricky one, because I also had mercenary intentions here, as I wanted to hold on to some of that traffic by providing the material they were looking for, to encourage visitors to stop by again.

I wrestled with it, but I couldn't do that for long; I had to make a quick decision if I was to capitalise on the traffic gains. It was an important moment, as it would set a precedent for the future. Berg's mother hadn't seen the video yet because she was also struggling to decide whether it would be right for her to watch it. In the end, I decided to post a link to an external site where the video was available, though not host it directly on my site. I didn't want to be known as a distributor of execution films.

Some media commentators have been predicting that the current Western penchant for reality TV programmes will result in continual upping of the stakes in the search for ratings until we reach a stage where people will be executed for entertainment: Snuff TV. What many of them fail to realise is that that threshold was breached in 2004.

Quite what Berg was doing in Iraq was a bit of a mystery. He'd been kidnapped in April, before the Abu Ghraib prison-abuse scandal broke, and this seemed to be a response. He was described as being a businessman from Philadelphia and being interested in picking up contracts to repair damaged radio masts. He'd been kidnapped after being released by US troops who'd detained him on suspicion of being a spy. Internet investigators turned up some evidence to suggest he had links with extreme right-wing groups and it was enough to get the rumour-mill working. Some started to suggest that he must have been working for an intelligence agency that was trying to infiltrate insurgent groups. Others suggested that the video was a fake produced by the CIA for propaganda use.

A Sunday newspaper contact had picked up on the speculation and he called me to see if there was any substance to the CIA conspiracy theory. I told him that I knew about the rumours but that

I'd have to scour through the video in detail and study the main planks of the arguments. He asked me if I'd do that and get a report together and I agreed. I'd hoped to stay out of this one because, up until now, I hadn't actually looked at the beheading section, though I'd looked at everything before and after. It wasn't for reasons of squeamishness; it was just that I didn't want to pollute my mind with unnecessary horror, if at all possible. I didn't want dead heads wailing at me in my dreams.

My contact was having very similar feelings, it seemed, as he'd obviously not watched any of it. He didn't have to now, as I'd agreed to do it for him and he'd pay me for my efforts. I felt like a bit of a hypocrite, initially, until I realised that the rest of the media had quickly left me behind and was already using those images to flog more papers and boost viewing figures.

The conspiracy theory was fuelled because the time-stamp in the right-hand corner of the screen switched between two completely different times, which indicated that the video had been edited. The plastic chair on which Nick Berg was sitting was said to be the same style as used in Abu Ghraib prison and the attackers appeared to be white-skinned. There was some comment on how Mr Berg looked like he might have been dead before the actual chopping off of his head took place, because when it happened there was little sign of blood. The most striking aspect of the case was his scream as the knife started sawing through his throat; it seemed woman-like, as if it had been dubbed on to the soundtrack.

I listened to that shriek over and over and it was odd and very disturbing, no doubt about it. But we were looking at a low-resolution digital Net video clip and you have to be careful in extrapolating too much from so little. I thought that one explanation for the voice might have been the severing of vocal chords. The other aspects were similarly inconclusive, yet people were claiming this as proof that the CIA had used Mr Berg and staged his execution inside Abu Ghraib in some dastardly propaganda move to detract public attention away from the prisoner-abuse scandal. I told the newspaper that all that could be proved was that the video had been edited, and that was no big deal.

Among the Western online jihad research community, the search was on to find the source of the video and to uncover who had uploaded it first and from where. The source was quickly traced to a computer server in a data centre in Malaysia, which had recently become a favourite haunt for jihadists. The heat had been turned up in the USA and fewer questions were asked of customers who hosted their sites in the Far East. Two known pro-al-Qaeda sites had moved to Malaysia recently, along with three that were linked to Hamas.

The plug was pulled on the site, called al-Ansar.biz, named after al-Zarqawi's group, though the registration details for the domain name were clearly false: 'New Dream Street, Denmark'. The location of the individual who uploaded the site was known only to people at the hosting company and they weren't talking.

That appeared to be the end of it, but no. One enterprising researcher had examined the server where the Berg video had been hosted and found that the same machine was also running the official website of Abu Hamza's Supporters of Sharia group. Further examination yielded a video clip that had been secreted there. Its presence was betrayed by one of the group's supporters in Sweden, who'd posted a link to a discussion forum with a comment along the lines of 'look, how cute!'

It was a film of young children re-enacting the Berg beheading video. One little girl in the footage was wearing an Islamic headscarf and she smiled as she watched a little boy, five or six years old, maybe, kneeling before two older boys whose faces were concealed with Arabic headscarves. They held mock rifles made from cardboard kitchen-roll tubes. After appearing to deliver a statement to the camera, like in the real film, the tallest boy grabbed the little one from behind and pretended to cut his head off. It looked like it had been filmed in someone's kitchen.

I got the feeling from watching it that the children had seen the video, and that made me ponder on the nature of parents who would expose young children to such horrors. One contact simply said: 'How incredibly, terminally insane.' The existence of the video was greeted with fury, especially after I sold the story to a newspaper, and the plug was pulled on the site, though it quickly re-emerged in Hong Kong.

If nothing else, the case proved that seemingly disparate militant Islamic groups were cooperating with one another, on the communications front, at least. It also hinted at a European connection, as site moves appeared to be coordinated en bloc, whether Hamas or al-Qaeda, and groups in London, Germany and Sweden appeared to be involved. It also suggested that al-Zarqawi's communications were managed from Europe.

I doubted the conspiracy theory, as there was obvious glee at the new development among those of a militant Islamic persuasion.

When the beheading video surfaced, Sheikh Omar Bakri Mohammed's al-Muhajiroun group issued a belligerent statement blaming the 'fascist' policies of the USA and the UK for the incident and claiming that the Abu Ghraib affair had made bin Laden's job 'much easier'. In case there was any room left for doubt about the sympathies of the group, the title of the press release made a clear and explicit impact: 'Don't lose your head in Iraq!'

The beheading strategy was soon adopted in Saudi Arabia. The American defence contractor Paul Johnson was kidnapped in mid-June. His captors, believed to be headed by the latest leader of al-Qaeda in Saudi Arabia, Abdul Aziz al-Muqrin, released a video on the Internet showing the blindfolded prisoner. He spoke to confirm his name and the reason for his presence in Iraq – maintenance of Apache attack helicopters – before the Saudi government was given 72 hours to release al-Qaeda suspects from its jails or the man would be killed.

The Saudi government reacted with a statement highlighting its policy of not talking to terrorists and it didn't look good for Mr Johnson. Saudi troops conducted a massive search for him and the kidnappers' hideout, but there were few leads – until the group was spotted trying to dump his decapitated body in a quiet street in Riyadh a week later. Photos of the body were posted on the Net before the gang set out to dispose of it.

Saudi security forces caught them in the act and a gun battle ensued. Four members of the group were killed, including al-Muqrin and the number two on the Saudi's most-wanted list, Rakan Alsaykhan, who'd been linked to the 2000 attack on the USS *Cole*. The two others, brothers Bandar and Faisal Aldakheel, were also on the wanted list. Al-Qaeda rapidly responded by announcing the appointment of yet another new leader.

WMD FOR DUMMIES

NOTHING CAME OF THE AL-QAEDA TRUCE OFFER, OR AT LEAST THERE was no spectacular attack to mark the expiration of the deadline for talks. In fact, July 2004 was one of al-Qaeda's quietest periods since 9/11. It had reached a point where people were saying, 'It's too quiet; I don't like it.' The lack of news and jihad chatter was like the lulls that had preceded the Bali and Riyadh bombings, though this seemed deeper.

Those underlying feelings of something being afoot were reinforced when the home secretary, David Blunkett, warned parliament of the dangers posed by 'sleepers' who were unknown to the authorities. Leading a double life and keeping below the radar, they were 'waiting their opportunity to wreak terror and death on innocent civilians'. He added, conspiratorially: 'In the United Kingdom, we've seen the superb work of our services disrupting and foiling potential attacks. Hidden, unspoken, unpresented work safeguards our interests across the capital and across the whole of the country . . . incidents where we do not hear publicly about what has happened.'

Perhaps instincts were right; he seemed to be hinting at heavy activity in the spook world currently, days before bin Laden's deadline was due to expire. The public, however, could be forgiven for being sceptical over yet more dire claims based on intelligence, though fears that a big terrorist strike was coming were reflected in high opinion-poll numbers. The publication of Lord Butler's *Review of Intelligence on Weapons of Mass Destruction* a few days later just added to the mixed signals.

Why should dark ministerial cautions about attacks in the UK be given credence when the intelligence was so spectacularly wrong on

Iraq? The Butler Review concluded that the WMD Iraq warnings were based on three main but unreliable human intelligence sources cultivated by MI6, who were often passing on third-hand information, or worse. There was also found to be an over-reliance on Iraqi dissident sources. It confirmed that the stocks of chemical and biological weapons components that the USA and UK insisted Saddam had held on to never existed.

Nevertheless, the risk of terrorism in the UK was deemed to be grave enough for the home secretary to announce plans to issue every household in the country with a booklet spelling out what to do in case of a terrorist attack or major civil emergency. It followed comments from anti-terrorism minister Hazel Blears a week earlier that advised members of the public to stockpile food and medicines in case of an emergency. News of the booklet was greeted with a certain amount of giddy derision in the media.

The last such booklet was issued in 1976, and infamously reprinted by the Thatcher administration in 1980, except the fear then was of nuclear war with the Soviet Union. Called 'Protect and Survive', it was infamous because the best advice it could give was for people to paint their windows white to help deflect the blasts and to hide under a table. The press was waiting for similarly useless advice in the terrorism booklet.

The new one was 22 pages long and called 'Preparing for Emergencies'. It was backed with an £8 million TV advertising campaign. The authors had obviously taken pains to ensure that there was no white-paint-type advice in there this time around; it was all very practical, although the resulting blandness was a bit baffling and it made you wonder why they bothered, as it was all couched in terms that could be described as calm-mongering rather than scare-mongering. Even the adverts were soothing, and government figures were assuring the media that it hadn't been published in response to any particular threat. Maybe it was, partially at least, a political arse-covering exercise.

If the government had been pleased that it had side-stepped any major criticism, that pride was soon dented when someone bought the domain name preparingforemergencies.co.uk and set up a spoof website. Thomas Scott swiftly received a terse email from the Cabinet Office asking him to remove the material, as it was claimed that people would be confused by the site and it adversely affected public safety, but the owner refused to bow to pressure. The site looked exactly like the real government site at first glance, and legal action was in the offing, until the media got wind of the story. On the fake site, the overriding advice was 'run like hell'. The introduction said:

> In an effort to worry the public and convince them to vote for us again next year, and because George Bush asked us to, this website includes the common sense advice found in the Preparing for Emergencies booklet, and information on what the government is doing to protect the country as a whole. (Hint: we're praying *really*, *really* hard.) National editions of the booklet will be available here when we can be arsed to get translators to put them into your crazy moon languages.

Within the online booklet, there was a message from 'Not Huw Edwards', saying:

> Helping to prevent a terrorist attack
> 'All information received by the hotline is researched and investigated before any police action is taken. Let us decide whether the information you have is valuable or not. And here's a hint: just because the Arabic man behind the counter at your newsagent looks shifty and has a cold, it doesn't mean he's stockpiling biological weapons, OK? Sheesh.'
> Not Huw Edwards, Deputy Assistant Commissioner, ACPO National Coordinator of Terrorist Investigations
> You can call the Police Anti-Terrorism Hotline on 0800 789 321. All calls will be treated in confidence, and we'll have a good laugh at them later.

It was a good example of Iraq-inspired scepticism, though some of the reasons behind the government's decision to publish may have emerged a few weeks later. In early August, the US administration announced that it was upgrading its terror-alert status in New York, New Jersey and Washington DC to orange, saying that it had received information that suggested al-Qaeda was planning attacks against financial institutions and that operatives had been conducting surveillance of key buildings, specifically: the New York Stock Exchange and the Citigroup headquarters in Manhattan; the Newark headquarters of Prudential Financial; and the Washington offices of the World Bank and the International Monetary Fund. The mode of attack would have been massive bombs concealed in limousines or large vans, which would be parked in underground parking areas and/or near highly populated building entrances. Unnamed US intelligence sources said that al-Qaeda had assessed security in and around the buildings, identified reconnaissance points, devised methods of making contact with employees in the buildings and noted traffic patterns and the locations of hospitals and police departments.

Media incredulity mixed with signs of public panic, as shops in the USA once more saw heavy buying of duct tape, plastic sheets and respirators. The FBI said there was no indication of the timing of the attacks, presumably to play down growing fears of an imminent spectacular. It was suspected that this was a show-boating move by the Bush team to boost its chances of staying in power in the upcoming presidential election, though it soon emerged that something big was happening.

Two days after the balloon went up in the States, anti-terrorism police in the UK launched a series of raids and took thirteen suspects into custody. The arrest of the alleged Azzam Publications mastermind Babar Ahmad came a day later. It begged the question: were all these arrests and so-called plots linked?

It transpired that the US alert was based on information gleaned after the arrest of a suspected al-Qaeda operative in Pakistan three weeks earlier. It also subsequently emerged that the British police raids were launched in haste, because the name of the suspect had been leaked by the Pakistani authorities. He'd apparently been tapped up and turned, and was cooperating and communicating with his associates under the beady eyes of intelligence officials. The British authorities were forced to leap out of the shadows and into action after the name came out.

The suspect was Mohammed Naeem Noor Khan. When his computer was examined, investigators found hundreds of images, drawings and plans of potential target buildings in the USA. Some of the material was years old, though some of it indicated that buildings had been under surveillance as recently as a few months back. He was also suspected of being a key link in al-Qaeda's command and control chain, as evidence was also found of a secret communications system where messages were relayed in code to operatives all over the globe. He was described as a 25-year-old 'computer engineer' who revealed under questioning that he'd been a frequent traveller to the UK, Germany, the USA and other countries.

The authorities had gone looking for him after a nephew of 9/11 master-planner Khalid Sheikh Mohammed and cousin of the 1993 World Trade Center bomber Ramzi Yousef, Abu Musab al-Baluchi, had been arrested in Pakistan in June. Khan spoke with a British accent, and that wasn't the only UK link: Khan's cousin was Babar Ahmad of Azzam Publications infamy. I'd heard mutterings about images on the Azzam website having been found to contain coded messages embedded in graphics there, using a method called steganography, though it wasn't something I'd looked into in any detail. That naturally raised the possibility that the two cases might be intertwined.

While Khan was acting as a double agent in a sting operation, he also ensnared another suspected al-Qaeda computer whiz in Pakistan, Ahmed Khalfan Ghailani, a Tanzanian. Known to use dozens of aliases, including 'Foopie', he was wanted for helping to construct the bombs used in the twin attacks on the US embassies in Kenya and Tanzania in 1998. He was number eight on the FBI's most-wanted list with a $5 million bounty on his head, and he'd reportedly been recently involved in the trading of blood diamonds.

As the media probed on in the days that followed, there had been some suggestions that photographs of Heathrow airport and details of underpasses near high-rise buildings in London had also been found on Khan's computer. The Pakistani government wouldn't comment, but there was no denial either. It was quite telling that the UK raids on 3 August 2004 took place at 3.30 p.m., rather than at dawn, which suggested they had to move fast. They took place at five locations across Britain. In Willesden, in north-west London, armed police burst into a barber's shop and dragged out one of the customers, and two people were detained after a high-speed car chase in Blackburn, Lancashire.

The suspects were taken to Paddington Green police station for questioning, and two of them were quickly released without charge. Scotland Yard was staying tight-lipped but, perhaps stung by accusations from the Democratic Party that it was a pre-election stunt, US sources told the media that the principal target of the British raids was one of the four people detained in Willesden and he was none other than the leader of al-Qaeda in the UK.

Codenamed Bilal, he was initially named as Abu Eissa al-Hindi, and subsequently known as Issa al-Britani and Dhiren Barot. Very little was known about him and I received several calls from newspapers asking if I could shed any more light on the subject. The lack of information returned by a quick Google search told me that this was going to be more than a bit difficult, though I told my contacts that I'd get on to it.

One of the first nuggets I found was that one of his aliases had been mentioned in the report of the official investigation into the 9/11 attacks. The panel's report revealed that he reported to Khalid Sheikh Mohammed, who'd disclosed under interrogation that bin Laden had sent Dhiren Barot to the USA in early 2001 to scope out targets for a follow-up wave of attacks.

I talked to contacts and scoured through my own files and the Web for potential leads, though it was a bit of inspiration that cracked it in the end. One of the nightmares of researching in this area is handling the long lists of alternative names and aliases used by al-Qaeda suspects to avoid detection, which is further complicated by Arabic names that can be spelt in several different ways. Having had no success in using the obvious methods, and fearing failure and feeling increasingly tense because of it, I took a guess at a possible misspelling of one of his forenames, and that threw up the name of an author of a book.

It was a guide to guerrilla warfare, based on his experiences of fighting jihad in the disputed Kashmir region between Pakistan and India. Called *The Army of Madinah in Kashmir*, it described how to plan operations using remote-controlled explosives, grenades and automatic weapons. More worryingly, it included a section on 'modern-day war stratagems', including 'germ warfare' and 'chemical warfare'.

It outlined some useful biographical information on the suspect. He was a Briton of Indian descent who converted from Hinduism to Islam at the age of 20. After fighting in Kashmir, he became a trainer at jihad camps in Afghanistan. In one chapter in the book, called 'A Day in the Life', the author describes the difficulties of operating in the mountainous environment of Kashmir.

> Enemy camps and bunkers are strewn across the entire area with parts where the Mujahideen cannot even walk across, such as man-made tracks or the soft sand to be found on the riverbanks. This is for fear of leaving distinctive 'stud' marked indentations in the malleable ground with one's footprints.
>
> In fact in many ways it can be said that the return trips are even more perilous than the ones to venture in. This is so because the weaponry which they emphatically struggled to bring inside initially will, rather than accompany them on

reverting, be buried in a cache, stashed away in some safe haven as a back up for those staying inside.

He added: 'Hence, it is this that renders each man returning to be equipped with either a pistol or a grenade and dagger. The guides will probably be the bearers of one or two rifles (AK-47) with minimal ammunition all round.' Another chapter, called 'The Realities of Indian Occupied Kashmir', claimed that Indian soldiers routinely gang-rape women.

The book was being sold for £4.95 by an Islamic bookshop called Maktabah al-Ansaar, based in Sparkhill in Birmingham, which was previously connected with Azzam Publications. I browsed through the catalogue on the shop's website and there was a booklet by Osama bin Laden called *Declaration of War*. A book written by Abu Hamza, called *Ruling by Man-Made Law*, could be bought for £1.75, as well as a number of audio recordings by him. A VHS video recording of the last will of one of the 9/11 hijackers was on sale for £7.50, which the shop recommended as a 'must view for all'. One DVD on offer for £7.50, called *Russian Hell Vol. 3*, included extensive 'war footage' of al-Qaeda-affiliated Chechen guerrilla fighters in action.

There was a wide range of jihad-related multimedia material being offered, including audio recordings of speeches by bin Laden and al-Qaeda propaganda videos. The shop had a bit of previous. It was opened in 1999 by Ashraf Thaher and was raided in November 2000 by the police and MI5 under the Prevention of Terrorism Act, although no charges were brought.

I packaged up the information under the headline 'UK al-Qaeda chief's murder manual on sale' and sent it out. The story was published alongside much hair-raising speculation about an attack on Heathrow airport having been averted and even that there was a plan to detonate a massive bomb inside a Tube tunnel beneath the Thames to flood the entire Underground network.

Four days later, the waters were muddied still further by the release of a court transcript in the States. It carried the news that a suspected al-Qaeda operative, called Mohammed Junaid Babar, who'd been detained in April, had pleaded guilty to collaborating with a British colleague in conspiring to send UK Muslims to a jihad training camp in the USA and supplying them with bomb-making materials to be used in a wave of bombings in the UK.

He was cooperating with the authorities, who were linking him with Bakri's al-Muhajiroun group. The UK bombing plot was being planned from December 2002 until about March 2004, according to the document. That appeared to link it to a series of raids in the UK on 31 March in which eight suspects, some connected with al-Muhajiroun, were arrested and 600 kg of ammonium-nitrate fertiliser were recovered from a self-storage depot in west London. Six were later charged with conspiring to cause explosions.

Three days after digesting this, on 17 August, came the announcement that Barot and seven others who'd been arrested in the latest raids – Mohammed Naveed Bhatti, 24; Abdul Aziz Jalil, 31; Omar Abdul Rahman, 20; Junade Feroze, 28; Zia Ul Haq, 25; Qaisar Shaffi, 25; and Nadeem Tarmohammed, 26 – had been charged with conspiracy to commit murder and conspiracy to commit a public nuisance by using 'radioactive materials, toxic gases, chemicals and/or explosives to cause disruption'.

Barot and Tarmohammed were charged with possessing a 'reconnaissance plan' for the Prudential Financial headquarters; Barot was also charged with having reconnaissance details for the New York Stock Exchange, the Citigroup Center in Manhattan and Washington's IMF building, along with notebooks containing information on chemicals, poisons and explosives. Shaffi was charged with possessing an excerpt from a terrorist training manual on manufacturing chemicals and explosives.

US officials said at the time that they were considering laying charges of their own against the suspects. They finally did so in April 2005, when charges against Barot, Tarmohammed and Shaffi were revealed after a grand jury indictment was formally unsealed. They were very similar to the UK charges, raising the possibility that they could face being extradited to the USA after they've gone through the British justice system. They were accused of physically conducting surveillance of the targets on or around 8 April 2001, and that included the use of video cameras.

This information filled in on some details as well; Barot was lead instructor at a camp in Afghanistan in 1998 and he made trips to the USA in 2000 and 2001. He and Tarmohammed travelled to New York on 17 August 2000 and went on later in the month to stay in Washington. Tarmohammed flew back to the UK in September and Barot followed on in November. Barot returned to New York on 11 March 2001, this time accompanied by Shaffi, who became ill and flew back to the UK on 3 April. Tarmohammed arrived in New York the following day, before both returned to Britain four days later.

This constituted a blizzard of terrorism news which, after a long lull, was a bit difficult to take in at the time. Several major attacks appeared to have been averted, including perhaps two or three waves of trademark al-Qaeda simultaneous spectaculars in cities in different continents, involving conventional and unconventional weapons. One wave may have comprised simultaneous attacks on the US and British mainlands, on the eve of the American presidential election perhaps, but not necessarily. Assessing the jihadis' goals in terms of judging what proportion of their ten million allocation of retaliatory deaths would have been used up is of course problematic, but I think it's likely that a large percentage would have been held in reserve, despite the rhetoric.

One key overall impression was that al-Qaeda is willing to bide its time in mounting mega-attacks and bin Laden had been planning follow-up attacks prior to 9/11. There didn't seem to be any shortage of volunteers from the UK; the country was clearly being used by al-Qaeda as a European HQ and its global communications system looked to be coordinated from Europe also, with the finger pointing at London as the main nexus.

The communications traffic suggested the involvement of al-Zarqawi's network in some capacity, not least because his speciality is believed by US officials to be poisons and gases, and that's been a theme running through many of the alleged plots. It's a difficult situation to sum up, as many parts of the picture are concealed or unknown, but that's the nature of the asymmetrical war that al-Qaeda is engaging the West in. Implicit in the design is compartmentalisation and secrecy.

I think of it as a situation that's similar to the illicit drugs trade, in that only a small fraction of the incoming shipments are intercepted by law enforcement. Most slip through the net. The main worry is those who've returned from training camps and who've followed their orders to blend in with society and lead an outwardly normal life until called upon; those who've not yet come to the attention of the authorities, the 'unknown sleepers' either awaiting activation – or already activated.

When the police pounced to break up the alleged Barot US/UK bombing circle, it was done in haste and not all of the cell members had yet been identified. The accidental release of Mohammed Naeem Noor Khan's name forced matters and, in the days that followed, unnamed American officials claimed that five al-Qaeda operatives had escaped the dragnet. They were now assumed to be on the run somewhere in Britain.

146

It was a sensational claim, and there was no outright denial from the police. One curious clue came from a press conference given to local newspaper reporters in Pakistan by the country's military spokesman, Major General Shaukat Sultan. He told them that Barot had secretly travelled to Pakistan in 'March or April' to the eastern city of Lahore to meet with Khan. He had an accomplice with him, an unnamed 'foreign explosives expert'. He seemed to be a sixth missing suspect in the case, as the five who'd slipped the net were all believed to be of Pakistani origin.

A security source told the media that all of them were believed to be still in the UK – somewhere. Barot was under surveillance by MI5 and MI6 as he travelled between the two countries, but he'd managed to give them the slip just before the news of Khan's detention in Pakistan. He'd told investigators in Pakistan that he'd met Barot on two occasions during trips to Britain. His role was to procure reconnaissance plans for Heathrow, while Barot would organise the attack, which would probably have been carried out using car or truck bombs. Khan also admitted that he'd visited Finsbury Park mosque and had met Abu Hamza.

Once Barot had been spotted again, it was decided that he should be nabbed immediately, rather than waiting to try to identify his unknown associates and risk losing him once more. He was presented as being the project leader for the operation, and certainly the surveillance cells looked to have been busted, so it was tempting to conclude that the others who were on the run were members of the attack team.

A story along the lines of 'large number of al-Qaeda suicide bombers on the loose' was something that the newspapers couldn't ignore. As expected, all the usual channels turned up zilch, and there was no discernable chatter about the guys on the run. Their names might have been on a list of suspects somewhere, but there were many thousands of possibilities.

One list I'd obtained had originated from the CIA, and it was a spreadsheet of suspicious individuals, companies and charities that had been distributed to major banks, though some of the details looked to be very outdated. There was also a supplemental list of thousands of Spanish names, along with telephone numbers and addresses, mainly in Spain and the USA. Nothing.

One thing I'm quite bad at doing is searching my own archives, which contain gigabytes of hairy and classified stuff, along with more routine items, such as copies of email messages, videos, images and saved Web pages. Ignoring my own previous research in the hurry to cover new ground is an error I've made before. I suck in a hell of a lot of data every day and it had reached a point where I could instantly call up a menu of background information from public and private sources on a subject without going online.

At the time, I wasn't even searching for anything, just browsing a list of file names and thinking of possible angles of attack based on any information I had relating to transportation, maybe, or airports. Several sites were known to have carried surveillance and targeting information, so I thought perhaps I might have something along those lines that I'd forgotten about. One significant phrase, link or email address could open up a colourful new world of possibilities.

As these thoughts were forming, my eyes were scanning down a list of emails from a recent conversation I'd had with a trusted contact. I remembered that he'd flagged up some threat involving public transport, though I couldn't recall the exact details initially. I thought it had involved a site with an odd name and that was about all I could dredge up. I took a closer look at those exchanges and was quickly flooded with excitement.

He'd stumbled upon his information in the first place, and now I'd stumbled upon his stumbling, so it was a doubly lucky find. During the quiet summer period, I'd been occasionally sending him emails, enquiring whether he'd been looking at anything of interest recently, and just saying 'hello', really. He did have something of interest: he'd been tracing email addresses and come across a British-registered site carrying a solitary document containing diagrams and chemical formulas. He'd thought it might be a plan for a chemical weapon of some kind, but he'd only just discovered it and was waiting for a translation of the text, which was in Arabic. The site wasn't listed on search engines and was thus 'invisible'. The document itself was in the form of a compressed zip file, which also afforded it some additional protection from discovery.

I remembered that I hadn't made any progress with it and, although I'd intended to go back to it when time allowed, I'd simply forgotten all about it. Unforgivable really, but at least I still had all the material, so I set about combing through it again. I recalled that the main diagram showed a large tin and four glass bottles. I located the page, copied the accompanying Arabic and translated it into English.

It was indeed a chemical device, although it was more than that:

the plans gave step-by-step instructions to making a miniaturised WMD. The text trumpeted the design as the very latest innovation in mass killing with unconventional weapons and the covert nature of the document was hinted at by a note which pointed out that the inventor couldn't be named. It sounded like he might be regarded as a hero, as a certain defiant pride shone through the words.

This was no student prank. The text looked authentic, in that it matched the language used in al-Qaeda material that I'd seen many times previously and all the right sentiments were expressed. Only the sickest of psychopath geniuses could have come up with this as a hoax. The devastating aspect of the design was the sheer simplicity of it. It also incorporated two different methods for delivering death in the most efficient, dastardly way.

The outer casing consisted of a large, three-kilogram tin of powdered milk, although the instructions said that any catering-sized tin would do the job. It was then drilled with holes. A cardboard collar was placed inside, encircling four glass cola bottles. Inside the bottles were three different chemicals which, when mixed together, produced two types of poison gas: cyanide and a chemical that attacks the lining of the lungs, causing victims to drown in their own blood. All that was needed to start the device was to break the bottles to allow the chemicals to mix and react and vent out through the holes in the tin. The document suggested that a one-gram TNT charge could be used to set it off, or the tin could simply be slammed down hard on the ground. The mini-WMD could 'easily' be constructed from materials that were readily available in high-street shops.

That was true enough – the document listed the products which contained the right chemicals and they could indeed be very easily obtained. The introduction said: 'The time has come to move in and engage with the Crusaders, who have exterminated thousands of children, women and sheikhs in Muslim countries and continue to do so.' It praised the development of this new weapon as 'simple', 'innovative' and 'creative' and, echoing the conclusion of the Saudi al-Qaeda WMD ruling, it went on to claim that use of chemical weapons against enemies of Islam is permitted by the Koran.

It also listed potential targets within countries that were participating in the occupation of Iraq. These devices could be used to greatest effect in and around schools, hospitals, churches, cinemas, restaurants, pubs, nightclubs and government buildings, it said. The instructions advised the operative to avoid using them on railway station concourses, because of the risk of being caught on CCTV, but said that deploying them inside train carriages was ideal. Similarly, it warned against placing them inside airport terminals, because of the risk of discovery by sniffer dogs, so positioning them near entrance areas was recommended. They could be used to greatest effect near to air-conditioning and ventilation intakes and emergency exits, according to the document. The author pointed out that the device had been designed with enclosed spaces in mind, although they could simply be thrown or catapulted into crowds in open areas, if necessary. He warned that operatives should take note of the wind direction and proximity of Muslim populations when using them out in the open.

The gas device was said to be effective over an area of one square kilometre, with the effects lasting for up to eight hours, although larger versions could be built to increase the killing zone. It was also claimed that one of the attractions of using this type of weapon is that a gas mask is no defence. One of the gases can be absorbed through exposed skin. The document said that this gas could lead to severe pain and paralysis in the neck muscles if a full protective suit wasn't being worn, and the effect would fool rescue workers into believing they were suffocating. This would prompt them to remove their gas masks and guarantee their deaths.

It was a fiendish plan by any standard, and it did seem to be a genuine step forward in weapon design. The way that this bomb produced a secondary gas reminded me of a controversial plot that was foiled by UK and UK intelligence agents on 6 April 2004. Operatives were planning to attack London using explosives mixed with a chemical called osmium tetroxide. It's highly toxic and attacks the eyes, lungs and exposed skin.

It wasn't clear if this was connected with the arrest of nine men and one woman in the previous week during a series of police raids around the country involving four hundred officers, although the timing was suggestive. Seven of the suspects, of Iraqi, Kurdish and North African descent, were arrested in Greater Manchester. The others were picked up in Staffordshire, the West Midlands and south Yorkshire. The move was said to have been made after mobile-phone calls had been intercepted at the NSA/GCHQ listening station at RAF Menwith Hill in Yorkshire.

The plot never came to fruition and there was much scepticism over the claim, after the media contacted experts who said they weren't convinced that the osmium would be able to cause much large-scale harm, though it was undoubtedly a dangerous chemical. One academic described it as a 'mild irritant', though the truth is that everyone was guessing, as such a combination has not been exploded in anger before. I've got no doubt that the inclusion of the chemical in an attack would have caused great panic, whatever its precise scientific dangers.

The authorities were cornered, as they were taking a lot of flak for acting pre-emptively to stop the alleged plot progressing, yet they would have got the same sort of treatment if a bomb had been detonated. It was another case of Iraq scepticism being unreasonably transferred to the al-Qaeda threat, and you would have thought from the coverage that the police were in cahoots with the politicians.

That would be quite a conspiracy, and it overlooks the fact that a range of public figures had stepped forward with statements warning the public that the threat was very real indeed. Even the head of MI5 and London mayor Ken Livingstone, who's not known for right-wing leanings, were singing from the same song sheet. MI5 director general Eliza Manningham-Buller had warned that Britain faced a 'serious and sustained threat' of terrorist attacks at home and abroad, while Livingstone had said earlier in the year that it would be 'miraculous' if London wasn't attacked.

The emergence of the new 'double death' chemical bomb confirmed in my own mind that there were probably several plans to attack the UK being worked on at any one time and that new innovations to catch out the security services were part and parcel of the planning. Limousine bombs, shoe bombs, invisible bombs, chemicals combined with explosives: this latest mini-warhead development appeared to be a natural progression. Building it would be simplicity itself. I could visit a few shops to buy the key ingredients and have it assembled within an hour. There, on my kitchen table, could easily be sitting the very thing that over 100,000 troops failed to encounter in Iraq. Only small quantities were required, so there was no question of risking arousing suspicion by calling up wholesale chemical suppliers. If I went on a shopping spree and made sure I went to a different town each time, I could easily have a couple of dozen devices stockpiled by the end of the week.

My contact who'd sniffed out the site where the bomb plan appeared said it was also linked to a Yahoo! discussion group which used the name of a website that had been distributing guerrilla-warfare and weapons manuals prior to the Iraq war. The operators appeared to be based in London, Riyadh and Mecca. One suspect was based in Saudi Arabia, though he was routing his email through an Internet account operated by a company in London that I'd never come across before. Others in this circle were doing the same thing.

A contact at the *Sunday Express* was very enthusiastic about my findings. It was a brand new angle on the escaped al-Qaeda operatives story. The communications links pointed to London and it was all exclusive and sitting up very nicely. It wasn't possible to tell if this was part of a plot to attack Heathrow or if it was part of an entirely separate plan and an unknown cell, but something serious was obviously brewing.

I wrote up the story and filed it by email and waited. I got a quick call asking me to provide the links to the document and my notes on those who might be involved, and I obliged. A few hours after that, I got a call to congratulate me in advance for making the front page in the next day's issue. It wasn't difficult to spot the paper when I went to the newsagent the next day, as I could see the ginormous headline shouting out 'CYANIDE TERROR OF COLA BOMBS'.

If there were any doubts about the lengths to which terrorists were prepared to go, they should have been dispelled by the Beslan school siege in Russia. It happened on 1 September 2004, following a resurgence of activity by the al-Qaeda-linked Chechen Mujahideen. A week earlier, two civilian airliners had crashed simultaneously in Russia, killing eighty-nine people, and female Chechen suicide bombers were suspected.

The airliner investigation focused on two women who'd bought last-minute tickets for the flights and the discovery of the explosive hexogen, which forms a type of plastic explosive when mixed with nitro-glycerine, in the wreckage of the aircraft. It was a type that had been used by the Chechens in the past and it was strongly suspected that the suicide bombers had been members of the female brigade of the rebel movement, commonly known in Russia as the Black Widows. They'd come to prominence two years earlier, making up half of the fifty or so terrorists who'd stormed the Moscow theatre and held seven hundred people hostage.

Beslan also happened the day after a Chechen woman blew herself up outside a Moscow underground station, killing nine people. This time, 1,300 people, mostly children, had been taken hostage at School Number One in the town, in the Russian republic of North Ossetia. It was jaw-dropping news.

The attackers stormed the school in two military lorries as the new term was just starting, killing five police officers and losing one of their number in the initial attack. Some 50 people managed to escape in the confusion and there was also uncertainty about the number of people left inside: the Russian government was insisting it was around 350 people, though eyewitnesses in the town said it was nearer 1,000.

Some of the terrorists were seen wearing what looked to be explosive belts and there was some sporadic shooting after they had seized control of the building. It was thought at the time that these were just warning shots to keep police at bay, but the investigation later found that the attackers' first move was to execute adult male hostages. That was what was behind the sound of gunfire; twenty bodies were dumped out of windows. The terrorists were displaying their anger at the Russian government's downplaying of the number of hostages.

The school was soon surrounded by a variety of army and police forces, including elite Spetsnaz (special forces) and other anti-terrorism troops. The world's media were also scrambling to get to the town, and soon it was being shown live on all channels. I spent much of the day watching the pictures, waiting to see what would happen.

The hostage-takers had herded everyone into the school gym, which they'd rigged with improvised explosive devices and surrounded with tripwires. They also issued a statement threatening to kill fifty hostages for every one of their number who might be killed during the stand off, and to blow up the entire school if it was stormed. Their central demand for the release of the hostages was the withdrawal of Russian troops from Chechnya, but it was almost inconceivable that their wishes would be granted.

President Putin was known for his strong line on the Chechnya issue and I couldn't see him agreeing to be totally humiliated. It would also break the cardinal political hard-man mantra about not talking to terrorists. That added to my feeling of doom, as it was a demand that couldn't be met, and maybe that was the idea. This had also been the demand during the theatre siege and it wasn't entertained then.

The government did, however, start negotiations with the terrorists, via an intermediary who'd assisted with mediation during the theatre siege. The terrorists refused to allow food, water or medical supplies inside and even refused permission to remove the dead bodies in the school compound. The conditions in the gym worsened and many children removed their clothing in the sweltering heat. Some ground was conceded when the hostage-takers agreed to release twenty-six women and children, though there were reports that mothers with two children were forced to choose just one child to take with them.

The rest of the second day was quiet, apart from the sound of two explosions, which turned out to be the attackers firing rocket-propelled grenades to remind the surrounding troops to keep their distance. Negotiations continued on day three and, in the afternoon, it was agreed that medical workers could enter the compound to take away the dead bodies. As the truck rolled into the school yard, it all kicked off.

What happened next is still a matter of dispute, although what appears to have occurred is that one of the terrorists accidentally triggered a tripwire and set off an explosive device that caused part of the gym roof to collapse. Many of the fathers outside the building who were waiting anxiously for their children's release were armed and mixing with Russian troops. On hearing the sound of the explosion and fearing that the endgame was under way, the fathers opened fire on the building. That prompted the terrorists to believe that the school was being stormed by troops, and millions of people watched as a great tragedy started to unfold live on TV.

Two medical workers were killed as the hostage-takers opened fire on them. They then gunned down several of about 30 hostages who had managed to escape from the gym after the explosion. The military's action plan was activated at this point and troops moved in to provide covering fire for the fleeing civilians. They were supported by helicopter gunships and a tank and a chaotic gun battle ensued as the troops, along with some armed civilians, started to advance on the school compound.

The militants made good on their promise and set off several large explosions, which destroyed the gym and set most of its remains ablaze. Special forces commandos set off two charges to blow holes in the building's walls to provide routes out for any hostages who might still be alive inside. After two hours of confusion, it was announced that troops were in full control of the school, though gun battles inside the grounds continued into the evening. Three terrorists had taken refuge in the building's basement, though all of them, and the hostages they were holding, were killed.

Thirteen of the attackers managed to break through the military cordon and escape, including two women who posed as medical workers. An unknown number were said to be holed up in a two-storey house some forty metres from the school gym, so the house was completely destroyed by tanks with flamethrowers. In the end, thirty-one attackers were killed, including one who'd been injured and then beaten to death by relatives of the hostages at a hospital. One was captured alive.

Some 331 civilians, mostly children, and 11 soldiers perished at Beslan. Around 434 people were hospitalised and 247 adults and 85 children were said to be in a critical condition immediately after the event. To describe it as a tragedy seems wrong, because it was more than that. There were reports that scores of children had been shot in the back, an 18-month-old baby had been stabbed to death, and the children were forced to drink their own urine, in the absence of fresh water. The suffering that people endured in that gym defies description; even 'hellish' doesn't seem right. One woman who'd escaped from the school committed suicide as soon as she returned home.

One aspect of the story that was played down, for fear of stoking ethnic tensions in the region and encouraging relatives to seek revenge, were reports that some of the older girls had been sexually assaulted in rooms adjoining the gym and that the attacks had been captured on video cameras. Others were said to have been violently raped in front of their parents, brothers and sisters and classmates.

It was all extremely depressing and distressing for any sane person, though praise for the terrorists was voiced in London. Universal condemnation greeted comments made by Omar Bakri Mohammed of al-Muhajiroun that Islamic terrorists would be justified in mounting a similar operation against a school in Britain, as long as women and children were not deliberately executed. He instantly made himself public enemy number one in the eyes of the press, although he spouted all the usual stuff about being quoted out of context, etc., even denying that he'd made such comments.

I got a lot of phone calls asking me if I 'had anything on him'. He'd previously played second fiddle to Abu Hamza in being al-Qaeda's most prominent supporter in the UK, but the spotlight was fixed on Bakri now. As with Hamza, he had been viewed as an absurdist clown but, as the media were starting to come around to realising that Hamza might be 'the real deal', I could see that Bakri was in for a rough ride. It emerged during the subsequent investigation that three of the Beslan terrorists had until recently been based in London, and had attended Finsbury Park mosque.

JIHAD BENEFITS

MORE EVIDENCE OF DEVELOPMENT AND INNOVATION IN KILLING methods and hostage-taking came hot on the heels of Beslan. On 16 September 2004, a 62-year-old British engineer called Ken Bigley was kidnapped in Iraq, along with two American colleagues, Jack Hensley and Eugene Armstrong. An unknown group had mounted a dawn raid on the house in Baghdad where they were living and had spirited them away.

It turned into a massive international news story when al-Zarqawi's group in Iraq released a video showing the three men blindfolded and sitting at the feet of a black-clad, masked kidnapper. The man read out a statement that threatened the prisoners with beheading unless all women held in American-controlled jails were freed within 48 hours. The video had been uploaded to the al-Zarqawi group website, which was being hosted by a company in the USA.

This website had been under constant attack by hackers and anti-jihad activists, which had forced it to move to new locations several times, although it often cropped up again within hours under a new name. Yet, it was always with the same mysterious hosting company, called Hostinganime.com, which seemed to be impervious to all the complaints that were being made about the site. The company's consistent refusal to respond to the criticism made some people think that maybe the site was being kept online by the authorities. It was, after all, just about the only source of leads about the whereabouts of the hostages.

This may have been another case of al-Qaeda-linked kidnappers issuing demands that they knew could not be met. The USA said

157

there were only two women in custody in Iraq – and they were both suspected of involvement in Saddam's biological weapons programme. One was Huda Salih Mahdi Ammash, a biotechnology researcher who was otherwise known as Mrs Anthrax. The other was Rihab Rashid Taha al-Azawi, a British-educated Iraqi microbiologist, known as Dr Germ. A joint report by the US chiefs of staff and the Defense Intelligence Agency in 1999 branded al-Azawi as the most dangerous woman in the world.

Prior to the Iraq war, she was often seen sitting alongside Saddam in TV images; now she was being held by the Americans at a secret location. Just before the invasion, she was named in the government's infamous intelligence dossier that laid out the justifications for going to war. No charges had been brought against her and, to start with, the UK was making favourable noises about the possibility of her being released. That suggestion, however, was shot down a day later by the American officials, who said it was out of the question.

A huge multinational effort was under way to try to secure the release of the hostages. The prime minister held talks with the new Iraqi interim prime minister, Iyad Allawi, and the Foreign Office made the unusual move of sending an official to appear on the Arabic TV station Al-Arabiya to appeal for information that could help in releasing Bigley.

In the al-Zarqawi video, the man reading the statement said that, if their demands were not met: 'By the name of Allah, these three hostages will get nothing from us except their throats slit and necks chopped, so they will serve as an example.'

As a reminder of the fate awaiting them, the group's website made available a video of the beheading of a Turkish hostage three weeks previously. This turned into an unprecedented international crisis as, at that time, 40 people were believed to be held by insurgent groups. They included eighteen Iraqi national guardsmen and two French journalists. Twenty-six others had been killed, and seven of those had been beheaded. Another 114 people had escaped, been released or rescued.

There were many rumours flying around about secret ransoms being paid by governments to secure the release of their citizens, and they often surrounded cases involving Italian hostages. The high numbers of people who'd been released by their captors without explanation indicated that there was a lot of covert activity going on – and the muted media coverage added to this impression. Lots of previously unknown groups were announcing that they were holding hostages and a new industry was taking shape. Word was out that foreigners could be sold for big money and there was some evidence that different groups were trading hostages with each other.

One organisation that wasn't known for accepting cash donations was al-Zarqawi's. In fact, other insurgent groups were issuing statements promising to hand hostages over to al-Zarqawi unless they got their money. Initially, it looked like the PR efforts of governments and the relatives of the three latest detainees were having some effect. The 48-hour deadline passed without incident and that was at least some source of hope.

That vanished on the fourth day of the crisis, when a video was posted on al-Zarqawi's Tawhid website showing the beheading of the American Eugene Armstrong. It was a now-familiar scene: he was bound and blindfolded and wearing an orange, Camp X-ray-style jumpsuit and sitting at the feet of five black-clad men. The leader of the group accused the USA of lying about there being no women in Iraqi jails and added: 'Since you didn't release our sisters, here's the first infidel.' He pulled out a huge knife and the other members of the group rushed forward and held the victim face down on the floor. Armstrong's head was sawn off and placed on his back. I don't remember hearing any screaming. The USA and the UK were told that they had 24 hours to meet their demands, otherwise another hostage would be killed.

Sure enough, two days later a statement was posted on an extremist website claiming that Jack Hensley had been killed, though a video wasn't immediately forthcoming, but a body had been found. It said that the British hostage Bigley would be next, though a deadline wasn't mentioned. The pressure was really on the prime minister, as Ken Bigley's brother, Paul, called on Blair to resign over the government's failure to secure his release. The Foreign Office was continuing to run appeals on Arabic TV, this time pointing out that there were no female prisoners in Iraq under direct British control.

The absence of another deadline encouraged me to continue to think that al-Zarqawi had no intention of releasing the hostages: he was more interested in embarrassing Western governments and garnering media coverage. The days that followed demonstrated that the group had a surprisingly in-depth knowledge of the current British political scene. That made me suspect that the Iraq group was responding to feedback from supporters in his European network.

The next video release, the following day, wasn't that of Hensley being killed, but of Ken Bigley pleading for his life. He stared into the lens and said: 'To Mr Blair, my name is Ken Bigley, from Liverpool. I think this is possibly my last chance. I don't want to die.' His family issued a statement begging the prime minister to meet the demands, amid criticism that he hadn't made a direct appeal to the kidnappers, as President Jacques Chirac had done in an effort to speed the release of the two French journalists who'd been captured earlier in the year.

Blair decided to address their concerns by doing an interview with BBC Radio Merseyside. By sheer coincidence, I was interviewed live on the same programme immediately before Blair was patched in to address the people of Liverpool. It was one of several radio interviews I did that day, and I remember seeing Radio Merseyside on the itinerary and making a mental note to be extremely careful with my words. It seemed that the entire city was following the story minute-by-minute, and vigils to pray for Ken's release were being organised by religious leaders.

I didn't know that Blair had followed me on the programme until I got home in the late afternoon. Perhaps I was keeping him waiting and having to listen to me ramble on was making him impatient and affecting his blood pressure. I was being piped in from a studio in the BBC's Portland Place headquarters in the West End of London, though the cramped room I was in was more like a cupboard under the stairs. I was simply ushered in and told to put on the headphones and wait. After beating back rising feelings of claustrophobia, I started to swing around on the chair, thinking during the initial eerie silence that spending time in a cupboard was an odd thing to be doing during the working day.

My media contacts were keen for me to get on to the Bigley case and I was keen to do just that, though most of the day would be taken up with interviews. The questioning from Liverpool was the most challenging of all, and I was on the back foot for a lot of the time. I was heavily self-censoring the words I was mouthing and I probably made a hash of it, at some points, because of the care I was taking.

The presenter opened up with some sceptical questions about the scale of the threat presented by al-Qaeda and I fielded those first, before he moved on to ask me what I thought about al-Zarqawi and his group. How serious was he? Was he linked to al-Qaeda? I replied that his group was very serious and that intelligence agencies believed it was aligned with al-Qaeda, though the precise details of those links were still a little unclear.

He then asked me what I thought of al-Zarqawi as a person. I knew this would be coming and I was trying to formulate an appropriate form of words as he was speaking. It seemed that the world had stopped turning during those few seconds as I pondered the options, recalling the voice of one newspaper contact who'd warned me not to do anything during my investigations that might endanger Bigley or any other hostage, like pretending to be a relative wanting to open direct negotiations, or something.

I was caught in a bind – should I soften my language in deference to the diplomatic efforts that were ongoing or should I be straight and honest? An entire city was tuned in and listening. Al-Zarqawi's group had a near 100 per cent capture-to-kill ratio and my job was to be honest and objective, I figured. I replied with something along the lines of him being as serious as they come and obviously a bloodthirsty psychopath. That was it, and then it was over to the PM. He said he would talk to the kidnappers if they got in touch with him, but he wouldn't negotiate.

Blair was under attack from all sides, and I suppose it was around about this time that it became quite apparent that he'd lost the trust of many voters, because of the Iraq war and the non-discovery of WMD and the lies that had been peddled. He'd flown in the face of the million or more people who'd marched in London to protest at the prospect of British involvement in a war in Iraq and he was now paying the political price. He was facing censure from his own supporters at the Labour Party annual conference in Brighton and it now looked like the hostage crisis would overshadow the whole event.

It did, and I found it hard to believe that this wasn't a deliberate ploy by the kidnappers. After days of speculation and rumour, on the final day of the conference another video was released. This time an exhausted and distressed Ken was shown chained up inside a tiny cage, dressed in an orange jumpsuit and sitting with his knees up to his chest. I just hoped that the cage was merely a prop for the camera. He was crying and said: 'Tony Blair is a liar. He doesn't care about me. I'm just one person . . . My captors don't want to kill me.' Speaking from the Labour conference in Brighton, Tony Blair responded by saying he was sickened by the footage and reiterated that everything possible was being done to try to secure Ken's release.

The prime minister was looking more haggard than usual. The Tories were in the lead in the opinion polls and supporters of Chancellor Gordon Brown were suggesting that Blair's days were well and truly numbered. Yes, self-inflicted, you might say, but few prime ministers in recent times could have been under the personal stress that Blair must have been feeling during these few days. When it was announced the following day that he'd undergone surgery to correct a heart problem, you had to wonder if this had been brought on by combined conference–hostage stress.

The crisis continued for another ten days until, on 10 October 2004, a video was posted on a Saudi website showing Ken being beheaded. He started to make a final plea to the government when, as in the previous execution films, he was suddenly jumped on by his attackers and decapitated with a large knife. There were no screams, just a final muffled cry of surprised anguish.

All efforts to save him failed, although the government said he had managed to escape at one point. MI6 had apparently made contact with one of the fighters guarding him, a Syrian, who gave Ken a weapon and allowed him to escape. He made a break for it, but was swiftly recaptured.

There was a second opportunity to save him that didn't make it into the papers. Many prominent members of the online anti-terrorism community became hot under the collar when Blair appeared to have suggested that the kidnappers would have to get in touch, when contact with them could in fact be just one email message away. Sites where videos were uploaded and discussion forums where al-Zarqawi's supporters hung out were well known. Why was the British government refusing to send emails to them?

Then came the curious case of a group of Dutch activists who, moved by Ken's plight, decided to scour the Net for traces of a direct point of contact with al-Zarqawi. After following numerous leads, they managed to come up with a telephone number. The day after Blair's hospital visit, they announced that they'd called the number and a foreign voice had answered the phone, at which point they'd decided to inform Ken's family and the Dutch authorities.

The home of Paul Bigley, who lived in Amsterdam, was visited by armed intelligence officers the following day. Material from his computer was copied and he was quizzed over the next 48 hours about allegedly contacting al-Zarqawi's group, though Paul denied he'd made any contact with them. It's still unclear whether this incident was linked with the Dutch activists' phone number and if the British government obtained this number – or whether they'd dialled it.

Some comfort for Ken Bigley's relatives came just before Christmas, when the interim Iraqi government announced that a senior aide to al-Zarqawi, who was head of the media department and in charge of filming the hostage beheadings and getting them to the outside world, Hassan Ibrahim Farhan, had been killed by Iraqi police. Two of his assistants, Khadi Hassan and 'Adil', were captured during the incident, though it wasn't disclosed where and when this had happened.

In early November, the USA launched a major offensive to seize back control of the city of Fallujah, thought to be al-Zarqawi's stronghold and the hiding place of his group of hostage-takers. The operation was successful and the building where Ken and the other hostages had been slaughtered was discovered, but, true to form, the chief suspects had vanished.

September 2004 had turned into a busy month. In the midst of the Ken Bigley saga, an officer from the Metropolitan Police anti-terrorism branch called to say that they wanted to pay me a visit. This is not an offer that you can turn down, really, so we fixed a date. They needed to take a statement from me about the cache of audiotape recordings featuring Abu Hamza that I'd handed over, via the *Daily Mail*, in April. I'd already outlined much of the content in my first book, but now the cops had suddenly decided they needed to know precisely how they came into my possession. The book was already on sale and it made me wonder, 'Why now?'

Hamza had been arrested in May of that year, after the USA had levelled 11 terrorism-related charges against him and applied for him to be extradited. There had been some disbelief and disappointment in the media that he was going to be handed over to the Americans and not be charged with offences in the UK. It looked like the government was side-stepping a difficult issue by letting the Americans have their way with him. It looked like political weakness and suggested that the police hadn't got anything on him, even though Finsbury Park mosque had been al-Qaeda's UK HQ under Hamza's tenure.

Hamza had, however, been arrested for alleged UK offences three weeks prior to the Met coming to my door. He was taken from HM Prison Belmarsh in east London to the high-security Paddington Green police station for questioning. Little was known about the nature of his perceived crimes, apart from them being related to 'suspicion of being involved in the commission, preparation or instigation of acts of terrorism'.

Most people felt that the time had come at last and that Hamza was about to be charged in the UK. British charges would take precedence over the US deportation case, which would be put on ice until he'd been dealt with by the British judicial system. The American request could be resurrected; he faced the prospect of serving a prison sentence in Britain and being deported to the USA to face the music there on his release.

After six days of questioning under the Terrorism Act, it was announced that Hamza had been 'de-arrested' and returned to Belmarsh. He'd been released without charge and it was seen as a police failure. It seemed inconceivable to many that, with all the plots and notorious characters that had been linked to Finsbury Park, the police had failed to come up with any evidence against him. After he was de-arrested, most in the media assumed that was that.

Three weeks after the visit, on 15 October 2004, it was announced that the Crown Prosecution Service had given the police the go-ahead to charge Hamza with terrorism-related offences committed in the UK. The news caused a sensation, as the media had assumed that the investigation had ended when he was de-arrested. I knew differently, but felt I ought to keep my mouth shut.

There was a mini phoney war and much speculation about what was happening for four days until it was confirmed that he'd been officially charged. There were sixteen charges, including ten of soliciting to murder. There were four charges of using threatening, abusive or insulting behaviour with intent to stir up racial hatred. Only one was under the Terrorism Act, which was possession of a document 'of a kind likely to be useful to a person committing or preparing an act of terrorism'. It was the final charge that really caught my attention, and it perhaps shed light on the sources on which the main charges were based: having threatening, abusive or insulting audio and video recordings.

Now that he'd been charged, reporting restrictions came into play, but the long arm of the Yard doesn't extend to America. There had been a lot of interest in Hamza there and in the London bureaus of the major US networks. I'd taken a call from CBS the week before, saying they'd like to film a report for broadcasting on the main evening news programme in the States.

I'd kept in touch with a producer I'd met earlier in the year, mainly because we seemed to be on the same wavelength and we got on. She'd expressed an interest in filming a story based around *Terror Tracker* when it was published. When she and the crew arrived at my house to start filming, she told me that her bosses liked the story a lot and they were now planning a two-part special about terrorism on the Internet, to be broadcast on consecutive evenings.

The first film centred on Glen Jenvey and it told the story of how he'd conned Abu Hamza by setting up a false website and proposing a joint venture between Hamza's group and his own fictitious Kashmiri terrorist group. The gist of the story was that anyone with an Internet connection could participate in the war against terrorists from the comfort of their own home.

I gave them some snippets from the copies of the audiotapes that I'd made before handing them over to the police. One of them was Hamza saying during one of his sermons: 'A land for jihad is in Afghanistan. If you are more courageous, you should do another Afghanistan in your own country.' The other key quote was: 'Our people should know that we should have intifada [uprising], also uprising in our own countries more than the Palestinians do in their own countries.'

I gave people a quick tour of the world of cybernetic terrorism in part two. I talked about orders being issued via websites, how bomb plans were available and how suspect sites were operated. The twist to the tale came when I said that a recent survey of the main militant Islamic sites had found that more than three-quarters of them were hosted on servers in the USA. They also filmed a quick interview with a former British intelligence officer, Crispin Black, who confirmed: 'It's quite clear that a number of terrorists certainly in the al-Qaeda network are frankly people that we would describe as computer nerds, and they're able to make evolutionary steps to keep one jump ahead of the authorities.'

It was a good shout and we reached, by my reckoning, some twenty-five million people in two swoops. It was the first time, to my knowledge, that a major US TV news network had taken time out to explain to a mass audience precisely how terrorists and terrorist support groups operate on the Net. It not only explained the technical details, it also highlighted the sheer scale of this new phenomenon.

I was curious as to how much traffic I could draw to my website, now that it was fully up and running. I'd spent too much time on it during the early summer, but I'd wanted to do the whole thing myself, just to prove that I had the expertise. It was a tedious business and in many ways I wish I'd got someone else to do it, though it was good knowing that I now had a new cyber-home that was halfway decent and that it was all my own handiwork.

Press attention shifted back to Hamza's colleague Omar Bakri Mohammed of al-Muhajiroun, as it was assumed that he was now a prime candidate for detention. Journalists had been digging around him for quite a while now, though Bakri had been more careful than Hamza in his choice of words when speaking in public.

The plug was pulled on the al-Muhajiroun website after Bakri's comments about the Beslan child murders, which was at least the second time in a year. Holding Bakri accountable for his comments was often problematic, as he had a habit of making his most outrageous remarks to foreign newspapers, then claiming that he'd been misquoted/mistranslated when the UK media picked up on what he'd said. After Hamza was charged, I expected to see a raft of angry statements threatening all sorts, but there was just a passing reference to him being 'kidnapped' by the authorities.

Reports from Belmarsh prison suggested that Hamza was continuing to preach his message to the other inmates. He continued to make headlines with stories about his activities inside jail, which weren't related to the charges levelled against him so they were not subject to restrictions on reporting. His famous metal hooks had apparently been taken away, as it was judged that they could be used as weapons, and new, specially designed aluminium ones had been provided at a cost of £5,000 to the NHS. He also had a personal nurse, who cost £30,000 a year. The other inmates called his male nurse 'Dirty Harry'.

It seemed that, initially, Bakri had decided to keep his head down to avoid going the same way. Just before Hamza was charged, he announced that al-Muhajiroun had been disbanded. It might have been a tactical move to avoid the organisation being officially proscribed by the government, though the statement mysteriously claimed:

> In light of the new reality after the blessed 9/11, the evil forces having united against the Ummah and Islam and fighting us all using the same bow – there is nothing left except that the sincere Muslims who fight with their lives, flesh and wealth unite for the sake of Allah.

He was soon back in the headlines, though, this time for calling on British Muslims to finance terrorism. In an interview with the Arabic newspaper *Al-Sharq Al-Awsat*, he advised people not to give donations to well-known Islamic charities but to 'the Mujahideen' instead. The group had been continuing to expand before the dissolution and had recently opened an office in Dublin, Ireland. Anjem Choudary, who'd been a senior leader of the organisation, told an audience at a debate at Trinity College that the hostages taken in Iraq were 'legitimate targets'.

He also refused to express any sympathy for Ken Bigley, and it became a big story because the UK was in the grip of another hostage crisis. This time, aid worker Margaret Hassan had been kidnapped and paraded on video. She was married to an Iraqi and had dual British and Iraqi nationality, and was clearly very distressed. It was feared that she had fallen into the hands of al-Zarqawi's group. Al-Zarqawi himself had just caused an international stir by officially pledging allegiance to Osama bin Laden and renaming his group al-Qaeda in the Land of the Two Rivers (al-Qaeda in Iraq). A second video emerged two weeks later showing Margaret being murdered with a single gunshot to the head.

I received lots of phone calls from media contacts who didn't believe that al-Muhajiroun was defunct, so I started patrolling. Members of the group had been spotted by the FBI at flight-training schools prior to 9/11 and this sprang to mind when, in November, it was reported that the police and security services had thwarted a plot to crash airliners into the office towers of London's Canary Wharf and Heathrow airport. The training of the suicide pilots had been disrupted, it said. The attacks may have been carried out simultaneously and it was one of 'four or five' such attacks on the UK that had been thwarted since 9/11. It was widely reported, even though there was no word on the timing of the planned attacks.

The news was anchored on the testimony of an unnamed 'senior authoritative source' quoted by the *Daily Mail*. The paper, which is traditionally hostile to the Labour Party, pointed out that its source 'has no axe to grind'.

In the New Year, Bakri upped the stakes and declared war on Britain. In an interview with the US news agency United Press International, he said Muslims in the UK had two choices: either leave the country or join the jihad. He claimed that the 'covenant of security' which had prevented attacks to date had been broken by the introduction of new anti-terror legislation and that Muslims

167

should consider themselves to be at war. Unless terrorism suspects held at Belmarsh were released without charge, 'the response from Muslims will be horrendous' and it may involve suicide bombings.

One of the few places where you could still find Bakri online was in a chat room on a network called PalTalk. This is an advanced form of discussion forum where, with the software installed and the right equipment, you can communicate with others via audio and video. I knew that Bakri appeared there every week, as his regular Friday sermons were broadcast there live. He talked via a mobile phone that was held up to a microphone. I kept meaning to drop in for a listen, but I kept forgetting to, so I was kicking myself when *The Times* went big on a story about remarks he'd made during one of these sessions. He'd allegedly encouraged young people to join al-Qaeda and referred to bin Laden as 'the emir [leader]'. A Scotland Yard spokesman said police were investigating to see whether a crime had been committed during the broadcast.

The media were really gunning for him now, as the police statement appeared to confirm that he wasn't such a harmless buffoon, and they sensed a Hamza-like situation developing. Embarrassed that I'd been scooped on my own beat, I thought I should pull out the stops and try to top that. I put out an all-points bulletin to my contacts asking for new information on Bakri and al-Muhajiroun.

Ideally, I was after a transcript of that sermon at least, but something totally unexpected came up. One of the mobile-phone numbers that Bakri used to talk to the press had appeared in a local newspaper advert. It wasn't really the kind of thing I was looking for, although I was sure we could have some fun with it, because it looked like he was a selling a car.

It wasn't the kind of thing that you'd expect someone who was subsisting on state benefits to be driving, as it was priced at £30,000. The nearly new silver Renault Espace seven-seat people-carrier had just 1,200 miles on the clock and had been bought in the second half of 2004. It had all the trimmings: electric windows, air-conditioning, electric sunroof, six-CD multi-changer, alloy wheels, anti-lock brakes, alarm and automatic gearbox. The two-litre turbo-boosted motor also had satellite navigation, cruise control and a DVD entertainment system.

The misspelt ad said the seller is 'neady for money'. I passed the lead on to a friend at the *Daily Star*, because I thought he'd appreciate this one. The *Star* called the number and was invited to view the car in Edmonton, north London, where Bakri lived. The young man who answered the phone said he was selling it on behalf of a relative and, when challenged about al-Muhajiroun, he conferred with someone in the background and said: 'I don't know anything about that.' Even so, he still wanted to know if the caller was interested in buying the car.

It was published under the headline 'BAKRI IS ARTHUR DALEY FOR THE JIHAD'. There was also a comment from the paper's motoring correspondent that advised readers to stay clear of the vehicle: 'The price sounds a bit steep to me. You can get it brand new for £28,075 and a dealer could discount it to £24,869.'

One of my contacts soon came up trumps, after she'd remembered that months ago she'd downloaded several recordings of Bakri's speeches. She has a habit of delivering the goods and I was delighted. When I'd tried in the past, the download links didn't seem to work and there had been long periods where the sites were offline. Luckily, someone had been a bit more diligent and I soon had the files on my hard drive.

There were just over six hours of speeches in total, all recorded in 2004, and I didn't really want to put myself through transcribing all that kind of material again – I'd done it with the Hamza tapes and had endured being mind-melded to him for weeks – but again it had to be done. It was rare material and at least there wasn't so much of it this time.

I was getting a little giddy from déjà vu right from the off, as the messages were very similar, even if the tone was different. Less than two minutes into the first speech, he declared: 'You cannot be a Muslim unless you reject and hate the kaffir [non-Muslim].' He was positively fizzing with energy and you could virtually hear him grinning widely as he set about putting the world to rights. It was as if there was an excited little boy inside him trying to burst out and that's where his charisma lay, I guess. It would have been endearing, were it not for all the war talk. Ten minutes in:

> You find today USA and its own global crusade against Islam and Muslims: even though they've got over 200,000 fighters, with all the artilleries, coming to fight Muslims – we know very well that if you have few number of people stood firm against [them], like the Mujahideen are now doing, God-willing, they will be defeated.
>
> They will be defeated in the battle of Afghanistan. They will

169

be defeated in the battle of Iraq, in the battle of Arabia. And
they will never themselves be able to win. They will be
defeated in the battle of Chechnya. And that is really the
promise of the Almighty.

I didn't transcribe every word, because I'd have been at it for days. I
tried to restrict myself to only transcribing the key segments. A lot
of what he was saying was well-worn talk on familiar themes. I
perked up, though, when I heard him leading prayers for the release
of Abu Qatada. His wish came true in March 2005 when Qatada was
among ten terror suspects who were released on bail and placed
under house-arrest conditions after the Law Lords ruled that their
continued detention was breaching their human rights. Qatada,
whom the Spanish anti-terrorism judge Baltasar Garzon called 'bin
Laden's European ambassador', was now back on the streets of
Britain.

Bakri was obviously in a buoyant mood when he delivered this
sermon, as he cracked a gag about defrauding the state-benefits
system, telling the followers that they should 'get Income Support,
the housing benefit, tax credit, child benefit . . . jihad benefit, you
know?' Perhaps he did have a bit of Arthur Daley in him, after all.

He went on to describe Osama bin Laden as a divine blessing
who'd been sent 'to strike fear into the hearts of crusaders all over'.
He claimed that US president George Bush 'can't bring himself to
mention his name' because 'he has become a phenomenon'. I could
hardly believe my ears when he started singing. It was a short verse
in Arabic featuring the word 'Osama' and it sounded like a line from
a jihad anthem, going something like: 'Oh, Osama! Leader of the
Mujahideen! We love you!'

It was a bizarre moment, and Bakri, clearly feeling relaxed after
exercising the lungs, went on to continue to praise 'Sheikh Osama
bin Laden' as the dignified leader of the Mujahideen. He then talked
candidly about how al-Qaeda operates, explaining that if you
couldn't get to the front lines yourself, you could help by supporting
the fighters, recruiting for them and using the media to promote
jihad and to 'strike fear' into the heart of the enemy on home turf.

He scoffed at suggestions that bin Laden was no longer in effective
control of the network, after he'd fled Afghanistan around the time of
the battle of Tora Bora. Bakri assured the audience that bin Laden was
still firmly in control and that al-Qaeda was expanding rapidly. Bin
Laden's statements ought to be studied very carefully, he advised.

His group had often been accused of recruiting foreign fighters for militant groups in Chechnya and Iraq, so I was interested to hear him recall the precautions that are taken when jihadi operatives are travelling. All digital devices are now removed from them to prevent electronic surveillance by the enemy, for example. The lesson of Afghanistan, where satellite phones had been overused and consequently provided the Americans with plenty of targeting opportunities when they invaded, had apparently been learnt. He wrapped up by claiming that there were secret mass graves in the desert of Coalition troops who'd been slaughtered by the Mujahideen and that casualties were far higher than was being reported in the Zionist media.

Bakri started the second speech by talking about suicide bombing. That term shouldn't be used, he said; the proper term is 'self-sacrifice operations'. The bombers were not to blame for any resulting deaths, because 'The cause of death is the almighty Allah.' They were guaranteed a place in Paradise, he said. He then joked about toying with the media and refusing to condemn suicide bombings: 'That's what they always ask you: "What do you think about the magnificent 19 who fly very high in the sky and hit the Twin Towers?"'

He went off on a bit of a tangent after that, declaring himself to be 'a Mujahid', claiming Aids had been sent by Allah to stop gays adopting children and raising them as homosexuals, and railing against politicians. He said: 'You want to call us extremists? Yes, I'm extreme – far from you, Mr Monkey Business, who follows the man-made law: the Monkey Parliament.'

We returned to 'self-sacrifice operations' and Bakri outlined what he thought was a perfect example: 'Somebody, he fly aeroplane and he decide to land the aeroplane over there, 10 Downing Street, for example, or in the White House; this another self-sacrifice operation.' He added: 'Those people who suicide like this for them are good people – are good people.'

Another reference to 9/11 came when he said: 'If you look deeply to the operation taking place in America, September 11, you can find it is very simple operation. It's not as sophisticated as people try to make out. It's not complicated at all: it's so simple.' He even cracked a gag about the attacks, provoking loud laughter from the audience: 'They make 911 call and it was too late.'

The victims were collateral damage, like those civilians who'd died in air strikes in Afghanistan and Iraq, he said. The distinction between civilians and non-civilians, he added, was a Western concept that did not exist in Islam.

Bakri's advice to those thinking of becoming suicide bombers was: 'Do the effort, clear your intention, go forward, never look backward, make sure you have nothing left behind you to think about or to cry for, and fight in the name of Allah.' For emphasis, he added: 'You make the effort; God makes the results.'

He sounded most jubilant when talking about Iraq and it being the perfect example of how a few Muslims can keep a much larger enemy at bay. Muslims had the right to cause 'maximum damage' to the invaders. 'They did not calculate that by removing the Iraqi regime so quickly we may open the doors for the Mujahideen to be free in Iraq and after that they will hunt you every day like birds. Every day! They dealing with invisible forces. They dealing with Mujahideen.'

Addressing the question of whether British Muslims could participate in a 9/11-style operation in the UK, he referred to the so-called 'covenant of security' that he claimed existed. British citizens couldn't participate because of that, though he left the door open on the question of assisting incoming foreign fighters. 'Muslims abroad are under no covenant to fight, so if they fight and they hit here, even if we've been caught in the target, my Allah accept us as martyrs,' he said.

'My Allah bless the Mujahideen, wherever they are, and in fact the ulema [Islamic scholars] agreed: self-sacrifice operations is the highest level of jihad, no doubt about it. The highest level of jihad, of the battlefield, is self-sacrifice operations, because those people been promised, in the Torah, in the Bible, in the Koran to get Paradise.'

Bakri was fond of talking about the 'covenant of security', as if he'd personally brokered a peace deal with the government. There was a kernel of truth in what he said, though. During the Thatcher era, a policy of tolerance was initiated, whereby militant Islamic and Saudi opposition groups were allowed to set up in London and operate without much official hindrance. The thinking followed the old adage about keeping your enemies close to you. It was thought to be better to monitor their activities rather than force them underground.

But for Britons wanting to go to fight abroad, the situation was different: '. . . then you want to fight in the name of Allah, so long as you fulfil the conditions; you are not under a covenant of securities and you are not killing women and children, nor your involvement in this type of operation of stealing and raping, that you have no problem after that'.

I sold the story to the *Daily Mail*, which focused on Bakri's 'jihad benefit' remarks, and I watched it being talked about in Web discussion forums. It's always good to be able to directly gauge the public's reaction to your work and I think it was typified by one guy who recommended that people read the *Mail* story, but only if they didn't suffer from high blood pressure. There was general incredulity over why he was still at large, though the home secretary had told parliament a few months earlier that 'every word' from the al-Muhajiroun leadership was being monitored.

After saying all of this, Bakri then claimed that the covenant no longer existed and declared war. According to Bakri's statement announcing the apparent dissolution of al-Muhajiroun, it was now open season in the UK, so anyone wanting to crash a plane into Downing Street was free to do so.

THE TRIALS

THE LATTER HALF OF 2005 HAD BEEN PREDICTED AS BEING A TURNING point in the battle to win public backing for the fight against al-Qaeda. The authorities had been confident that, when terrorist suspects started coming to trial, the Iraq-tainted public scepticism over the scale of the threat posed by terrorists on the domestic front would begin to wane. The trials have indeed started to flow, though it hasn'r been plain sailing for officialdom and the police have been stung by yet more criticism of their handling of the cases. The public were more inclined to believe in the conspiracy theories which claimed that al-Qaeda was a figure of the imagination of the intelligence services, and some 'experts' were adamant that bin Laden supporters in the UK were incapable of mounting large-scale attacks.

The start of a flood of new insights into the real nature of the terrorist threat to Britain came on 8 February 2005 with the arrest of a suspect at Heathrow airport. Salahuddin Amin, 29, a British citizen from Luton in Bedfordshire, was arrested at Terminal Four after arriving on a British Airways flight from Pakistan. When he appeared at Bow Street Magistrates' Court in central London on the Monday, he was charged with conspiring with others to cause an explosion in the UK between 1 October 2003 and 31 March 2004.

Amin was remanded in custody pending a trial, and his solicitor issued a statement on his behalf that alleged he had just endured ten months of being tortured by British, American and Pakistani intelligence officers while being detained in Pakistan. 'My only crime is that I took it on myself to provide water and food and shelter to the widows and orphans of the Afghan war,' he said.

He was accused of conspiring with men who'd been arrested and charged after being detained in raids during March 2004, when a large amount of ammonium-nitrate fertiliser was discovered in a self-storage depot. The men included Anthony Garcia, 21, of Ilford, Essex; 20-year-old Jawad Akbar from Crawley, West Sussex; Omar Khyam, 22, of Crawley; and Waheed Mahmoud, 32, also from Crawley. They were alleged to have conspired with a 17-year-old youth to cause an explosion in the UK. Garcia, Khyam and Nabeel Hussain, 18, from Horley, Surrey, were charged under the 2000 Terrorism Act with possession of an article for purposes of terrorism.

The group was being linked with another suspect, Mohammed Momin Khawaja, a 29-year-old computer software programmer who had been detained in Canada after the UK raids. He was subsequently charged with involvement in the activities of a terrorist group and facilitating terrorist activities and there was speculation in the media that the arrests resulted from intercepted emails. Police impounded computers at an Internet café in Langley Green, Crawley, near where three of the British suspects lived.

Khawaja became the first person to be charged under Canada's new anti-terrorism laws. His father, who was living in Saudi Arabia, was arrested at the same time by the authorities there. The Canadian charges indicate that Khawaja was involved in a car-bomb attack that was being planned and that the target was a prominent building in or near the City of London.

One newspaper quoted Bakri at the time as saying that he recognised 'three or four' of the names. He said they were members of a group in Crawley, numbering around 40 people, and it had broken away from al-Muhajiroun, claiming it wasn't extreme enough.

That wasn't the only al-Muhajiroun link to the case. Also implicated was Junaid Babar, a naturalised US citizen originally from Pakistan who pleaded guilty in August 2004 to five charges of involvement in terrorism. He admitted to smuggling money and military supplies to a senior al-Qaeda figure in Pakistan, setting up a jihad training camp in the US and assisting with a bomb plot in London. He was believed to have been an active member of al-Muhajiroun's branch based in the New York borough of Queens.

A few days after Amin appeared in court in the UK following his arrest at Heathrow, the French authorities announced that they'd foiled plans by Islamic extremists to attack the Eiffel Tower, a shopping centre and a range of other targets inside the country. Several dozen people had been detained during a long-running judicial investigation into links between Islamic groups in France and the militants in Chechnya. It was claimed that attacks on Russian targets in France with chemical weapons were being planned as a show of support.

Then, on 28 February 2005, came the bombshell news that a terrorist suspect, 25-year-old Saajid Badat, from Gloucester, had admitted conspiring to blow up an airliner with a shoe bomb. He'd been arrested in November 2003 but the full details of the case had been wrapped in much secrecy, until he entered a plea of guilty at the Old Bailey. He was charged with possession of explosives in early December 2003 and conspiring with the convicted shoe-bomber Richard Reid.

In September 2001, he'd been travelling between Europe and Pakistan and, on 11 September 2001, he went to the British embassy in Brussels, Belgium, and falsely claimed to have lost his passport. He was issued with a new one. Reid did the same thing three months later. American charges against him, which were unsealed six months earlier, claimed that on an unknown date, Badat had gone to Afghanistan and obtained improvised explosive devices concealed in footwear. The devices were substantially similar to those that Reid had been given.

Between September and November 2001, Reid and Badat created numerous email accounts to coordinate their activities. Reid's target was American Airlines Flight 63, which was due to depart from Paris bound for Florida on 22 December 2001. Some 197 people would have died that day if a flight attendant hadn't famously noticed Reid using a match to light the fuse in his shoe.

Badat was due to bring down a second airliner around the same time as Reid, but he sent an email on 14 December indicating that he wanted to withdraw from the plan. He'd booked a ticket to fly from Manchester to Amsterdam, where he would have boarded an America-bound flight, though he didn't take that trip. Instead, he enrolled at the College of Islamic Knowledge and Guidance in Blackburn.

His role in the plan came to light when Belgian telephone cards were found on Reid. They'd been used to contact his and Badat's al-Qaeda handler, Nizar Trabelsi, who was now in prison in Belgium. A former professional footballer, Trabelsi was sentenced to ten years in jail after admitting to planning a car-bomb attack on a NATO airbase in Belgium.

Badat was arrested after surveillance operations by the police and

MI5 and, when his home in Gloucester was raided, one of the devices he'd brought from Afghanistan was found there. The fuse and the detonators had been separated from the plastic explosive TATP (triacetone triperoxide), though 100 people in surrounding properties were evacuated as a precaution while it was removed. The fuse and detonator were found in a suitcase and the explosive was found rolled in a ball inside a sock in a second suitcase. He'd had them there for nearly two years, which was suspicious, though he said that was because he wasn't sure how to dispose of them.

His guilty plea came as a surprise and, after being given credit by the judge for having the good sense to withdraw from the operation, he was sentenced to 13 years in prison. The judge said it would have been 50 years if he had not backed out, and it marked the first successful conclusion to a major anti-terrorism case in Britain since the 9/11 attacks.

Like Hamza, Badat had also been indicted in the States, so he too faces the possibility of serving time in a British prison before being deported on release to face terrorism charges in the USA. That wasn't the only link with Hamza: Badat, Trabelsi and Reid had all been visitors to Finsbury Park mosque.

Although the scraggy face of former criminal Richard Reid has been etched into the mind of the public as a typical example of an al-Qaeda operative, he was an exception. Badat was more typical than Reid. Considered intelligent and mature at a young age, he grew up reading the Koran at a local mosque in Gloucester while attending the Crypt Grammar School for Boys. One of his neighbours described him as 'a walking angel'. He excelled academically and was offered places at two universities, but he decided he wanted to become an Islamic cleric and he instead embarked on a three-year tour, taking in India, Saudi Arabia, Pakistan and Afghanistan.

How and why he came to embrace Islamic fundamentalism is still unclear, though it's a fair assumption that Finsbury Park mosque must be part of the answer. It's believed that he became a worshipper there while studying at university in London in 1998, before he suddenly quit the course and travelled abroad. Intelligence sources said that they believed he'd been trained in the use of explosives at bin Laden's Khalden training camp in Afghanistan, where Reid and Zacarias Moussaoui had trained, before he was sent on to the Derunta camp to be trained for the shoe-bomb operation.

Some light on what might have happened emerged during the

trial of one of Hamza's closest associates in the USA. James Ujaama used to run Hamza's websites, until he was arrested in his home city of Seattle on suspicion of aiding the Taliban. It's a case I've covered in detail previously but, in a nutshell, Ujaama changed his plea to guilty after a video clip from the Hamza tapes collection was played in court and he agreed to testify against Hamza.

In Ujaama's original indictment, the Americans claimed that Hamza was able to provide 'letters of introduction or sponsorship' for those seeking jihad training at al-Qaeda camps in Afghanistan. Both were also accused of involvement in a plan to establish a jihad training camp in the USA, on a ranch in Bly, Oregon. It was designed to act as a base where new recruits could be taught the very basics before being sent on to Afghanistan. During the brief period when the camp was in operation, the document noted that on one occasion, after firearms practice, a group of recruits watched a video on the use of improvised poisons.

In the subsequent indictment against Hamza that sparked his arrest, the USA claimed again that he arranged for new recruits to travel to jihad training camps in Afghanistan. The indictment describes how he put Ujaama in contact with an unnamed man who would arrange safe houses and lodging in Pakistan and entry into Afghanistan, using money taken from the Finsbury Park mosque charitable fund. Ujaama and the second man, 23-year-old south London computer student Feroz Abbasi, who was later captured and interned at Guantanamo Bay, travelled to Pakistan in November 2000 and crossed over into Afghanistan separately.

Others linked to the mosque include Djamel Beghal, an Algerian associate of Moussaoui, who is serving a ten-year prison sentence in France for plotting to blow up the American embassy in Paris. Two of Beghal's alleged conspirators, computer expert Kamel Daoudi and Jerome Courtailler, were also believed to have been Finsbury Park attendees. Abu Zubaydah, currently in US custody and one of the suspected chief planners of the 9/11 attacks, was said to be the ultimate mastermind behind the embassy plot.

In mid-March 2005, Pakistan's president, General Pervez Musharraf, revealed in an interview that Pakistani forces had had Osama bin Laden surrounded in a hideout in the tribal border area between Afghanistan and Pakistan in April and June 2004. His location had been established from information gained during interrogations of al-Qaeda suspects and through 'technical means', though the al-Qaeda leader managed to escape somehow. Musharraf admitted that the trail had since gone cold. The USA had resorted to running a campaign of TV ads in Pakistan in order to generate some new leads.

Another key fugitive who was still at large was the suspected mastermind behind the Madrid train bombings, Syrian Mustafa Setmarian Nasar. He had a $5 million bounty on his head and documents found in the flat he used in Madrid indicated that attacks on other targets in Europe were being discussed. A long-time associate of al-Zarqawi, he was now believed to be in Iraq, while two other fugitive members of the group were known to have used forged British passports in the past and might have been in the UK.

That stoked fears that an attack timed to coincide with the upcoming general election might be in the offing. Nasar had recently been sighted in Britain and he used to live in north London in the mid-1990s. What concerned the authorities is that, much like al-Zarqawi, he had a record of leaving sleeper cells behind him during his travels. He was also wanted by the Spanish authorities for allegedly aiding the hijackers in the run-up to 9/11.

After Badat's shoe-bomb admission, the prime minister faced allegations that he was over-hyping the threat posed by al-Qaeda when he remarked that there were 'several hundred people in the UK plotting terror attacks'. That assessment – the first time a number had been put forward – was, however, backed by the police. The new Met police commissioner, Sir Ian Blair, said the following day: 'Yes, I am aware of the fact that there are very many people who came back from the camps in Afghanistan and who are therefore potentially a threat to the United Kingdom. And I agree with the prime minister's assessment, on that basis, that there are hundreds of people who came back from the camps and are now in the United Kingdom, and that is a very dangerous issue for us all.'

Germany was also seeing increased activity among extremist groups, who were supplying fighters to al-Zarqawi in Iraq and providing false documents and medical supplies, according to the security services there. The Netherlands was cracking down on mosques that had become centres of extremism, and had detained three clerics to face deportation. Those efforts had been given extra impetus in November when the film-maker Theo Van Gogh was murdered by an Islamic militant. A similar situation existed in Belgium, also.

Meanwhile, Abu Hamza was reportedly having a rough time in prison. *The Sun* newspaper splashed with a story from one of his associates who claimed that Hamza had been attacked by a fellow inmate in Belmarsh Prison and he regularly received death threats. A statement from Supporters of Sharia went even further, claiming that his cell was raided several times daily by officers accompanied by snarling dogs. It was claimed that the heating to his cell was switched off every night and he'd been refused a request for extra blankets. Prison officers encouraged inmates to threaten Hamza and assault him, it was alleged. This amounted to torture, the group claimed. Muslims at the prison had mistakenly been offered spicy pork chops as an evening-meal option one day during the previous year and his supporters insisted that that was no accident. Belmarsh was Britain's Abu Ghraib, they maintained.

Supporters of another detained terrorism suspect, Babar Ahmad of Azzam Publications, were also stepping up their efforts. His deportation case was due to come to court in April and the campaigners, who counted a large number of far-left, anti-globalisation types among their number, were preparing to hold demonstrations outside the court. Some 200 people had protested at his 2 March hearing, including former British Guantanamo Bay detainee Martin Mubanga. Ahmad was communicating with them via letters published in *Socialist Worker* and his case was also being championed by the Workers' Revolutionary Party.

'It's the hinge that squeaks that gets the grease,' as Malcolm X said. 'All over the country, and in fact all over the world, people are waking up to the horrors being perpetrated by the tyrants of power and authority,' he said in one letter. 'I have been thrust alone into a battlefield against the most powerful country in the world with my arms tied behind my back. As if that is not enough, my own government has stabbed my tied arms deep into my back. So much for the "Land of Hope and Glory!"'

His case was controversial because he was facing extradition to the USA under a new fast-track treaty that was non-reciprocal, meaning that any UK citizen could in theory be plucked from the street and deported to the US on the basis of minimal evidence. All the American government had to prove in court is that all the paperwork had been completed satisfactorily, basically. Ahmad would be the first person to be deported under this treaty and it was a test case. It had been adjourned until April after his defence team claimed that he couldn't be deported because he could face the death penalty in the States and that was in contravention of his human rights.

I was asked to contribute to a BBC *Newsnight* film which was broadcast the night before the hearing. I'd first come across Azzam Publications in 2001, so I was well acquainted with the case – especially as I'd now just finished writing the second chapter of this book. I emailed the reporter, Peter Marshall, and told him: 'Funnily enough, I've just written 6,000 words about him.'

He and the cameraman arrived at my house a few days later and we spent a couple of hours chatting in the kitchen and poring over Azzam Web pages that I'd saved many moons ago. They were the original documents that were referenced in the US charges against Ahmad and Peter hadn't seen them before. We scoured through them all in detail while the cameraman focused on the monitor. Peter had been talking to members of Ahmad's family before he came to see me and we chatted off-camera about what they'd told him before we got on with the formal interview shots.

The family's main argument was that it was a case of mistaken identity, though they'd refused point blank to discuss the technical, computer-related evidence that had been outlined by the USA. Was it possible that a mistake had been made? I said that you couldn't rule out Keystone Kops syndrome, but hard drives with Azzam documents on them had been found in his office at Imperial College and on floppy disks in his room at his parents' house. They would have to show that this evidence had been planted or fabricated for their defence to bear any scrutiny, I replied.

The Azzam material was found on encrypted sections of hard drives and that indicated that he was aware of the gravity of what he – or the real operator, if not him – was doing. There were legitimate reasons for using encryption, I added, such as protecting personal privacy. However, combined with his possession of the documents, it didn't look good. For the US government's part, there'd been criticism that the evidence produced to back their case was flimsy, and I had to agree with that, because superficially it did look that way. However, I pointed out that the case against him didn't have to be proved at this point; the Americans simply had to demonstrate that there was a case to answer.

I gave him a sound bite along the lines that the evidence was flimsy, though I made a slip of the tongue that made it a bit too unequivocal. I meant to say it *looked* flimsy. If the family could make some mileage out of that, then fair play to them, I thought. I'm no fan of extradition treaties that mean that I or any other British citizen could be 'disappeared' on the vague whim of an American official.

I realised right from the start that I was being used to outline the prosecution's case, because no one in officialdom would talk about it. The broadcast report was biased in favour of the relatives, but I didn't mind really – someone had to review the evidence against him and he deserved a little elbow room, because of the inequities of the treaty.

After the March hearing, in a media interview, the US government's lawyer, John Hardy, claimed that Ahmad had travelled to Phoenix, Arizona, in 1998 to meet a terrorist suspect called Yaser al-Jhani and others who claimed to have access to bin Laden. He'd expressed interest in setting up a jihad training camp there: 'That is, a training system, in effect for the Mujahideen to visit and train to fight abroad,' said Hardy. Details of the visit were contained in a report that the Americans were preparing to enter as evidence, he said, though there was no suggestion that the plan came to fruition.

Another forthcoming courtroom shocker was presaged by a report in a monthly German political magazine which had quoted German intelligence sources as saying that they feared al-Zarqawi was planning a major chemical attack in Europe. There had been reports that members of his network had visited the former Soviet republic of Georgia to get hold of arms components. 'We in Europe have been afraid that a big bang is coming sometime and that al-Zarqawi is planning it,' said one official.

There was a sense of the jitters in the air, especially in the UK, with a general election looming large. This unease was stoked when it emerged that a white Nigeria-born Briton, Zayead Christopher Hajaig, 35, had been arrested by the Met anti-terrorism squad at his home in Essex. He was being held pending extradition to the States, after a 'special-alert bulletin' had been issued by the FBI. He had taken flying lessons in 2002 at the same airport near Atlanta where two of the 9/11 hijackers, Mohammed Atta and Marwan al-Shehhi, had learned to fly. He'd recently raised suspicions because of his rude and abusive behaviour at the flight school when he tried to upgrade his pilot's licence and accelerate his training, despite his licence having been revoked due to him missing a medical examination.

It came a day after the USA unveiled its charges against Dhiren Barot, Nadeem Tarmohammed and Qaisar Shaffi over the alleged plan to bomb financial institutions in the US. They were awaiting trial on similar charges in the UK. That story soon faded because the London ricin poison plot hit the headlines.

Details of the conviction of Kamel Bourgass came from nowhere, because there had been a complete reporting ban out of fears that details might affect other ongoing trials. That was lifted on 13 April 2005 when the judge sentenced him to 13 years in jail for plotting to spread ricin through the streets of the UK. It transpired that the 31-year-old al-Qaeda suspect was already serving a life sentence after being convicted of stabbing Detective Constable Stephen Oake to death while resisting arrest in a raid in 2003 in Manchester.

The raid had been launched after the discovery of a suspected chemical-weapons laboratory in a flat above a shop in Wood Green, north London, in January 2003. As I've revealed previously, I'd come across a document that was published on a website called the *Mujahideen Poisons Handbook* which contained instructions on how to make ricin from castor-oil beans, just before that discovery took place.

Bourgass had been betrayed by a colleague who'd been detained and interrogated in Algeria and had been cooperating with the authorities. Information provided by Mohammed Meguerba had led the police to the flat, where they discovered instructions for making explosives, and equipment and recipes for making ricin, cyanide, botulinum and other poisons, along with castor beans.

As the details emerged and controversy raged over the following days, one fact stood out like a sore thumb. It was known that Bourgass had stayed for a period at Finsbury Park mosque, but the police now revealed that forensic tests had shown that the poison recipes were photocopies that had been made inside the mosque.

Although the police hailed the conviction as a great example of a catastrophe being averted, they copped fierce criticism over the fact that four men had been cleared of any involvement in the plot. The jury was discharged after its members failed to agree on a verdict of conspiracy to commit murder after four weeks of deliberation. One of the accused was the guy who'd operated the photocopier at Finsbury Park mosque. That had led to a second trial of four other alleged conspirators being abandoned.

The police can tend to distrust juries, and that's down to the control-freaky nature of the job; they resent having to hand over effective control of the outcome of cases to a dozen randomly chosen herberts from off the street. It's an understandable suspicion and, in subsequent media interviews, it was clear to me where the police were laying the blame for this, because it was so barely disguised: cretinous members of that jury.

There was much scepticism in the media about the manufacture of ricin, because none was actually found in the flat in Wood Green. This was seized on by sceptics, who claimed that the threat had been exaggerated and that a climate of fear was being deliberately created. Meguerba in Algeria had said two batches had already been made and they were in round, blue Nivea face-cream containers, but the police had found only one empty container. For critics to seize on this and claim that there was no actual ricin plot was going a step too far. The police could only assume that Bourgass had disposed of it after he'd abandoned the flat in Wood Green. After all, he had admitted to making it, though he claimed that it was to be used by militant groups in Algeria.

There was also consternation over the details of the plot, which didn't involve ricin at all; it was actually to spread nicotine poison on car-door handles along Holloway Road in north London. That sounded more like the actions of a lone nut, rather than a well-planned al-Qaeda spectacular. Perhaps the police made a mistake here, as they later explained that they believed that the real target was the Heathrow Express rail link. Bourgass was planning to spread ricin on handrails in the carriages and in the toilets. They'd found maps of the route but the evidence was not disclosed in court, out of fear of causing public alarm or inspiring copycat attacks.

It was not even certain that Bourgass was his real name. He also used the name Nadir Habra and he arrived in the country clandestinely in a lorry in 2000, later telling immigration officials that he'd been born in Algeria in 1973. He wasn't deported and he lived in bedsits in London and Manchester and had spent nights sleeping at Finsbury Park mosque. Meguerba said that he'd first met Bourgass at an al-Qaeda training camp in Afghanistan in the late 1990s and that Bourgass had been hand-picked by senior al-Qaeda figures to go on to receive specialist training in poisons.

Meguerba said he'd met bin Laden twice and also spoke of his association with Nizar Trabelsi, a Finsbury Park visitor and the handler of the two British shoe-bombers, Reid and Badat. The camps in Afghanistan where they had all trained were under the command of the alleged 9/11 masterplanner Abu Zubaydah, who is now in US custody. Bourgass was part of a network of North Africans, mainly Algerians and Tunisians, headed by Abu Doha, a senior al-Qaeda operative who was arrested in the UK in February 2001 to face extradition to the States on charges of involvement in a plot to bomb Los Angeles airport on Millennium Eve. He was detained at

Heathrow airport just before he was due to board a flight to Jeddah in Saudi Arabia.

Doha had been a senior member of the Salafist Group for Call and Combat (GSPC), a terrorist group which has carried out terrible atrocities in Algeria. According to a US indictment, bin Laden granted a request from him in 1998 to set up the Khalden training camp in Afghanistan for Algerians and other North Africans. Hundreds of Mujahideen recruits were trained there. Many were sent to fight in Chechnya, while others were sent to Western countries as sleeper agents.

According to Meguerba's evidence, bin Laden dispatched another senior al-Qaeda commander, Rabah Kadre, to assist with the British poison plan. He came to London via Slovakia, where he'd hidden for a year with a false French passport, and took up the position of librarian at Finsbury Park mosque. He was arrested along with Doha at Heathrow, though Kadre was released without charge, only to be rearrested a few days later to face extradition to France on terrorism charges.

He was accused of involvement in a possible plot in France, after the authorities had discovered that four suspects, three Algerians and a Moroccan, arrested in Paris in December 2002, had had contact with him. They'd been found with a large amount of cash, extremist Islamic literature, a computer, electronic circuitry that could serve as a component in bomb detonators, and two phials of an unknown liquid, as well as a protective nuclear, biological and chemical weapons suit. They were all said to have trained at camps in Afghanistan and Chechnya.

On 21 March 2003, the French authorities announced that they'd found two small flasks containing traces of ricin in a left-luggage locker at the Gare de Lyon railway station, while a suspected terrorist cell was busted in Germany on suspicion of planning an attack to mark the start of hostilities in Iraq. The French ricin find came on the same day that two men 'of African origin' had been arrested on suspicion of recruiting fighters for Chechnya and preparing chemical attacks on Russian interests in France.

The US secretary of state Colin Powell told the United Nations Security Council, during his infamous Iraq presentation, that the Algerians had been sent to the UK by al-Zarqawi. It might have been one of the few truthful things he said during that speech. A few days after the Madrid bombings, a statement was circulated in the name of al-Zarqawi which praised the attack and claimed it on behalf of al-

Qaeda, warning Europe to expect more of the same. His precise affiliation with al-Qaeda remained unclear until October 2004, when he announced that he'd pledged allegiance to bin Laden. I suspected the mystery over his link with al-Qaeda was deliberately engineered to sow confusion in the minds of the enemy and those in the West who doubted that the network was operating in Iraq.

That was firmed up on 21 April 2005 when the USA claimed that they'd intercepted a communication between al-Zarqawi and bin Laden, in which bin Laden asked al-Zarqawi to start planning attacks within America. He was also linked to the discovery of the half-tonne of ammonium nitrate and the arrest of al-Muhajiroun supporters in police raids in April 2004. Those, according to US reports, had been prompted by an email message that appeared to contain instructions for an attack, which had been sent by an associate of al-Zarqawi to al-Qaeda commanders in Pakistan and associates in the UK.

It wasn't until late April 2005 that it emerged that al-Zarqawi had narrowly escaped being captured by US troops during a raid two months earlier. Acting on a tip-off that said he was due to travel to the city of Ramadi for a meeting, troops were deployed along the route he was due to take and Predator surveillance drones circled overhead. As US soldiers stopped a car being driven by one of his bodyguards, a pick-up truck one kilometre behind made a sudden turn and sped away.

Al-Zarqawi was inside. He jumped from the moving vehicle as it passed under a bridge, to escape detection by the Predators above. He made it to Ramadi on foot, though he left his laptop computer behind in the truck. This was analysed by the US military and it led to the arrest of several of his key associates. It might still also shed further light on his associates in Britain.

One of the many threads running through the ricin affair – and indeed this whole book – is Finsbury Park mosque and Abu Hamza. I've had to be careful when mentioning him here to navigate around the *sub judice* laws, as he's yet to come to trial. Perhaps the tone of this forthcoming event was set during his last pre-trial hearing in January 2005, where he refused to appear at the Old Bailey via video link, claiming that he couldn't walk from his cell because his long toenails made it too painful.

The heat was back on Bakri in May. The *Star* story about him selling his car hadn't gone unnoticed by *The Sun*. I didn't follow up on the original, but *The Sun* had been watching out for subsequent developments and, hats off to them, they came up with another nice exclusive. After selling his previous vehicle, Bakri had bought a new people-carrier, a top-of-the-range Toyota Previa with leather upholstery and all the extras. It cost £28,000, and this is where the controversy lay, because it was paid for by the state. He was receiving disability benefit and he was entitled to the car under the motability scheme. There was a quote from the manager of his local dealership, describing how they were dumbstruck when Bakri and his entourage swept into the showroom and issued demands.

Bakri phoned a radio talk show in London the following day to vent his fury and claim that he 'deserved' the car. He freely admitted to never having a paid job during his 19 years in the country. 'Nobody deny that I live off benefits. I am working, you see – I am commanding good, forbidding evil,' he said.

Bakri appeared to drop out of sight after that. I tried to find out where the group had moved to. It seemed likely that they had adopted new names and new websites, as they'd done in the past. They were known to have used over 80 different titles for what was, in essence, the same network.

Using various methods, I established that this was indeed the case, and the group seemed to be operating under the new guise of the Al-Ghurabaa Foundation. They had two new websites and I zeroed in on the first one. I could immediately see that there was some potentially naughty material on there. It looked like they hadn't banked on being rediscovered so quickly. The multimedia section there was well stocked with audio and video material and I could see at least four recordings of Sheikh Abdullah el-Faisal. He was serving a long stretch after being convicted at the Old Bailey of soliciting to murder. The case centred on tapes of his sermons, which were actively sold and distributed.

In the ones focused on in court, he was calling for the murder of Jews and the use of chemical and nuclear weapons in the jihad against non-believers. Abu Hamza was due to appear as a witness in his defence, though el-Faisal's team apparently concluded that it might be counter-productive, so he wasn't called. There were also a number of Hamza's sermons there to download.

Bakri was making a big mistake here if he was distributing material that had already been judged to be criminal. It took hours to copy everything. There were dozens of files of interest there, but my attention was grabbed first by a video titled 'Tranny Attack'. The juxtaposition of jihadism and transvestism was new to me.

It was self-shot footage of a demonstration held by the New York City branch of al-Muhajiroun the previous year. I could see banners and placards, and then a woman who was obviously taking issue with the group of bearded men there. She grabbed a placard from one of them and stood on it. I could see that a crowd of passers-by had gathered opposite to watch what was happening. One of the men then retrieved it by pulling it out from under her feet, which sent her sprawling, before a police car arrived on the scene. That was it, so I looked further and found out that she was charged with damaging property. She complained in an interview that the police should have arrested the demonstrators, not her. The al-Muhajiroun members were jubilant and they twisted the knife further by putting out a gleeful statement claiming that the police had messed up because she wasn't a woman at all, but a 'she-male'.

The earlier cause of the dispute was shown in another video. The camera was pointed at the feet of the protestors and soon an American flag laid out in the road came into shot. The demonstrators slowly started to gravitate towards it and stand on it. Then they started shuffling around and stamping on it, until eventually it was ripped into shreds by hand amid frenzied shouts of joy and jubilation.

I turned to the files credited to Bakri and they all looked like they might be recent. I chose the latest, which looked to be the most interesting, mainly because it was a video clip. Footage of his sermons was a rare commodity; I'd only seen one previously. It was over an hour long and Bakri's opening comments confirmed that it was recent, having been made only weeks earlier, on 24 May 2005. It was a video of a sermon he was giving to a room full of supporters. There were no real clues as to the location, except a very low-flying aircraft could be heard at one point. The camera was set in a fixed position in front of Bakri, who was seated behind the widescreen laptop in front of him, which looked huge because of the perspective. During his sermon, his eyes were frequently downcast and it looked like he was reading incoming emails as he talked, judging by the frequent 'ping' noise that could be heard in the background. It was an impressive demonstration of multi-tasking, if nothing else. As I watched the first few minutes, I was struck by how informal he was; he was obviously feeling very much at home among his own people and this relaxed attitude may explain his consequent lack of discretion.

His demeanour in private differed from his public persona. He started by talking about a statement put out by al-Qaeda in Iraq, confirming that al-Zarqawi had been injured during a gun battle with US troops near the Iraqi city of Ramadi. It called upon Muslims worldwide to pray for his recovery. Bakri summarised: 'So they ask for Muslims worldwide to ask Allah to give him recovery and Allah to give him complete remedy and make him the strong knife in the throat of the enemy and grant victory for the Muslim Ummah [Islamic nation].' That alone was a pretty good start. Al-Zarqawi's injury was 'an honour for all of us and an honour for him'.

He then continued to read the rest of the statement, which said that al-Qaeda had stepped up its attacks in retaliation. Bakri told the group that over the past 24 hours, the group had mounted a record total of 120 operations in and around Baghdad, and he was drowned out by loud shouts of celebration and 'Allah-u-Akhbar!'.

Al-Zarqawi had wiped the smiles from the faces of the Americans, he said, before going on to talk about plans for a demonstration to be held outside the American embassy in London. The purpose was to 'incite people to do jihad, incite people to hate the new pharaoh [President Bush]' and show solidarity with the insurgents. He seemed to think that the plan for the day, which was being done cooperatively with other radical groups, didn't go far enough. It was all too timid. He suggested, 'Why not do more – maybe take over the embassy?' He went on: 'Our call for jihad is to send a message back to Muslim Ummah, to the Mujahideen: "We are with you." There's people around the world who have the same voice like you, the same stand like you.' The West needed to be told: 'We have enough ammunition in Islam, we can hit you, hard; so don't play with fire. We know who you are.'

The 'covenant of security' that had supposedly protected the UK from terrorist attacks in the past was off now, he reiterated. The 'new reality', as he saw it, was conflict between Muslims and non-Muslims: 'Nowadays, people they really want to be devil worshippers; the devil's assistants and the devil followers and the devils will fight us . . . If they follow us believing what we believe, they become our brothers. If they follow us fighting us, we will fight them back.'

Fostering racial hatred seemed to be the new goal of the group. He smiled and said: 'That is the natural and the healthy relationship between both of them . . . Not to be brotherhood, interface and – not that.' Muslims must hate the non-believers and steer clear of them, and 'rise against him whenever you can and kill them'.

That sounded like the money shot. That's soliciting for murder, surely, I thought. He grimaced and leaned forward with clenched fist as he growled the words 'kill them'. I think he realised that he'd gone too far, because he said straight after: 'You'll have to put what I said between two brackets. For you to make interpretation. It's nice to make interpretation sometimes.'

He then moved on to the main theme of his talk, which was the definition of a good Muslim, though he soon digressed and warned his followers not to pass on news from British newspapers. He mentioned articles in the press about Abu Hamza and Abu Qatada and urged Muslims not to spread 'rumours' put out by the kaffirs. 'So you need to verify the news, especially nowadays we're living in kuffar society. I mean, the kaffirs by default hate the Muslims and that is healthy.'

He again paused to make some announcements about the forthcoming US embassy demonstration, before returning to elaborate on the depth of hatred required for non-Muslims: '. . . Allah says don't feel sorry for the kaffir. I don't feel sorry for the kuffar, especially if they die. What? Attacking Muslims? In Islam, it is not allowed to call the kaffir innocent, you know that? The term "innocent" is haram [forbidden] to be applied to the kaffir. Allah said those who do not believe in Allah, they are liars; not only kaffir, liars! That way anyone he say to you something, even if it was true, take it and still say, "You are a liar."'

He referred to his appearance on the LBC radio talk show after the *Sun* car story, and it seemed that his woes were doubled. I didn't hear the programme, though Bakri said that the presenter, Nick Ferrari, had taken the trouble beforehand to contact the Department of Social Security to offer Bakri a job with LBC. Unless he accepted, he faced seeing his state unemployment-benefit payments stopped. Bakri laughed it off, however, and joked about how he could feel some back pains coming on. He smiled widely and declared proudly: 'They hate me . . . Last week, I was speak about car and satellite dish and jacuzzis and it was now give me job.'

He was talking about the *Sun* car story and a subsequent visit to the car showroom. 'They said to me: "You still want to take car?"'

'I said: "If car offer to me limousine with jacuzzis, with satellite dish, I will take it, and leave for you the Ford Fiesta."'

'He said: "What are you talking about?"'

'I said: "I am a Muslim. I ride horse. I'll leave the donkey for you. In Islamic state, no kaffir can ride horse, you see, in front of Muslims. We know it. Kaffir not allowed to ride horse!"'

190

Bakri went on to explain that non-Muslims had a social standing equal to animals, as a kaffir was forbidden to ride a horse in the presence of a Muslim. In a final swipe at the newspaper, he proclaimed: 'Because, if you worship *The Sun*, we worship Allah who created the Sun and the Moon! The highest! So don't play with us, you kaffir.'

He turned towards the particular types of kaffir who could be legitimately killed. After initially saying that women and children were exempt, there was a corollary. They were exempt only if they hadn't elected a government that supported the invasion of Iraq. In that case, all civilians in that country were legitimate targets. 'If she supports by even voting for George Bush, that's her, get dismissed. Finish!'

Bakri started to wind up by telling his audience that, as well as respecting Osama bin Laden, they should be holding al-Zarqawi in similar regard. 'We must have as we love Sheikh Osama bin Laden, Sheikh Abu Musab al-Zarqawi, and the Mujahideen and the mujahids, for the sake of Allah . . . We respect them, we love them a lot, we make dua [prayers] for them, and Allah honour them.'

He ended by denying rumours that he was a spy for MI5 and suggested that his colleague Abu Hamza was a better candidate. The fact that he, Bakri, hadn't been detained in custody, despite being arrested and released 16 times, was proof that he enjoyed divine protection, he claimed.

His trashing of *The Sun* made this paper the obvious first port of call for me. They immediately acknowledged the importance of this find and ran a story on the front page and an inside page under the headline: 'WARPED BAKRI'S CRY FOR MURDER'. The Labour MP Andrew Dismore, disparaged by Bakri as 'Andrew Dismal', had tabled nearly 200 parliamentary questions about him and al-Muhajiroun and he called for him to be prosecuted. 'This sounds like incitement to murder,' he said.

I think it was the following day that *The Sun*'s crime editor phoned to say that he'd been invited to Scotland Yard for a chat with the anti-terrorism branch. They wanted a statement from him and would I mind if he mentioned my name, as they might want access to an original copy of the 'kill them' video. If they, as a media player, had decided it was right to cooperate, then I supposed it was reasonable for me to assist also. I agreed to let my name be put forward.

I soon got a call from an anti-terrorism branch officer to arrange to come and visit me the following week. He wanted the video and I started to worry about the possibility of my computer being taken away for examination, albeit it with me chained to it. I was worried enough to contact a solicitor for guidance on the issue, and was put through to the solicitor's secretary. 'The anti-terrorism squad are coming to see me and I need some advice on what the correct procedures are,' I explained. There was a little gasp of surprise at the other end of the line. 'It's all right – *I* haven't been arrested or anything.'

The solicitor phoned me later in the day and reassured me that they couldn't just walk off with my computer. There was no technical reason why it would need to be removed from my house. I should make it clear that I was not prepared to hand it over voluntarily, though I was willing for the particular files of interest to be copied at my house, or under my direct supervision. She gave me a clear warning: 'They'll try to take it away and, even though they'll say they'll only copy those files, they'll copy the entire hard drive. Don't let them do it.'

We arranged it so that she would be available to conduct negotiations over the phone, if required, when the meeting was due to take place. It was virtually plain sailing in the end. The officer and I watched excerpts from the video together and, on hearing the 'kill them' comment, the officer asked if I'd be prepared to give a statement and provide copies of the video. I was warned that I might be called upon to give evidence in court, if charges were brought.

I agreed and we spent some time working out the text of the statement, which he wrote down by hand, after we'd reached agreement on each sentence. He had come armed with blank CDs and I copied the files onto these under his supervision and they were labelled and noted. He said if charges arose, they might need to come back and take my hard drive away for forensic examination, but the CDs would suffice for the moment. It might be a good idea if I bought a new hard drive, in case anything happened to the original files in the meantime, he suggested.

I started working through the rest of the material I'd acquired. It was going to be an arduous process, because some of the videos were nearly two hours long, so I decided to go through only the four most recent sermons and leave the other twenty-five or so for another time. The police's interest in the video convinced me it was worth pressing on.

In the first one, Bakri was directly urging people to physically fight jihad. It started on a familiar note: 'No, we don't obey the law of the land. Allah says don't obey the law of the land.' After asserting that it is the destiny of Muslims to control the earth, he told his followers: 'So, it's very essential for you to know that is the thing which can give you green card to Jannah [Paradise] is al-jihad, in the way of Allah . . . let your death occur when you are on the battlefield; is the best way to die. In others words, go and fight . . . fight and die for the sake of Allah.' He added: 'If you cannot go, send your children.'

On the next one, he was also encouraging his followers to back the US embassy demonstration plans: 'Come out publicly, openly, declare it – give them headache!' If all Muslims came out on the street to vent their anger, he claimed, it would shake the Western establishment and the entire world. The uprising could be funded by the government as a kind of war booty.

The UK state-benefits system needed reform, so that payments went only to those fighting jihad. He said: 'Some of them, because they take Income Support, they want to give the allegiance to the Queen, because of the Income Support, whereas in the first place, you should take it without them saying even to filling application. At the first place, the words belong to Allah and nobody should enjoy it but the Mujahideen.'

On the third recording, he seemed to be giving his audience a final pep-talk before the much-anticipated demonstration outside the US embassy the following week. The remit didn't stop at mere vocal support for the Mujahideen: 'When we speak about demonstrations, we're speaking about supporting, we're speaking about helping . . . when they seek support, you must support them, verbally, financially, physical. If they ask for help, they must help. If they ask you, you know, to fight, they must fight.'

This upcoming demonstration seemed to be very important, as a lot of time was being spent on it. The sermon was entirely devoted to the subject of demonstrations. There seemed to be an internal debate over the wisdom of contributing to protest marches, as if the ranks thought it was not radical enough. Bakri appeared to be struggling to convince some that participation was critical. 'But a demonstration which is carried out to command good and forbid evil, expose enemy, supporting the Mujahideen, highlight, you know, the, highlight serious situations of the Muslim Ummah [nation] – is nothing wrong with that,' he argued. 'For God's sake, we need ourselves to be, we need ourselves to be clearly, you see, to be clearly, that form of demonstration is there. So, are we going to leave all this? It is a particular means, you see, to boosting the moral of the Muslims or the Mujahideen, or those who are in captivity. Plus, the demonstration will help train the people to go out, come out and express their anger. Do you know why? To cause anarchism, on the right time. You were trained in how to cause anarchy. You will train the Ummah to come out, how to say "no" to the evil in his eyes. Say "no" to the oppression. We'll motivate them: it's got a lot of positive outcomes, a lot of positives.'

Then something very curious happened. Bakri was talking in a multimedia Internet chat room, using a system called PalTalk, which allows groups to talk to each other in real time using microphones and Web cams. He'd got into hot water when *The Times* delved in there and caught him telling people that they should join al-Qaeda. He'd now learned his lesson and made his cyber-pulpit private, so access was restricted to keep out the media and the spooks. He was crowing about the 'fresh list' of vetted participants and how he was now impervious to monitoring. You could hear him, or an assistant, clicking away to respond to messages and approving access requests. It was like a switchboard, and he'd stop every now and then to greet someone he knew and patch them in.

Bakri sounded like he was having a bit of an uphill struggle in convincing his followers that they should attend the demonstration, and he became a bit flabbergasted. It was as if he'd patched someone in to try to settle the debate. Without introduction, a new voice started talking. It said: '. . . I am a student of Mufti Nizamuddin Shamzai, the one who was made shahid [martyred] last year. And [my] higher studies under him, completed my studies, in Jamiat-ul-Uloom Islamia in Karachi, which in the West is known as The Terrorist Institute.' He told everyone that participating in the demonstration was 'the command of Allah'.

A very involved, curious and tedious discussion then evolved for the next 30 minutes on the role of women in protests. It was much in contrast to the usual apocalyptic jihad talk and I wondered if there was some kind of subtext to the discussions. The session ended with a prayer for the release of Abu Qatada.

The intervention of the Terrorist Institute man got me thinking. His mentor, Shamzai, was one of Pakistan's most respected Sunni clerics and one of the most radical. His Jamiat-ul-Uloom madrassa (religious school) was renowned as the place where many of the leaders of al-Qaeda and the Taliban were first indoctrinated. It was the nearest thing there was to an al-Qaeda university and many thousands of students had passed though its gates. He'd been gunned down and killed by four attackers after he left a TV studio twelve months previously. The attackers escaped in cars and on motorcycles and rioting broke out in several districts of the city when news of his death was announced. No group claimed responsibility, though it's been suggested that his demise might have been linked to his agreement to involvement in a plan to broker a peace deal between the government and militants in the South and North Waziristan regions in the semi-autonomous tribal borderlands.

This is where al-Qaeda leaders are said to have relocated after the US-led invasion of Afghanistan. Shamzai had previously led a delegation of Pakistani clerics to Afghanistan during the rule of the Taliban and he'd urged Mullah Omar not to hand bin Laden over to the Americans. It seems that his subsequent involvement in the peace effort might have been perceived as betrayal and swiftly dealt with, as would any threat to bin Laden's safety.

Here we had a virtually self-confessed al-Qaeda-aligned terrorist, probably Pakistan-based, participating in Bakri's chat session – with his approval. It wasn't illegal, but I sensed that there was more to this than just a demonstration. He'd been put online in an attempt to silence dissent in the ranks, that was for sure, but the stilted conversation that followed looked suspicious.

The al-Muhajiroun successor group was operating at least two new sites, though I was one of only a handful of non-Bakri followers who was in on the locations at the time. The second site featured another heavily populated media section and I'd sucked in all of those files as well. Among them was a video of the long-awaited demonstration, shot by a Bakri devotee, and running to over 90 minutes.

While, ostensibly, it was organised to protest against allegations that the Koran had been abused at the Guantanamo Bay detention centre in Cuba, all the talk was of Iraq. The event was designed to show solidarity with other Muslims around the world who'd rioted in several countries over the report in *Newsweek*. Several people had died, which was made even more tragic when the magazine retracted the story, saying it couldn't back up the claim. Nonetheless, the damage had been done and there was an air of hostile indignity at the demo. They were rowdy and chanting threats against the UK, USA, Tony Blair and George Bush. Many of

195

the attendees were wearing scarves around their faces to conceal their identities from the surveillance teams watching them.

The central message was a promise that retaliation for the UK's participation in the invasion of Saddam Hussein's Iraq was coming – and it was coming soon. The demonstration opened with a scene showing a large crowd outside the embassy, behind crash barriers, chanting: 'USA, you will pay! Aeroplanes are on their way!' Other lines over the next ten minutes included: 'USA, watch your back! Mujahideen are coming back!', 'Tony Blair, watch your back! Osama is coming back', 'Bomb, bomb UK! UK, you will pay!' and 'Muhajiroun are coming back!'

Two speeches followed, one given by Bakri's spokesman Anjem Choudary, who told the crowd: 'The only language that we speak today is the language of jihad.' He was followed by the former Guantanamo Bay detainee Martin Mubanga, who spoke about how he witnessed the Koran being mistreated there.

The protestors, now in a very agitated mood, were chanting: 'Nuke, nuke USA! Nuke, nuke USA!', when the main speaker arrived. Clad in white and escorted by a man wearing an Arabic headscarf to conceal his identity, Omar Bakri made his majestic entrance. He was wearing a mock ID card with a picture of Omar Abdul Rahman, the mastermind of the 1993 World Trade Center bombing, to demonstrate his solidarity with the jailed cleric.

He was given the microphone and it was fighting talk all the way, delivered with a solemnity to underline the seriousness of his message. He started off by telling the crowd that Islam has 'a very sharp sword; it's called the sword of jihad'. To subsequent shouts of 'Allah-u-Akbar!', he urged the faithful: 'Believe on it [the Koran], implement it and fight for the sake of Allah!'

Bakri then referred to the murder of the Dutch filmmaker Theo Van Gogh, who was stabbed to death by an Islamic militant who was outraged at the portrayal of the Koran in his most recent work. The murderer was a mujahid, he said, and went on: 'Don't play with fire! Because the fire will bring nothing for you except fire.'

Minutes later, a shocked Bakri is interrupted and he ducks and takes cover as a fireball erupts from the middle of the crowd. There is much movement and confusion until the crowd parts to reveal the cause of the blast: there was a burning American flag on the pavement and someone had been a bit overenthusiastic with the petrol. How ironic that, in warning the West not to play with fire, Bakri nearly got set ablaze by his own followers.

I viewed the scenes that followed as ominous, however. After the flag-burning, several people decided to burn the placards they were holding, as they featured images of George Bush. The burnt cardboard disintegrated or dropped to the ground, leaving the protestors holding aloft flaming wooden crosses. The protestors obviously realised the symbolism of the burning crosses and waved them around with great pride. It's not a sight I'd seen before at a gathering of Muslims; it was more reminiscent of the Ku Klux Klan, the US neo-Nazi group. It was hard to tell if this was an unintended consequence or pre-planned, but that image alone served to sum up the entirety of the message on the day.

There were several still images of these scenes, taken by somebody else with a digital camera. The demonstration was a gathering of the different factions in the UK jihad community and I noticed that the file names of the photographs contained the word Tajdeed, which indicated the participation of the followers of the London-based Saudi dissident and long-term enemy of the Saudi royal family, Muhammad al-Massari. He was rumoured to have been involved with talks with Ken Bigley's captors.

Bakri thanked the overall organisers, the Islamic Observatory Center, which was headed by Yasser al-Sirri, an Egyptian asylum-seeker whom the US had accused of helping Omar Abdul Rahman to communicate with followers in Egypt. Also there was a contingent from Abu Hamza's Supporters of Sharia group. This was now headed by his chief assistant, Abu Abdullah, while Hamza remained in prison.

During the burnings, Abdullah had taken the mike and, as the crowd started to settle, he addressed them. Looking towards the embassy, he said: 'How can there be peace when you violate us to the limits beyond boundaries, beyond understanding, pushing humanity, pushing Muslims over the edge? Then expect retaliation. Expect retaliation. Expect retaliation.' He then reiterated: 'For you, and your democracy is pushing Islam over the edge. Islam is a peaceful religion, but when it's pushed and it's denied its rights, expect retaliation. So, I put it to you, Mr Bush and Mr Blair, you proclaim to believe in democracy, and yet you deny Islam its freedom of speech, and my evidence of this is my honourable beloved brothers in al-Islam, that are in Guantanamo Bay, that are in Belmarsh prison, that you've released nine, but you're still humiliating my brothers and placing them under house arrest. Where his liberties? Where is it that you want to debate and have some kind of unity for you to understand and accept what we believe in?' His message to non-believers was: 'You may embrace Islam or die by the sword.' He added: 'Stand firm, because the day is coming, the day of judgement . . .'

The mike was returned to Bakri and he thanked Abdullah for reminding everyone about our 'beloved brother, Sheikh Abu Hamza' – 'the time it will come when they be punished . . . whenever the time is right, I don't think any Muslim he will hesitate to do his duty.'

Bakri wound up by saying: 'That's why, my dear Muslim brothers, let the truth prevail; go back home and do your own homework, study the book of Allah, implement it yourself and be part of the global struggle, the global jihad.' The event ended with Bakri leading the chanting of 'USA, you will pay! Bin Laden is on his way!'

OPERATION BURNING CROSS

'LITTLE FUCKERS,' WAS MY FIRST THOUGHT ON THE MORNING OF 7 July 2005, on hearing the first report of an explosion on the London Underground. If I'd thought 9/11 was hard work, then that paled into insignificance when compared to 7/7. The nightmare scenario had arrived and few were prepared for it. The entire British media immediately went onto a war footing.

Up until then, there had been maybe a couple of hours of confusion, as the initial cause was cited as a power surge. Then came the first report of an explosion. Bombings made a lot more sense than power problems, considering the scale of the apparent chaos. I built an instant mental snapshot of what might have happened and sensed that, on the balance of odds, this was a very British terrorist operation.

As well as the start of the summit of the G8 leaders in Scotland, the other big event of the day was supposed to be the formal start of Abu Hamza's trial, though that was later adjourned until 2006. It was difficult to get off the phone and get some work done; everyone wanted anything and everything and they wanted it exclusively. All the scepticism about sleeper cells and even the existence of al-Qaeda vaporised. The *Power of Nightmares* brigade, those who'd belittled the scale of the threat posed by Islamic terrorist groups and argued that it was nothing more than a myth peddled by politicians, became redundant.

The covert coalition of sympathy between al-Qaeda and those in the West with leftist political and anti-globalisation leanings really did now seem to be woefully misplaced. A sympathetic kaffir is still a kaffir, as members of al-Muhajiroun demonstrated when they

199

disrupted campaigning in east London during the last general election. The threat from al-Qaeda would be the same even if everyone in the Middle East decided tomorrow to lay their differences aside and live in peace.

On the day and over the weeks that followed, hundreds of journalists, maybe thousands if you include the foreign press, were leaving no stone unturned in trying to find that exclusive nugget of information about what was clearly going to be the biggest police investigation in fifty years. It was agonising, because there was nothing to be had and I knew that there wouldn't be much until there were some results from the forensic examinations of the bomb sites.

There was a paucity of intelligence on the activities of terror cells in the UK, obviously. On 8 June, MI5 had put out an advisory note to businesses, informing them that the terror-threat level had been downgraded from 'severe general' to 'substantial', meaning that it knew of no active plots. I posted the story on my website at the time. It had been prompted by the conclusions of a terror-threat assessment by the Joint Terrorist Analysis Centre, run by officials from the intelligence services, Customs and the Metropolitan Police. It said that there were currently no groups with the intention or the ability to mount terrorist attacks in the UK.

I'd suddenly become a consultant to several media organisations and I bashed the phones and pestered all the usual suspects and stretched my imagination to come up with non-usual sources like everybody else, though there was nothing on offer beyond silence and mere speculation. Some key contacts had certainly been warned not to talk to the media. The police had a complete lock on the situation and nothing was leaking – mainly because there was nothing to leak.

A bit of light was shed when I found out, on very good authority, that the word in the US intelligence community was 'the Brits have nothing'. Apparently, phone taps showed that prominent jihadists who were under surveillance had expressed surprise at what had happened. Much of the subsequent jihadi chatter in the UK mirrored this surprise. US operatives in the field had picked up on some signs that al-Zarqawi's network could be involved, but that was doubted by analysts.

Perhaps it didn't have any relevance, but two days previously the Jordanian authorities had arrested al-Zarqawi's spiritual mentor, Sheikh Abu Mohammed al-Maqdisi, also known as Issam Barqawi.

This came to mind because the suspected al-Zarqawi supporters who were operating the document-repository website, and who were staked out by the *Sunday Times* at the house near Heathrow months previously, had named the site after al-Maqdisi.

The day before the attacks, a group called the Global Islamic Media Front (GIMF) had put out a five-minute-long video celebrating martyrs who'd died in suicide bombings in Iraq. It showed footage of attacks filmed by the militants themselves along with rousing anthems and, unusually, English subtitles. Towards the end there were images of al-Zarqawi and bin Laden. The final frames showed a photograph of bin Laden, taken on the battlefield during the Soviet–Afghan war. Wearing a helmet, fatigues and clutching a radio, he smiles widely into the lens and waves with the other hand, as if he's bidding people a fond farewell. His image then slowly fades away.

Just after news of the first casualties started to emerge on 7 July, a statement claiming responsibility for the attacks was posted on Qal3ah.org, or 'The Fortress'. Aaron Weisburd at Internet Haganah had said that the site was a front operated by a prominent Saudi dissident in London called Saad al-Fagih, though al-Fagih denied any involvement when confronted by reporters. I was familiar with him, as he headed an organisation called the Movement for Islamic Reform in Arabia (MIRA), which campaigns for the overthrow of the Saudi government. He had been associated with al-Qaeda since the 1990s and was named by the USA as a Specially Designated Global Terrorist in 2004. The US Treasury claimed that al-Fagih had contact with bin Laden, via an intermediary called Khaled al-Fawwaz, reputed to be bin Laden's representative in the UK. They both shared an office in the late 1990s and it's been claimed that, in 1996, al-Fagih bought a satellite phone using his own credit card and sent it to bin Laden, via Fawwaz. The same phone was used by one of the suicide bombers days before the 1998 attacks on US embassies in East Africa.

The US Treasury specifically referred to the MIRA website: 'The messages are intended to provide ideological and financial support to al-Qaeda-affiliated networks and potential recruits.' Al-Fawwaz was later arrested pending deportation to the USA, though neither America nor the UK took action against al-Fagih.

One of the most notorious contributors to al-Fagih's website was an author who called himself 'Lewis Attiyatullah'. In April 2004, the site published a letter by him titled 'Yes, Blair, this is a historic war'.

Described by the USA as an 'al-Qaeda-affiliated author', he warned of 'an incoming huge and spectacular [event]' as punishment for Britain's involvement in Iraq. For inexplicable reasons, that letter was re-released in May 2005 by the GIMF propaganda group, which produced the eve-of-7/7 video.

Another of al-Fagih's key associates has been named as Mustafa Setmarian Nasar, also known by a range of other aliases, including Abu Musab al-Suri. A Syrian national, distinguished by his fair complexion and red hair, he'd been named as al-Qaeda's suspected chief of European operations and the suspected mastermind behind the Madrid train bombings.

Nasar had settled in Neasden in north-west London in 1995, before he moved to Afghanistan in 1998 to become a trainer at the al-Qaeda camp in Derunta and another known as al-Ghurabaa in Afghanistan, latterly specialising in teaching new recruits the use of poisons and chemicals. He was in the process of establishing his own European network before he fled Afghanistan ahead of the US-led invasion. His current whereabouts were unknown, though there was some suspicion that he was now in Iraq. He was named in the press as one of five chief suspects for masterminding the London bombings, mainly because of the superficial similarities with the Madrid attacks. He was indicted in Spain in 2003 for allegedly training al-Qaeda sleeper cells for deployment there, and in Italy and France. Although Nasar was out of sight, he'd certainly been active recently. He'd set up an al-Qaeda jihad training camp on the Web.

Nasar is a man of foresight because, before he left Afghanistan, he'd taken the trouble to commit his entire jihad indoctrination course to videotape. The tapes, amounting to 24 hours of continuous footage, had been digitised for distribution on the Net. His supporters had been hacking into innocent websites and hijacking server space to host the videos.

I watched a few samples from the several hundred megabytes in the collection and all the scenes looked pretty similar: Nasar standing in front of a whiteboard full of Arabic, talking and pointing, sometimes holding up documents to show to the class. I asked my translator to take a look, and she confirmed that he was talking about the history behind the global jihad.

In December 2004, links to a 1,600-page e-book by Nasar called *The International Islamic Resistance Call* were posted to jihad sites. In it, he called for war against the enemy on all fronts and proposed that groups operating under the al-Qaeda banner needed to switch from a classic pyramid-shaped chain of command to a 'secret-gang structure' consisting of numerous semi-autonomous cells. He also talked about the 'third generation of Mujahideen' – the youngest post-9/11 converts – which was 'still in the process of being defined'.

He was helping to nurture the next generation, and the virtual jihad camp was part of his contribution. It was an ingenious idea, as anyone, in their own home and in bite-sized chunks at their own leisure, could undergo the same course they would have been put through in an al-Qaeda camp in Afghanistan. The risk of discovery was minimised, as it greatly reduced the need to travel abroad or attend meetings of activists.

The last known location of the virtual camp had only been discovered and shut down by anti-jihad activists a few weeks earlier. It had been a game that had been going on for some time; as soon as the cache of videos was discovered, a new host site would be hacked into, so it could reappear literally anywhere, effectively at random. The task of the pursuers had been to detect its re-emergence, which would have seemed almost impossible, were it not for the fact that there was great ingenuity on both sides.

Weeks before the 7/7 attacks, the online jihad camp resurfaced on a website registered to a lady in Norwich. Her details had been used to set it up and she got quite a surprise when she took a phone call from the States and was informed that a suspected al-Qaeda operative had stolen her identity. The details of the case were passed on through official channels to London, though it's unknown what, if anything, was done about it.

The first call on 7 July – well, email actually – was from a producer working for the BBC's *Panorama* programme. They wanted me on board as a consultant, as they were planning a special programme on the bombings for broadcast in four days' time. Everyone was scrabbling around in a vacuum in all-hands-to-the-pump mode and I agreed, though I wondered how I'd be able to juggle that with all the other jobs that were bound to come in. Later in the day, I was also on board as a consultant to NBC News and their top investigative team was flying into London to take over the bureau's coverage.

The BBC wanted me to cover the cyber perspective and reactions to the news of the bombings in the online jihadi community. During the afternoon, I took a look at one of the biggest sites, run from London, and, sure enough, there were messages of praise for the bombings. The first described them as the 'blessed attacks', proclaiming that God is great and describing it as retaliation. Another called on the prime minister to pull troops out of Iraq immediately.

The thing that actually struck me was how muted the celebrations were. Yes, there were messages of praise, but it wasn't as if the boards were lit up with them. I was also asked to check out a few stabs in the dark as well. In the absence of any other leads, a media manhunt had got under way for a man who'd been linked to a foreign terrorist group, but I wasn't aware that he was a significant player of any kind – if at all – and strongly suspected that the information was a 'bum tip'. He was eventually tracked down and, sure enough, he strenuously denied any involvement.

He was said to have been a student of the radical preacher Abu Qatada, and then someone started a rumour that Qatada had issued a fatwa authorising the attacks. I thought that was just as unlikely, as I'd never heard of such a thing and he was under house arrest and subject to intense monitoring. I was asked to track the fatwa down, but I knew it probably didn't exist.

The publication of the statement of responsibility did throw up some very interesting links. According to Spanish court documents, al-Fagih's former associate and bin Laden representative Khaled al-Fawwaz was a close associate of Abu Qatada. Qatada was editor-in-chief of a magazine called *Al-Awsar*, which was the official publication of the GIA Algerian terrorist group, while Nasar was a director of the publishing company during the mid-1990s. Al-Fagih was connected to this circle, if only because the last known location of the hacked Nasar virtual jihad camp site was first announced on his private, invitation-only email group.

The hunt for the mastermind of the bombings was under way, though the first decent new lead emerged the day after the attacks, when a video surfaced on the Internet celebrating them. It was crude and looked like it had been done in a hurry. It consisted of BBC news footage of the attacks that had been spliced together with captions and a voiceover.

It was odd to watch, as the carnage in London and the thrown-together treatment of the material was eerily reminiscent of scenes of fighting and suffering on the dusty streets of Palestine or Iraq. It started with a shot of the bus in Tavistock Square, where 13 people had died, including the bomber, 18-year-old Hasib Mir Hussain. The Arabic voiceover said: 'We pray to God to take revenge from our enemies before we die, from Jewish, Christians and their soldiers and all those who torture Muslims. May our weakness be our power over them and their own power be weakness against them.'

A written message on the screen said:

> The murderers had to pay the price for the massacre and crimes they have committed, and today the Muslims are happy for God's revenge after the blasts which made 39 victims and 700 injured, and the number is still escalating.
>
> God is great.
>
> Thursday, 7 July 2005

A second, longer and more elaborate celebration video emerged the following day. The central section simply comprised footage from a pre-Iraq bin Laden speech. He said: 'You will be killed and attacked the same way you killed and attacked us.' In essence, the message the video producer was sending out was 'you had been warned'.

I'd been asked to be on the lookout for videos of the last wills of the bombers, though I didn't think that was a likely prospect in the short-term. One doesn't necessarily follow straight after the other. It was a year after the event before Hamas released the wills of the two British suicide bombers who set out to blow up Mike's Place in Tel Aviv, for example. These groups do not release anything that may provide clues while an investigation is ongoing.

I'd asked my translator if she'd transcribe everything said on the two post-7/7 videos, to see if there were any signs of who might have produced them. A lead along these lines might provide pointers towards those involved in the bombers' support network. Neither of the videos looked like they'd been pre-prepared, so I didn't get the feeling that the producers would have been involved directly.

She came up trumps when she emailed to say that both of the videos were credited to GIMF. I hadn't been keeping tabs on this group recently, so I emailed a few people who had been to see if they could refresh my memory. I asked one contact: 'Is this group the real deal?'

'Yes, GIMF is the real deal,' came one response.

The explanation and the details were recounted in a world-weary fashion, as this group had been operating unhindered for years, under various differing names, and was around before 9/11. Despite numerous complaints and reports to the authorities, nothing had been done. People were apparently sick of banging their heads against the wall of official indifference. One long-time contact said:

'Odd they haven't caught them, since they have been around forever now . . .'

GIMF was the leading producer and distributor of pro-al-Qaeda multimedia propaganda on the Internet – flash movies, videos, graphics and illustrated weapons guides. The organisation had very good connections, as it had access to the raw footage shot by terrorist groups and the source of their communiqués, and it was thought that it could be hooked up with operational units and handling their PR. It appeared to be an international collaborative effort and the suspected ringleaders were based in the UK, Canada, Saudi Arabia and Tunisia.

One possibly very significant fact emerged from all the background: the group appeared to have been behind a series of threats to bomb underground stations in the Swedish capital Stockholm on 29 April. If true, that would have been the first sign that attacks on transport systems in Europe were being considered by al-Qaeda followers. The threats had been posted to two notorious jihad discussion forums and I took a look at those pages.

Sure enough, they were filled with a couple of dozen different banner-type graphics threatening attacks in Sweden. The precise grievance wasn't clear, though there were mentions of the government having insulted Islam in some way. One of the graphics consisted of a map of the city, a shot of an underground station and a bomb with a timer that displayed 'so:on'. Below this were the words: 'I choose the train because it's full of Swedish, just like what happened in Madrid.'

It was a bit mystifying, because Sweden wasn't involved in Iraq, though its troops were present in Afghanistan. The only explanation I could come up with was that the threats had been aimed at pressurising the Swedish government into not acceding to a request for the deportation of a terrorist suspect there. Oussama Kassir, a Lebanese-born Swede, was one of two men who'd travelled from London in November 1999 to meet James Ujaama in the USA and scope out the site of a proposed jihad training camp in Bly, Oregon. The USA alleges that they were sent by Abu Hamza. When he introduced himself, Kassir described himself as a hit-man for Osama bin Laden, according to court documents. He was so angry at the poor state of the facilities, he threatened to shoot Ujaama. He'd since returned to Sweden, where he was found guilty of weapons violations in 2003 and spent ten months in prison after illegal weapons were found in his

Stockholm house. Charges alleging that he was planning a terrorist attack were dropped.

He was a free man now in 2005, and he later gave an interview to a local paper in which he denied that he had anything to do with the London bombings, though he described the bombers as 'martyrs'. He admitted being an assistant to Abu Hamza, but he claimed he was only acting as a nurse. I knew Hamza's Supporters of Sharia group had a branch in Sweden, so it seemed likely that this guy might be connected with that.

The GIMF UK connection looked to be much more promising. The presumed leader of the group was notorious and known to be a computer wizard of the highest order. Those who'd followed his activities described his specialities as 'surveillance, security and counter-intelligence', and his online identity was Irhabi007, which translates to 'Terrorist007'.

I knew that name, as he'd first posted a link to the video of the hostage Ken Bigley being beheaded on al-Zarqawi's website. I'd looked into his activities at the time and was told that he'd been gathering and posting military intelligence on potential targets in Iraq, the USA and Israel. He'd also been providing detailed instructions on an array of techniques and technologies that could be used to evade detection online, as well as distributing jihad manuals and 'how to' material.

A profile of him had started to emerge: he was judged to be a native English speaker who had just started to learn Arabic, to a level which was described as 'poor'. He'd been working with a group of Italian-speaking extremists and a French-speaking collaborator, though he could not speak those languages. Irhabi007 was also a suspect in numerous incidents where vulnerable Web servers had been hacked into and used for covert file-sharing. In 2004, the FBI opened an investigation into his activities when he was linked to the 'hijacking' of a Web server belonging to the government of the State of Arkansas. I checked to find out what happened, but it seemed that the case had been dropped without a resolution. 'Perhaps now that there's a morgue full of bodies in London, someone will decide that this guy is a problem after all,' said a source.

I spoke to one of the investigators involved in the Arkansas server hijacking case and asked if there was any specific evidence in the files linking Irhabi007 to the UK. My contact said he'd scour through the files and get back to me. I waited a few days, and the reply was worth it. Irhabi007 was known to be a master of disguising his location but he'd made a couple of minor errors recently. A team who'd been tracking his online activities had managed, using some good old-fashioned detective work, to trace his true whereabouts. He'd been caught out using a BT broadband Internet account from a location in Ealing in west London. What's more, he'd stolen the ID of the lady in Norwich in an attempt to resurrect the al-Suri virtual training camp. He was the dominant figure in the global jihad communications network and his group's involvement in the London videos was the first tangible indicator that the bombers were al-Qaeda supporters.

The police started giving out signals that the attacks were indeed suicide bombings on 12 July, ahead of a press conference, during which the bombers were named. It was the historic moment the media had been waiting for and virtual confirmation that Britain has been a breeding ground for suicide bombers. The police avoided using the word suicide.

A journalist friend who works for one of the daily papers later called me with some startling news: he'd parked his car at Luton station and boarded the same train that the bombers took. He'd ridden the suicide-bomb train, but was feeling guilty because he couldn't remember seeing anything suspicious and, consequently, he hadn't contacted the police. He may have parked next to the car where the nine unexploded bombs were later found, for all he knew, he said. None of the faces from CCTV images rang any bells with him, but, he asked, did I think he should go to the police? I told him he probably should, just to make himself known.

There was a double coincidence, because I was due to meet a couple of TV producers in Luton on the morning that the bombers' car was discovered in the station car park. I was having problems with my car, though, and I wasn't confident that I'd be able to make it as far as Luton, so I phoned them first thing in the morning to suggest that we meet at my house instead. In the intervening period, before we met at lunchtime, the news broke that Luton station had been cordoned off. When they arrived at mine, they insisted that I must have had prior knowledge of the announcement and that was the reason why I'd suggested switching venues.

The following day, I had to go to King's Cross for a TV interview. The Tube journey was certainly grimmer than usual, and at one point I recalled a cameraman – a Caucasian Australian with a handlebar moustache – telling me that, as he regularly carried bags bulging with cables, he'd had to show his press card a couple of times to avoid being attacked by packs of have-a-go passengers. A message on the BBC's website summed it up perfectly for me: 'One guy in the train had a Walkman wire hanging out of his pocket and everyone left the carriage at the next stop.'

After the interview, with the pressure off and enjoying the early evening sunshine, I decided to walk from King's Cross to Euston, along the route of the No. 30 bus that was destroyed by Hasib Hussain. It seemed like a good opportunity to have a wander and sample the post-bombings atmosphere. It certainly smelled the same: regular wafts of stale fast food. The scene was pretty usual, bar the TV cameras and lights set up on street corners. I passed two nattily-dressed presenters who were preparing to go live on air and it was an absurd sight to see them lit up on little platforms covered by gazebos whilst normality bustled all around them.

I was hungry and I thought about going into McDonald's opposite the station, as I was passing it, but decided I didn't have the time and pressed on. Weeks later, the police said that, instead of getting on a Northern Line train with his bomb, Hussain exited the station and went into the same McDonald's, where he ate whilst frantically trying to get through to his three other colleagues on the phone. He left messages for them, saying that he couldn't get on to the Northern Line, and pleaded for advice. It dawned on him that, having got no response, they must have gone through with the plan. Rather than having second thoughts, it seems that he was intent on dying that day. He walked out of the restaurant and chose a target at random: a passing bus, which was packed with commuters who'd been evacuated from the Tube.

There was much talk on the day about the cross-shaped formation of the bombings. I took the trouble of plotting the bomb locations on Google Earth and it was more coat-hanger-shaped, geographically speaking. Schematically, according to the Tube map, it looked different and would have looked like a cross if Hussain had headed north, as it's thought he was originally intending.

There has been press speculation that the intention was to etch a 'burning cross on the heart of London', which I was more willing to consider than I would have been if I hadn't heard the promises of impending retaliation and watched the flaming crosses being brandished outside the US embassy a few weeks previously. It was a cross-shaped concept, in any case, as each member of the squad headed for a different point of the compass, starting from King's Cross.

When I reached the junction with Tavistock Square, I paused to see what was occurring. There were quite a few TV crews and reporters there waiting to film the bus being removed, but I guessed that the grisly forensic work was still ongoing. The steps of the church on the corner of the street in front of the hoardings that were masking the crime scene were neatly bedecked with hundreds of bunches of flowers, and behind, in the rear courtyard, I could see several identical, unmarked red vans parked.

There was a poster tied to a lamp-post appealing for information on a woman who hadn't been seen since the bombings, complete with her picture and a telephone number. Minutes earlier, opposite King's Cross station, a woman had rushed past me, sobbing and scouring the crowds desperately, as if she'd lost someone. I wondered if the poster was her work, as I'd read that the relatives of some of the presumed victims had refused to accept the inevitable and were clinging to the notion that they may have been injured and were maybe wandering around in a daze, or perhaps in hospital suffering from amnesia. I was moved enough to think about writing the number down, just in case, before I came to my senses.

It was just out of sight, but the image of the day that touched me the most was a picture of the British Medical Association building immediately adjacent to the bombed bus. A conference was being held in the building at the time, so 14 doctors and a nurse were immediately on the scene and it became a mini-hospital. There was a blue plaque on the front of the building, commemorating it as one of the homes of Charles Dickens, and the white stone around it was splattered with blood and human remains. Dickens was my first close encounter with journalism, around the age of seven, as the junior school I attended was built close to another of his former residences. A bust of him had taken pride of place in the assembly hall. The picture of the devastation at Tavistock Square resonated with me for that particular reason, and it also seemed succinctly to summarise the nature of the changed times we were now living in.

The following day, I found myself in the bizarre position of making a televised call for calm among the people of Aylesbury. ITV Central called and asked me for an interview, as one of the bombers, Germaine Lindsay, had lived there and it was on their patch. Born in Jamaica, he had changed his name to Abdullah Shaheed Jamal after converting to Islam. He was named as the bomber who'd killed 25 people on a train on the Piccadilly Line, when he detonated his bomb between King's Cross and Russell Square stations. During the interview, the reporter asked me what my message to the people of Aylesbury would be. I was a bit flummoxed initially, as I had no idea what kind of a town it was, or its ethnic make-up. I told him that people should remain calm and shouldn't treat anyone any differently, meaning: don't abuse Muslims or attack mosques. 'That's exactly what these people want,' I argued.

I had also been commissioned to write a couple of opinion pieces on the bombings. Making predictions at that stage seemed precarious, because there were so few facts to work with. As I pondered on it all over the next few days, though, it seemed that some new conclusions could be drawn. Events before 7/7 suggested that plots to attack the UK were in constant development, so it seemed safe to suggest that the bombings were part of a long-running campaign that had already been started.

The ultimate aim of militant Islamic groups was the overthrow of democracy and the establishment of a Taliban-style Islamic government. It's all too easy to scoff at such ambitions, and that was the core of the problem: the militants were serious and determined and they had been underestimated. In order to create the conditions necessary for revolution, they needed to foment civil unrest.

In effect, the militants had won the first battle, which I concluded was designed to ratchet up racial tensions. All the recent rhetoric from these groups had encouraged hatred of kaffirs, who were all portrayed as murderous oppressors. It all helped to create a siege mentality among their followers, and the next logical step would be to transfer that siege mentality to the general Muslim population. Every suspicious glance at another passenger on a Tube train would add up from now on in.

The Muslim Council of Britain received 30,000 hate emails in the days after the attacks. Reported attacks on Muslims and people of ethnic minorities rose 500 per cent in the three weeks after the bombings. At least seven mosques and Sikh temples were attacked. My appeal for calm in Aylesbury was only partially successful, as someone attempted to firebomb Germaine Lindsay's house.

Fleet Street swarmed all over the backgrounds and family connections of the bombers for the next week or so. Somewhere along the line, it was mentioned that one of the bombers had recently been watching Internet videos of terrorist attacks in Iraq and it was suggested that this may have finally pushed him over the edge. I started fielding calls about jihad websites and bomb-making manuals. There was particular interest in the type of explosive detected at the suspected bomb-making factory in Leeds, nicknamed Mother of Satan by al-Qaeda operatives. It's easily made from two chemicals found in household products and may explain why Germaine Lindsay spent an estimated £900 frantically buying specific types of men's aftershave in Aylesbury two days before the attacks. I told reporters that they may have been extracting the alcohol for use in bomb-making, while others suggested that a quantity of aftershave might add an extra napalm-like effect to boost the effectiveness of the devices.

Later, I preferred to consider the possibility that this was connected to a final, eve-of-attack cleansing ritual. The 9/11 hijackers are said to have performed a Koranic ritual to prepare themselves for death, and that involved applying perfume to the skin. Witnesses have commented on how several of the 9/11 hijackers reeked of aftershave on that day.

As their backgrounds came to light, the official explanation, that these were people who were previously unknown to the authorities, started to look decidedly shaky. There were press reports that security officials in the US had confirmed that the self-confessed al-Qaeda operative Junaid Babar had admitted knowing the eldest of the bombers, Mohammed Sidique Khan, 30, the presumed leader of the group and killer of himself and six other passengers at Edgware Road. Babar, who reportedly had links with Bakri's al-Muhajiroun, had pleaded guilty the previous year to conspiring in a plot for a wave of bombings in the UK targeting pubs, train stations and restaurants.

Whitehall sources defended their 'clean skins' line and were quoted as saying that the link between Babar and Khan was 'indirect', even though the US reports said both had met in Pakistan. A French newspaper claimed that Khan had been on the target list during a string of raids in the UK connected to the Babar case but he was one of the five suspects who'd 'escaped'. Officials responded by saying only that he'd been subjected to a routine assessment by MI5 the previous year but he was deemed to be on the periphery of the alleged plot and not to be a threat. Germaine Lindsay was said, by US sources, to have been on a watch list, though the British had lost track of him. The Leeds bombers were banned from three mosques in their area for 'unacceptable behaviour', though it appears that this hadn't come to the attention of the authorities.

There was much speculation about the Leeds bombers' connections to a terrorist suspect called Haroon Rashid Aswat, formerly a senior aide to Abu Hamza. The papers carried quotes from anonymous sources fingering him as the chief suspect for masterminding the attacks. He grew up in the same Dewsbury area of Leeds as Khan, the bus bomber Hasib Mir Hussain and Aldgate bomber Shehzad Tanweer, 22, who killed six people.

The Times quoted intelligence sources as saying that Aswat had phoned two of the bombers twenty times and that Khan had spoken to him on the morning of the attacks. He was said to have visited Britain and toured the home town of the bombers and scoped out the targets in London, before flying out of the country hours before the attacks. British sources, however, claimed that someone was using a phone registered to Aswat and that it may not have been Aswat making the calls.

There was confusion, as US sources were flagging up Aswat while the British were downplaying the reports, suggesting it was a case of mistaken identity. *The Times* reported that he'd been arrested in Pakistan and the story was widely circulated – it was even said that he'd been detained with $17,000 in cash and wearing a belt of explosives. Yet, there were conflicting reports from Pakistan on the veracity of the story.

Aswat was wanted by the USA over involvement in the plan to establish a jihad training camp in Oregon, along with James Ujaama and Oussama Kassir. While the other two had busied themselves with firing weapons and watching a video on the use of poisons during a visit to the camp, Aswat spent most of his time reading the Koran. His re-emergence was doubly puzzling, because it had been thought that he'd been killed in fighting in Afghanistan. It looked like he'd switched IDs with a dead colleague – or someone had done that for him.

It seemed like a no-brainer when the Pakistan government revealed that three of the four bombers had recently spent three months in the country. Khan and Tanweer arrived in November 2004 on a Turkish Airlines flight and left on 8 February 2005. Hasib Hussain arrived in July 2004 on a Saudi Arabian Airlines flight, but the date and port of his exit had not been established. All three men had been secretly filmed by a system called Pisces, which monitors everyone entering the country legally.

Photographs were released to the media and the calm, blank expressions on their faces reminded me very much of the CCTV images of the 9/11 hijackers just before they boarded their flights. There was no hard information on their movements inside the country, though local press reports claimed that they'd visited a radical religious school, or madrassa, with links to the al-Qaeda-aligned group Lashkar-e-Toiba. Another report said that Tanweer had travelled to Faisalabad to meet Osama Nazir, a suspected member of another banned militant group called Jaish-e-Mohammed.

Aswat was said to be in Pakistan, but that was later shown to be a myth when it was announced that he'd been detained in Zambia on 21 July. He was quickly extradited and flown to the UK, where he was arrested on landing. There had been sceptical noises emanating from Scotland Yard about Aswat's possible role in the bombings. The USA submitted a request for his extradition to face charges of involvement in the Bly jihad camp plot, but there were no charges relating to London.

Several suspects had been arrested during the post-7/7 crackdown on militants in Pakistan and some 600 people in all were detained in the weeks following the attacks. President Pervez Musharraf later ordered all foreigners to leave madrassas in the country, a move that was estimated to affect some 1,400 people. Pakistan's madrassas have long been regarded as the crucible of the global jihad, but Musharraf later retorted that Britain needed to put its own house in order before criticising others.

As the media spotlight started to swing towards the recruiters and inciters, a fatwa approving of the London attacks emerged on the Internet. It was published on 12 July, though it was five days before it was picked up, as the site it first appeared on went offline soon after, so it wasn't in wide circulation. It set out to refute other fatwas that had been issued to condemn the bombings. It was titled: 'The Base of Legitimacy for the London Bombings'.

It argued that there was no need for Muslims to defend their religion with a fatwa each time an attack took place on enemy soil. The author's prime message was the prohibition of any sympathy for the enemy – on the contrary, Muslims should celebrate with joy every tragedy that befalls the infidel oppressors. Britain was described as an infidel country and an enemy of all Muslims: 'As long as it remains an enemy, it is a Muslim duty to terrorise it . . . they are the allies of the worst devilish idol of our times – the USA and the Jews – and do their utmost to support them.' The fatwa argued that every British citizen who voted for an MP should be regarded as an attacker, or at least an assistant, as major political decisions are based upon public support voiced through parliament. It continued:

The division between civilians and soldiers is a modern one, and has no basis in Islamic law . . . where every healthy male above 15 years old is a potential soldier . . . In the USA, the UK, and Israel, even the females are recruited to the military, and hence they are not innocent civilians too.

Therefore the United Kingdom is an infidel country, which fights against Islam and the Muslims, with every criminal means possible . . . The Muslims should use every means possible, approved by the Prophet . . . including destroying their houses and terrorising them . . . Allah, may you destroy the United Kingdom and the United States and their allies; kill them and do not leave them a remain. May Allah humiliate the UK and terrorise it . . . Show us in the USA, the UK, and their allies your might and wonders of your power.

Ideologically, the counter-fatwa echoed the arguments of the previous Saudi WMD fatwa. It was unsigned, though there were indications that the author was a Saudi scholar living in London. It contained an Arabic phrase which is often used to refer to clerics living in London – 'the awakening sheiks' – and the fact that the author didn't feel he could put his name to this suggested that he feared pursuit by the authorities.

The reference to males above 15 being potential soldiers is a line that has been used by Abu Hamza, so that to me reinforced the impression that it originated in London. It also included quotes from the April 2004 fatwa by Lewis Attiyatullah, which warned that a spectacular attack on the UK was in the making. The evidence pointed towards the Saudi dissident al-Fagih, as the warning was first published on one of his websites and Attiyatullah was a regular contributor.

The other suspect was Muhammad al-Massari, who ran an almost identical organisation to al-Fagih, called the Committee for the Defence of Legitimate Rights in Saudi Arabia (CDLR), also known as the Party of Islamic Renewal, and he was also a close associate of Omar Bakri.

Al-Massari was one of the figures being investigated by a police officer who was jailed for spying for the Saudi embassy. Both al-Fagih and al-Massari shared an al-Qaeda association in their past relationships with Khaled al-Fawwaz, bin Laden's now jailed personal representative in London. They assisted al-Fawwaz in running al-Qaeda's media office during the mid-1990s.

One of al-Massari's group's websites, called Tajdeed, could only be described as UK Jihad Central and it had been operating freely for years. It was one of the main outlets for the GIMF, the producers of the London celebration videos. In the discussion forums on the site, there was everything a potential terrorist could wish for: propaganda videos, statements of responsibility, military manuals and even tips on the best routes into Iraq from Syria.

Al-Massari caused widespread outrage when, in a television interview, he defended the posting of a video of an attack on British Black Watch troops in Iraq. Three soldiers, 22-year-old Scott McArdle, Paul Lowe, 19, and Sergeant Stuart Gray, 31, died when a suicide bomber drove a car at them near Fallujah in November 2004. Some of the video was played during the interview, but the end of it would have been too gruesome to show. I remembered watching it months earlier and being repulsed at the final scene, which showed one member of the attack team kicking the severed arm of one of the dead soldiers.

Al-Massari was unrepentant, claiming that they were legitimate targets, as they were attacking Muslims in Iraq, so he instantly became a main media target the following day. The government was in a bind because it couldn't deport him to Saudi Arabia, where he might be subject to torture, and it seemed his online activities couldn't be stopped under present legislation. He also operated a radio station (Al-Tajdeed Radio) that beamed jihadist programming into Saudi Arabia and Iraq 24 hours a day, but that was out of reach also, as programme tapes were sent from London to the Netherlands and broadcast via satellite.

The signs that al-Massari was pioneering jihad via the Internet went back to at least 1998. After the cruise-missile attacks on bin Laden in Sudan and Afghanistan, a statement was circulated on the Internet calling for all Muslims to rally to the aid of bin Laden. A British newspaper questioned the author of the statement, Mohammed Sohail, and he said he worked for a London-based group called the Global Jihad Fund, 'helping with things such as recruitment and fund-raising for organisations involved in jihad'. He added: 'I work for two people, really: Mr Massari and Osama bin Laden.'

Sohail worked as an executive for the company then in charge of managing Britain's rail network, the much-maligned Railtrack. In 1999, the company launched an investigation into his activities when it was found that he'd been using its computers in a campaign to recruit volunteers to fight jihad in Afghanistan, Kashmir, Pakistan, Kosovo and Chechnya. He also operated a website called the Islamic Gateway, which distributed the propaganda of several militant Islamic groups, including Omar Bakri's al-Muhajiroun.

More recently, in 2004, one of al-Massari's two sons, Majid, was detained in the USA and held on charges of immigration violations. The grounds were that he had an undisclosed drugs conviction and he was facing deportation to Saudi Arabia. There were some mutterings in the intelligence community about his father's alleged involvement in an undisclosed plot to assassinate the crown prince of Saudi Arabia, though al-Massari senior maintained that Majid was being held hostage in a campaign to silence him.

Majid was a computer security specialist working as a technician at the University of Washington and it appears that his brother, Anmar, has since taken over the reins of the al-Massaris' online empire. To me, the al-Faqih and al-Massari circles seemed to be the obvious places to look for clues about the support network behind the London bombers, as well as the true identity of Terrorist007 and those behind the GIMF.

Scrutiny of potential recruiters and inciters stepped up an order of magnitude after the failed repeat bombings of 21 July. A squad of suicide bombers was on the loose and it was another day of sensation, phone calls and interviews. I, and others I spoke to, were physically flagging from the long hours and weeks already spent frantically chasing post-7/7 leads. The big question, of course, was: were there any links between the two cells?

It seemed to me that the second group of bombers may have at least taken their cue from the 'success' of the first group and put a long-standing plan into action. They wouldn't have had to know each other if this was a network of sleeper cells operating along the lines of the 'secret gang' structure advocated by Nasar, and I found it hard to believe that these might have been two spontaneous and completely unrelated events.

One curiosity about the second attacks is that the first unplanned bus bomb was copied the second time around, which suggests that the second team mistakenly thought that that was part of the original plan. It adds to the theory that the two teams were entirely unconnected and if there was any command and control at a higher level, it must have been distant and something along the lines of 'when you hear the news, you go for it'.

Thankfully, only the detonators exploded and not the main

charges, and that suggested to me that they were the work of a different bomb-maker this time. He'd obviously made the same mistake in all five bombs, or there was a flaw in the plans he was working to. A massive police hunt got underway and 6,000 detectives flooded the Tube system to dissuade any other cells from mounting further attacks.

The news broke the following day that a suspected suicide bomber had been shot dead by armed officers at Stockwell station. It didn't make me feel any safer to hear a police officer on TV tell viewers that, if you want to avoid being shot dead by police on the Tube, simply stop when challenged and cooperate. Within hours, it developed into a scandal of the highest order, as it became clear that an innocent man had been killed. Jean Charles de Menezes, a 27-year-old electrician from Brazil, had been mistakenly identified as a suspect after he emerged from a block of flats that was under surveillance.

In race-relations terms, it is difficult to dream up a more damaging scenario. The radical preachers were going to latch on to this and claim it as concrete proof that the kaffirs were gunning down innocent brown-skinned people like they were stray dogs. For the militants, it was a recruitment-driving gift.

A call from a Muslim woman to report suspicious goings-on at a house in Birmingham led to the arrest of the suspected would-be Warren Street suicide bomber, Yasin Hassan Omar. He was arrested with the aid of a Taser stun gun, and that attracted implied criticism from the chief of the Metropolitan Police, Sir Ian Blair, who pointed out that 'an incredible risk' had been taken, because the electric charge could have set off explosives.

The other prime suspects were in London two days later. One, Hussain Osman, the suspected Shepherd's Bush bomber, was arrested in Rome. The 27 year old, also known as Hamdi Isaac, was traced via calls made to his brother, who was living in Italy, and was tracked by the authorities as he made his way across Europe. He told the Italian police that he never intended to kill anyone and that the goal had been merely to frighten people and draw attention to the issue of Iraq. He said they had been spurred into action by watching videos shot by insurgent groups in Iraq that were circulating on the Internet.

One of the leaders of Stockwell mosque in south London said he had warned the police in 2003 about a gang of youths who were harassing moderate Muslims, but nothing was done. Mosque trustee

Toaha Qureshi said Osman was named specifically in a letter written to the deputy borough commander of Brixton Police, Malcolm Tillyer, as a member of the group who had been 'inciting racial and religious hatred in the community'. It claimed that the group were spreading extremist views and literature and had been targeting moderate leaders of the mosque for abuse.

Qureshi said: 'We could not have been more explicit. It was put in such a manner that it should have been taken seriously. If they had done something, then I don't know how many lives we could have saved.' He added: 'They [had] an agenda to turn this centre into another Finsbury Park mosque.' Osman was believed to have been a regular visitor there, until the government moved to oust Abu Hamza. There were reports that investigators were looking at the possibility that all of the suspected bombers originally met at Finsbury Park mosque.

And that's about as far as I can legally go, thanks to the Contempt of Court Act. As soon as proceedings are started against a suspect, the case is subject to reporting restrictions which mean, by and large, that the media are banned from reporting on any information that might influence the outcome of any trial. In effect, a huge rusty iron curtain slams shut and secrecy prevails until the trial is over. It's one of the most draconian laws on the statute book and means that the British people will be kept in the dark about the precise circumstances of the 21 July bombings until the trials are over, which could be years. Until then, all the media are able to report is basic information, such their names, ages and the charges against them.

The British media were warned that they could face prosecution under the Act if they published photographs of the 7/7 bomb sites. The police argued that publication could compromise ongoing investigations, and so the British public were denied the opportunity to view those scenes of devastation on the Underground. The restrictions did not, of course, apply to the foreign media.

In the USA, the media are free to report on cases without restriction. You could almost hear gaskets blowing inside Scotland Yard when pictures of the bombed trains and the devices found in the car in Luton appeared on US TV. Anyone with an Internet connection could now see the pictures, making a mockery of the law and the arguments of the police. If the Met had been in charge in New York on 9/11, images of the attacks and the resulting damage would have been suppressed, and views of the World Trade Center would have been quickly blocked by the Mother of All Hoardings. Is that really the way we're going to carry on in the future: terrorist attack followed by State-imposed media blackout? That's utter madness, but it's still the law in Britain in the twenty-first century.

Whilst debate raged over the possible motives and precise affiliations of the bombers, it was quelled to an extent with the broadcast on Al-Jazeera of a videotaped statement by al-Qaeda's deputy leader. These are too often dismissed as sabre-rattling efforts, but militant Islamic groups do take these as guidance from the central leadership. One analyst noted that in his various speeches, bin Laden had named 23 countries as targets for retribution and all had been attacked in one way or another.

On 4 August 2005, Ayman al-Zawahiri, sitting by the obligatory propped up AK-47, claimed the London attacks in the name of al-Qaeda. He named Tony Blair and his policy towards Iraq as being the cause. 'We exploded volcanoes of anger in your countries,' he said. 'To the British, I am telling you that Blair brought you destruction in the middle of London and more will come, God willing.' In his last appearance, in early June, he warned that Muslims should not rely upon peaceful protests and demonstrations to bring about change; it could only be achieved through the use of violence.

I was drinking a glass of milk and gagged on it when I read that the home secretary, Charles Clarke, had denied that Britain has long been a hotbed of Islamic militancy. Prince Turki al-Faisal, Saudi Arabia's then ambassador to the UK (now ambassador to the US), responded by saying that he'd been going around in circles in trying to warn the government of the danger posed by Saudi dissidents in the UK. It had being going on since 1996, he said, and his two chief grievances were the presence of al-Fagih and al-Massari and their activities in London. 'When you call somebody, he says it's the other guy. If you talk to the security people, they say it's the politicians' fault. If you talk to the politicians, they say it's the Crown Prosecution Service. If you call the Crown Prosecution Service, they say, no, it's MI5. So we have been in this runaround for two and a half years,' he said.

The police had also hinted that the CPS had been a stumbling block, when it pointed out in response to media enquiries that only one attempt to prosecute radical preachers for inciting hatred or violence had been successful – out of a total of twenty attempts. The firebrand imams, such as Bakri and Hamza, were regarded by many as harmless loudmouths, and that perception lingered on even after 9/11.

What greater failure of government can there be than to allow a secret army, bent on overthrowing the state, to build up unchecked for so long? Just consider the numbers: it's estimated that there are 100,000 people in the UK who know how to operate an AK-47. An estimated 10,000 of those can strip one down blindfolded. Similarly, 10,000 are trained in the use of explosives. A May 2004 government report suggested that there are 16,000 people in the UK actively engaged in terrorist activities and some 3,000 who've passed through al-Qaeda training camps.

Behind every suicide bomber is a support network, and here the figures are even more alarming. A YouGov poll of British Muslims, the results of which were published in the *Daily Telegraph* days earlier, found that 56 per cent of respondents said that they understood why the bombers did what they did. Six per cent said the bombings were justified and another six per cent weren't sure. Thirteen per cent sympathised with the feelings and motives of the bombers. Ten per cent said they would not report an imam who was radicalising young Muslims and preaching hatred towards the West. The official 2001 census figures put the size of the British Muslim population at just under 1.6 million people, which looks to be an underestimate. Other figures put the real size at between 1.8 million and 2 million. Even taking the official census figures, it can be deduced that the would-be martyrs could count on some 10 per cent, or 160,000 people, for assistance, of varying degrees, in mounting terrorist attacks inside the UK.

That's a pretty impressive fifth column already by any standard and, largely because of Iraq and Net-powered propaganda, the numbers are steadily clocking up. The only morsel of comfort for Labour politicians is that the policy of accommodation started during the Thatcher era. There were no doubts by now that the country was looking at domestic insurgency by militant Muslims of unknown scope.

Britain was the newest land of jihad and the base of a third generation of al-Qaeda operatives. We had young, home-grown recent converts, self-trained and operating in small and largely autonomous groups. The previously headline-grabbing militant groups had splintered and gone underground. Young preachers were now inciting and recruiting in makeshift mosques in basements and garages.

Nasar's vision will be complete when those who have fought in Iraq come to the UK, bringing their technical knowledge and war stories with them. British Muslims will have a panoply of jihad martyrs and Mujahideen heroes to choose from. Some analysts have expressed the fear that those returning will become the field commanders in a domestic insurgency, but the government assures us that the British contingent of the Iraq insurgency is close to negligible . . .

The root cause of the problem is state failure stretching back decades, particularly within the education system. The whole story took a very personal turn when I read a story quoting an ex-school colleague of one of the 21 July suspects. I recognised the name of the school and it dawned on me: the bomb suspect and I had attended the same school. Contempt of Court fears prevent me from being specific, but I was completely unsurprised and instant comprehension came from the knowledge. We were many years apart, but we shared the same heritage. I'd survived the place and managed to turn my life around, but I could well believe that the school has been breeding potential suicide bombers, having been through the grinder myself.

I was born in the same borough and, like him, I'm the son of an immigrant. My father is Irish and he came to Britain in the 1960s to escape the crushing poverty there, when it was common to see signs outside boarding houses saying 'no blacks, no dogs, no Irish'. He was forced to sleep rough on the streets of Manchester because of that, before he made his way to London.

In 1977, he had a run-in with the police that embittered him for years to come. He was returning home on the Tube one evening, leaving the carriage of a Piccadilly Line train at King's Cross, when he was suddenly bundled off the train by four plain-clothes police officers and slammed into a wall. He was ordered to stretch out his arms and legs, and the contents of his bag were tipped onto the floor. Inside the bag was a brown paper-covered package and it was unceremoniously ripped open and examined. There had been a spate of IRA bombings and it seemed that the officers had overheard him talking to a fellow passenger, noticed the Irish accent, and that he was carrying a bag and wearing an Irish tartan flat cap. They put two and two together and got five. Inside the package was a digital alarm clock that he'd bought for my mother as a birthday present.

He was soon released, though not without an exchange of words during which one of the officers indicated that he wouldn't have got off so lightly in less public circumstances. They walked off, leaving him scrabbling around on his hands and knees on the floor, retrieving the contents of the bag. It was humiliating and he was left feeling as if he should be ashamed to be Irish, even though he wasn't an IRA supporter. The same thing happened again two years later.

The concept of a suicide bomber was unknown then, otherwise who knows what might have happened. He was sure they were armed and wouldn't have hesitated to gun him down if he'd looked like he might make a run for it. The nastiness and the officers' clear belief that all Irish were guilty was what really rankled him.

I remember the night well. A digital clock was a novelty then and we gathered together to marvel at the impressive blue glow of the LEDs. My parents didn't let on about the drama which had preceded that innocent little family event until years later.

The Irish were generally regarded as scum in those days. The headmaster of the junior school I went to in the same area was from this school of thought. Whenever we made eye contact, he seemed to have a peculiarly disdainful sneer that was reserved just for me. That had always puzzled me until, again, years later, my mother told me that he was well known for having a thing about the Irish.

The morning assembly should have been a big clue. We trooped down the gloomy Victorian staircase, lined with glazed, shit-coloured bricks, and into the hall every day, accompanied by the scratchy sounds of Elgar playing on the record player. Every day, we waited for the headmaster to walk through the door dramatically at the appropriate moment and take his place next to the flag, and we would all have to stand up in time for 'Land of hope and glory . . .'!

It was during the song that I noticed he was watching me with that look of disapproval. Beyond the title, I didn't know the rest of the words and I don't remember being taught them. We went through that ritual every morning, and I was just mystified as to why this song was deemed to be so important. I was soon plonked into the class reserved for the divs, ethnics and misfits. It didn't deter me, however, as I was naturally bookish and spent most of my time outside school reading or browsing in the local library. I'd often have three books on the go at once, yet I was in the dustbin class.

The situation got immeasurably worse when I moved on to the local comprehensive and graduated to the Suicide Bomb School. It had the reputation for being the worst of the worst and the whole experience was traumatic. The school existed to serve a single purpose: to prepare us for our future lives as street cleaners, checkout assistants, drug dealers and suicide bombers. The teachers weren't interested in my ambition to become a British Airways pilot: they didn't do the vision thing.

Standards may have improved there very recently, but it was too late for me and the bomb suspect, despite the wide time difference that separated us. Even in 2001, according to the school's last Ofsted report, its examination results were judged to be 'well below average', compared with the national average. During our time, it must have been somewhere around the 'Jesus wept' mark. It was a factory farm for kids who were expected to go nowhere and there was an almost wilful lack of care at the place. With over 1,000 pupils on the roll in soul-destroying conditions, teaching methods that relied heavily on dictation and little in the way of diversion or enthralment, it made for perfect conditions for gangs to coalesce. There was a naturally tribal atmosphere and the inmates made their own amusements. Truancy was rife and it was tolerated and even encouraged by the staff as an easy method of reducing classroom disruption.

The State failed me and I've no doubt that the suspect got similar treatment, along with millions of others. There's now a British Mujahideen in our midst and it's been State-nurtured and funded. The education system has been turning out rebels without a cause for decades. Many have now found one, so State apathy has put us in a position where national security is at serious risk.

Armies of the rudderless have been created; people who've had their childhood aspirations brutally knocked out of them and been brainwashed into believing they should expect no improvement in their lot. This has provided the extremists with a vast recruitment pool. Some young Muslim men are bound to be attracted by the possibility of a new life, fighting for the truth and rescuing the oppressed – naturally.

The change can be rapid. It's alarmingly easy to brainwash human beings; one of the 7/7 bombers had only converted to Islam two years previously. The Internet means that indoctrination and training can be carried out unobtrusively in private; plans can be discussed securely, using a variety of Net-based methods, and all the chemicals are available in local shops. The government doesn't want an official inquiry into the Summer of Bombs, and that isn't surprising: the State has failed us all on every level.

EPILOGUE

AS I WAS POLISHING OFF THIS BOOK, OMAR BAKRI FINALLY FLED THE UK, to avoid possible deportation to his native Syria. He decided to take an extended holiday in Beirut, as he holds Lebanese citizenship and his mother lives there. Bakri jumped before he was pushed, as the government announced that 'the rules had changed' in the official delineation between free speech and incitement to violence.

He denied it, but a newspaper had claimed to have caught him on tape referring to the 7/7 bombers as the 'fantastic four', just as he'd referred to the 9/11 hijackers as the 'magnificent nineteen'. It had sparked another huge media furore and a reporter had called for some quotes in reaction to the news. I pondered briefly and concluded: 'It looks like the game's up for him.'

Official action against him seemed imminent, come what may. The government was consulting opposition parties on new anti-terrorism measures, which included suspending the Human Rights Act, if necessary, to purge the country of 'preachers of hate'. New guidelines for the deportation of undesirables were proposed and they included those making speeches in support of terrorism.

This would apply to statements already on record, so Bakri would have been snared one way or another. The following day, the news broke that he had done a runner. The quote looked prophetic, in retrospect, though he insisted he'd gone on holiday to avoid media harassment and would soon return to have £8,000-worth of heart surgery on the NHS. The Home Office locked him out at the end of the week, saying that he wouldn't be permitted to return as his presence wouldn't be 'conducive to the public good'.

Soon, ten remaining radical clerics, including Abu Qatada,

Muhammad al-Massari, Saad al-Fagih and Yasser al-Sirri, were said to be on a government list of prime targets for deportation. Officials had been negotiating with other countries to gain guarantees that the deportees wouldn't be subject to torture on their return, in an attempt to quash any human rights objections. Agreement with Jordan, Qatada's home country, had been reached and Egypt was set to follow.

Al-Massari's case looks to be the trickiest, not least because the former home secretary David Blunkett has previously ruled that there is insufficient evidence to justify his deportation to Saudi Arabia. Al-Massari pledged to fight the government in the courts, though he closed the controversial jihad discussion forum on his Tajdeed website in response to the changing conditions. Visitors instead were confronted with a statement castigating Tony Blair as a war criminal trampling on people's right to free expression.

A hundred or more others further down the food chain were also said to be under similar scrutiny. It was all good PR that would show the politicians as being virile and tough on the causes of terrorism, but the reality was that the headline deportations hardly mattered. Those people had already done their jobs.

The prime minister also announced that al-Muhajiroun, its successor groups and Hizb ut-Tahrir would be outlawed. The jihad movement had already splintered and retreated underground, where a new and younger generation of preachers had taken over the reins. One jihad-oriented website had been muzzled, but there were many others still distributing training materials and propaganda.

The pause was short-lived, however. After the storm of controversy that greeted the unveiling of the government's proposed new anti-terrorism measures, the extremists came back online with a vengeance. The promised swift deportations of 'preachers of hate' didn't materialise and there was something akin to mild uproar amongst the press and public over the plan to outlaw the 'glorification' of terrorism, because it was too vague and could ensnare the innocent.

It was a little better than the early hints after 7/7 about simply making it an offence to even visit a pro-jihad website. I remember discussing it with several colleagues and none of us could see how that could be effectively enforced in the first place, never mind the Big Brother aspects. It would have meant that journalists working in this area would also be potentially criminalised. 'It's impossible,' I concluded.

We agreed that it wouldn't stop us doing our jobs, but it would mean that the government and police would hold a very big discretionary stick over us. The focus on banning then changed from users to suppliers, and the glorification offence was proposed, which would cover statements on record going back 20 years. Critics pointed out that those who supported the anti-apartheid struggle in South Africa would be labelled terrorists under this law.

The home secretary scoffed at the suggestion that Nelson Mandela admirers would be pursued, because the powers were discretionary, but that made it even more worrying, to my mind. That was the giant rift in the whole plan: the potential for misuse against critics of the government. That then morphed into 'glorification with intent' to incite acts of terrorism, which many argued was little better.

Sensing that the danger to them had receded, the extremists returned to business as usual. In fact, it was more than that as, at the time of writing, there is more al-Qaeda material in circulation than there was before the 7/7 bombings – far more.

Even though a crackdown was said to be on, a convicted terrorist was still recruiting inside jail. Incredibly, the would-be shoe-bomber Saajid Badat was allowed to conduct weekly prayer meetings in the high-security Whitemoor prison in Cambridgeshire. This only came to light when it was reported that a small bomb had exploded inside the prison. The device was believed to have been made from materials readily available inside the prison, and Badat and three other inmates were segregated when they tested positive for traces of explosive.

The lack of arrests relating to the support network for the 7/7 bombers gradually refuelled ideas that there may be no direct connection with al-Qaeda, and this generated conspiracy theories within the Muslim community that people other than those named were behind the bombings. Apparently, the so-called bombers were innocent patsies in a CIA–MI6 operation designed to scare the population into conformity.

Lots of cold water was poured on these ideas with the broadcast on Al-Jazeera, on 1 September 2005, of the last will of Khan, the 7/7 Edgware Road bomber. In the five-minute video, he said the attacks were retaliation for the UK's involvement in Iraq and blamed the British people for supporting the government's foreign policy. 'We're at war and I am a soldier,' he said, promising that attacks would continue.

The tape was designed to demonstrate that 'Mother al-Qaeda' was still operational and not fatally wounded as the generals and the politicians would have us believe. More than that, the organisation appeared to have fully recovered from the setbacks of Afghanistan and built up a network of cells in Europe, a third generation of operatives composed of young, recent converts.

Many of the new recruits are likely to have been procured via a European network that al-Zarqawi had started to establish prior to 9/11. Khan's praise of al-Zarqawi, after bin Laden and his deputy Ayman al-Zawahiri, was significant. Towards the end of 2004, radical preachers such as Bakri started urging their followers to regard al-Zarqawi in the same light as they would bin Laden.

It seemed likely that the bombers were spirited away to an al-Qaeda training camp during the Pakistan visit to undergo final training and indoctrination. The release of the video followed the pattern of propaganda after 9/11, when videos of the hijackers in training and giving their final wills and testaments to the camera were drip-fed to Al-Jazeera and jihadist websites. It seemed to be reasonable to expect the release of further videos, showing the London bombers undergoing training and reading out more last wills.

If the preparations for the London attacks followed the same pattern as 9/11, then the bombers may have met with bin Laden, al-Zawahiri or another senior leader. Past history shows that bin Laden personally selects the participants in centrally planned spectaculars, who then, after final training and videotaping their last testaments, spend a lot of time in his company before heading off on their missions.

These final pep talks are designed to linger in the mind to counter any second thoughts the operatives might have on the day. For recent converts, meeting bin Laden or a leader of his stature would be an overwhelming experience. Perhaps it was these memories that came to mind when bus bomber Hasib Hussain sat in McDonald's trying to contact his colleagues after being unable to get on to the Northern Line as planned, before he steeled himself and looked for the nearest alternative target.

The involvement of al-Qaeda's London-based communications cell and Terrorist007 was likely, if Khan's section of the video had been produced in the UK: the London cell was certainly involved in distributing it online after the Al-Jazeera transmission. The video had all the hallmarks of having been professionally produced, as

Khan's words were carefully scripted and its format conformed to al-Qaeda's 'house style'.

The carpet seen in the background was just about the only clue to follow in determining the origin of the film, along with the acoustic echo that indicated it was recorded indoors. I mentally noted that Germaine Lindsay had worked in a carpet shop in Aylesbury until recently. Also, the lack of an AK-47 propped up behind Khan's right shoulder looked to be telling. The style, however, was very much that of al-Qaeda's media production unit, known as As-Sahab, which pointed towards a location in Pakistan or Afghanistan. That was likely to be in or near the North and South Waziristan tribal badlands bordering Afghanistan. This is where al-Qaeda central has relocated, as bin Laden enjoys rock-solid support among the people there.

There are often rumours that bin Laden has been seen there, and stronger evidence has emerged for the existence of training camps. It has been a battleground, as the Pakistan government has tried to root out extremists, but success has been limited, because of the remoteness and inaccessibility of the area. Al-Qaeda is also not without supporters inside Pakistan's military and intelligence agencies.

Khan's last statement was followed by a message from al-Zawahiri, who said that the 'blessed London battle' was a 'slap' to the policies of Tony Blair, implying that the network is capable of delivering uppercuts in the future. His call to transfer the guerrilla war in Iraq to the homelands of Western countries was more concerning. He announced the opening of a new phase in the global jihad, and, amongst the jihadi community, these messages do not fall on deaf ears.

The impression given by the video is that al-Qaeda's new generation is firmly plugged in to al-Qaeda central and al-Zarqawi is on the board of directors. There is no new al-Qaeda, just a bigger version of the one that existed before 9/11.

It seemed that the indications that al-Zarqawi's network was active but largely unmapped in the UK and Europe were correct when figures emerged from the US in October 2005. Unnamed counter-terrorism officials estimated that al-Zarqawi's network now operated in forty countries and encompassed two dozen terrorist groups. They also admitted that little was known about how he and his group in Iraq coordinate activities outside the country.

The multiple suicide bombings in Bali that month came as a

reminder that the threat of repeat attacks on London remained. In the four months that followed the 7/7 attacks, there was little visible evidence of progress in investigation.

It wasn't until November 2005 that the reasons for the official reticence to talk about the 7/7 bombings started to emerge. One newspaper, quoting police sources, claimed that all of the bombers had been under surveillance for several weeks 12 months before the attacks took place, but they were discounted as a threat because there was nothing suspicious about their activities; they appeared to be living normal lives. The ringleader, Khan, was said to have been filmed meeting a known al-Qaeda fixer, but no action was taken. That version of events has not been disputed by the authorities.

Neither has it been disputed that the bombers were among the five people who'd escaped during the hastily launched 3 August 2004 raids to break up the alleged US/UK bombing plot, after details of the capture of computer expert Noor Khan were leaked to the media in Pakistan. The subsequent front-page story I wrote at the time about bombers being on the loose and preparing to strike against public-transport targets turned out to be all too true. The London bombings could have been prevented, and the error meant that the attackers had a clear run at the target.

INDEX